PRAISE FOR *WHISK*[...]

An *Oprah Daily* "Best New Book" and "Riveting Nonfiction and Memoir You Need to Read" • A *New York Times* "New Book to Read" • An *Esquire* "Best Nonfiction Book" • A *Washington Post* "Book to Read" • An *Elle* "Best Book" • A *Zibby Mag* "Most Anticipated Book" • A *San Francisco Chronicle* "New Book to Cozy Up With" • *The Millions* "Most Anticipated" • An *Electric Literature* "Books by Women of Color to Read" • An Amazon Editors "Best Book of the Month" • An *Esquire* "Best Book" • *Publishers Weekly* "Top 10 Memoir and Biography"

"[A] vibrant memoir." —*The New Yorker*

"Indeed, while some reviewers have already qualified her book as a 'Native memoir,' Taffa's story is in fact distinctly American, full stop, and one that a country afraid of its own history needs to hear." —*Washington Post*

"I was completely taken by *Whiskey Tender*: its gorgeous sentences, its searing observations about identity and loss and inheritance, and its exploration of generational and terrestrial traumas. This is a strong and special book."
 —Carmen Maria Machado, bestselling author of *In the Dream House*

"What makes Taffa's version exceptional is her visceral prose and sharp attunement to the tragedies of assimilation. This is a must-read."
 —*Publishers Weekly* (starred review)

"We have more Native stories now, but we have not heard one like this. *Whiskey Tender* is unexpected and propulsive, indeed tender, but also bold, and beautifully told, like a drink you didn't know you were thirsty for. This book, never anything less than mesmerizing, is full of family stories and vital Native history. It pulses and it aches, and it lifts, consistently. It threads together so much truth, by the time we are done, what has been woven together equals a kind of completeness from brokenness, and a hope from knowing love and loss and love again by naming it so."
 —Tommy Orange, bestselling author of *There There*

"The result of a lifetime, Taffa's remarkable debut stands out from other contemporary memoirs and Native American literature." —*Booklist* (starred review)

"In a memoir populated by dreams but legislated by family and culture and reality, Deborah Taffa suggests that if we are going to heal we need to be able to remember our wounds. In a style that is by turns measured, then biting, then humorous, then humble, then soaring, Taffa has a personal and moral conversation with an untold history. This story—which centers around being both Native and American at the same time—is a great lesson for how we can hold, and even embrace, our divisions and our tensions to create a new mosaic for the future."

—Colum McCann, National Book Award winner and author of *Apeirogon*

"Rich and wise." —*Los Angeles Times*

"This book is about inheritance, but it is also about reclamation. It's about the history we can't change and those futures that we're shaping despite their pings from the past. And in her graceful, compassionate, bold, and humorous debut, Taffa explores how to navigate this rift with insights of breathtaking beauty and depth."

—John D'Agata, Guggenheim Fellow and author of *The Lifespan of a Fact*

"Taffa's work is a testament to the power of and need for intergenerational story-telling and a reminder that neither the history, identity, nor future of Native Americans is a monolith. She succeeds in creating a memorable celebration of 'our survival as a culture, as well as the hope, strength, and grace of my family.' A searching and perceptive Native memoir." —*Kirkus Reviews*

"A single life can be the wellspring for an entire mythology, and Deborah Jackson Taffa's *Whiskey Tender* flows like water over desert earth. We are given the life of a people, their history borne of and defining American history. We are given a story, singular and impossible to put down."

—Jai Chakrabarti, author of *A Play for the End of the World* and *A Small Sacrifice for an Enormous Happiness*

"The many strands of narrative coalesce to form a visceral story of family, survival, and belonging, flooding the field with cleansing light."

—*Esquire*

"A memoir of exquisite detail and honesty, *Whiskey Tender* is a quintessentially American story in which Little Debbie snack cakes and *The Price is Right* are every bit the birthrights of Deborah Taffa as the legacies of Indigenous displacement,

oppression, and murder. Taffa's moving book reminds us that capital-H history never ends with travesties but carries through specific individuals in real time, and that while America can take and take, it can never kill off the truth or the spirit."
—Joshua Ferris, author of *Then We Came to the End*

"In *Whiskey Tender*, Deborah Taffa examines, courageously and compellingly, the many forces that made her. Her extraordinary, hard-working father; her complicated, beautiful mother; a childhood divided between Quechua and Navajo territories; and her own bullheaded, indomitable spirit. A deft and engaging weave of personal narrative, generational trauma, US policies of exclusion and erasure, and Taffa's unquenchable desire to find her way back to the mystery that always has been and is still at the center of existence, this superb memoir of place, culture, and finding power will open your eyes as well as your heart."
—Pam Houston, author of *Deep Creek: Finding Hope in the High Country*

"Screaming from the heart, Taffa's confiding memoir pierces generations of colonial harm . . . a mature, illuminating text that will also appeal to coming-of-age readers."
—Cynthia Leitich Smith, American Indian Youth Literature Award winner for *Hearts Unbroken*

"In this finely drawn memoir, Deborah Jackson Taffa has written an essential story of America. A meticulously researched and critical look at self and country, *Whiskey Tender* breaks your heart and then makes it soar."
—Kelli Jo Ford, author of *Crooked Hallelujah*

"Taffa's nuanced, compassionate descriptions of her attempts to overcome bullying at school or her family's struggles after trading the connection and support they enjoyed in Yuma for a modicum of upward mobility in Farmington are engrossing."
—*San Francisco Chronicle*

"*Whiskey Tender* is a gem that is a deeply personal story, but also sheds a light on the injustices faced by Indigenous people past and present. It is a must-read."
—*Durango Herald* (Colorado)

"In Deborah Jackson Taffa's memoir, transparency is laced with humor and heart."
—*Santa Fe New Mexican* (New Mexico)

WHISKEY TENDER

A MEMOIR

DEBORAH JACKSON TAFFA

HARPER PERENNIAL

NEW YORK • LONDON • TORONTO • SYDNEY • NEW DELHI • AUCKLAND

For my grandchildren,
who will one day look for themselves in this story

HARPER ● PERENNIAL

A hardcover edition of this book was published in 2024 by Harper, an imprint of HarperCollins Publishers.

WHISKEY TENDER. Copyright © 2024 by Deborah Taffa. All rights reserved. Printed in the United States of America. No part of this book may be used or reproduced in any manner whatsoever without written permission except in the case of brief quotations embodied in critical articles and reviews. For information, address HarperCollins Publishers, 195 Broadway, New York, NY 10007.

HarperCollins books may be purchased for educational, business, or sales promotional use. For information, please email the Special Markets Department at SPsales@harpercollins.com.

FIRST HARPER PERENNIAL EDITION PUBLISHED 2024.

All images are courtesy of the author unless otherwise noted.

Designed by Nancy Singer

The Library of Congress has catalogued the hardcover edition as follows:

Names: Taffa, Deborah Jackson, 1969– author.
Title: Whiskey tender : a memoir / Deborah Jackson Taffa.
Description: First edition. | New York, NY : Harper, [2024]
Identifiers: LCCN 2023020169 (print) | LCCN 2023020170 (ebook) |
ISBN 9780063288515 (hardcover) | ISBN 9780063288539 (ebook)
Subjects: LCSH: Taffa, Deborah Jackson, 1969– —Childhood and youth. | Yuma Indians—New Mexico—Farmington—Biography. | Pueblo Indians—New Mexico—Farmington—Biography. | Yuma Indians—Fort Yuma Reservation (Ariz. and Calif.)—Biography. | Pueblo Indians—Fort Yuma Reservation (Ariz. and Calif.)—Biography. | Farmington (N.M.)—Biography. | Fort Yuma Reservation (Ariz. and Calif.)—Biography.
Classification: LCC E99.Y94 T34 2024 (print) | LCC E99.Y94 (ebook) | DDC 978.9/8200497572092 [B]—dc23/eng/20231012
LC record available at https://lccn.loc.gov/2023020169
LC ebook record available at https://lccn.loc.gov/2023020170

ISBN 978-0-06-328852-2 (pbk.)

24 25 26 27 28 LBC 5 4 3 2 1

✠ ✠ ✠

Long ago when the people were given these ceremonies, the changing began, if only in the aging of the yellow gourd rattle or the shrinking of the skin around the eagle's claw, if only in the different voices from generation to generation, singing the chants. You see, in many ways, the ceremonies have always been changing.

—Leslie Marmon Silko, *Ceremony*

we need a god who bleeds now
whose wounds aren't the end of anything.

—Ntozake Shange, *From Okra to Greens*

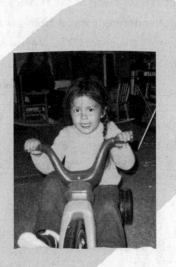

The author on her
childhood Big Wheel
in Yuma, Arizona,
circa 1973.

CONTENTS

✜

PART 1

PART 2

PART 3

PART 4

PART

1

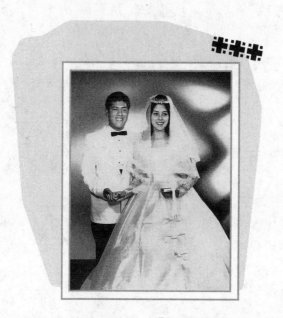

Edmond Jackson III
and Lorraine Lopez
Herrera, the
author's parents,
on April 6, 1963, in
Yuma, Arizona.

The last time I went home to the reservation was for my mother's funeral. My father was driving, and as we crossed the southern Arizona desert following the transport van that carried her body, I fell into a sandstorm dream. Dust blew, obscuring the highway, and small pebbles pecked the car like hail. I was driving alone in my dream and wanted to keep up with my mother, but the wind blew the sand so thick it darkened the earth, and I had to slow down because the steering wheel pulled through my hands. Though I knew the car might crash into the badlands, I did not feel afraid. Instead, the sand flying into the headlights mesmerized me, making me forget who I was, where I was, why I started on this journey. There was no transport van with my mother's body before me. Just the wind and darkness and a sense of wonder, the same feeling I had in my earliest years when the earth and the elements and the tiniest creatures were miracles.

The storm stopped and I descended from the car. The sun hung high and blazing, and I looked down the highway to spot a lake, shimmering on the empty road. Awake, I would have known the water was a mirage. But in my dream, I was thirsty and walked toward it, still believing with the faith of a child. I grew up in a homeland favored by the Fata Morgana. Long before I understood illusions, I would see Spanish galleons floating over the horizon. For years, many of my ideas about the world were tricks of the environment. "We're here," my father said, waking me. We got out of the car and went to my mother in the transport van. Her eyes had reopened in transit, and she stared at me, as if acknowledging that I'd spent a lifetime doubting what I saw. I felt her chastising me with her gaze, as if she were saying I could no longer stay small and invisible, as Indian kids are. I was a fifty-year-old woman now, and it was time to grow into more than a ghost child in love with, and afraid of, mirages.

ANIMAS

(1981)

T he highway to Silverton, Colorado, is an ear-popping ascent with hair-
pin turns and missing guardrails. Dad hugged the mountainside with
the van as we climbed, tapping his horn before each blind curve to warn
truckers of our presence. We had left the hellish reservation border town
we'd just moved to behind and were headed to a vacation paradise located
past a ski resort named Purgatory.

As soon as Dad pulled into our favorite camping spot on the Animas
River, I jumped out of the van and ran down to the water. At the age of
twelve, I was still knobby-kneed and tube-socked, my brown skin splattered
with mud. How lucky it felt to be a kid, unhindered by a woman's body.
My bones remained hollow and birdy that summer, boyish and inconse-
quential for a few more blissful months.

Tell me your favorite childhood memory, and I'll tell you who you are.
I remember the laughter my sisters and I shared as we tossed tiny balls of
bread to see-through fish along the shoreline. I remember Dad fiddling
with the worms he used for bait, and Mom asking a kayaker about a rapid
called Mandatory Thrashing. I remember all of us working together to
pitch the tent and make a temporary home.

Our time on the river felt like spiritual repair. Dad grilled the trout
we'd caught during the day. He whittled long marshmallow sticks, and we
sat around the fire, listening to his reservation ghost stories—the fog wall

that rose one night when his buddies chanted Indian songs, the mountain lion girl that scared him as a kid. Dad burned with energy, and long after the moon rose in the sky, he kept talking. We'd go to bed exhausted, knowing that in the morning he would heat our shoes by the fire he stoked at sunrise.

Nostalgia plays tricks on memory, and the Animas River is consistently sepia tinted in my mind. Dad was always my hero anyway, so when I remember him at the river, I remember his bonfire stories, or the way he used to let us touch the dent in his skull where he got shot by his brother's arrow—I don't stop to think about his anger, or his strict rules, or how often he was gone. I don't dwell on his workaholic ways or consider the overbearing weight he and Mom placed on us to excel.

Remembering the river helps me forget, at least for a moment, the challenges, fears, and feelings of inadequacy I experienced in my childhood. *Memoria praeteritorum bonorum,* my own set of rose-colored glasses. A trick of the mind that helps me highlight the peaceful days, the quiet ones that punctuated the violence, pressures, and confusion of being a Native girl in a northwestern New Mexico town where cowboys still hated Indians—three white teenagers had murdered three Native men just before my family and I moved there for my father's new job, when I was six years old. Navajo people marched in the streets that April, and though we missed the protests and backlash, the town's tension remained consistent, even after the Civil Rights Commission came in to keep the peace.

My early childhood took place in an era when good Native families didn't move off their home reservations, because close friends and relatives called relocation a betrayal. It was a time of conflicting choices, when young people like my father and his siblings, who grew up on the reservation, faced a dilemma that pitted high reservation unemployment and double-digit inflation against the desire to belong to their tribe. In moving from our Quechan (Yuma) reservation in California to the Navajo reservation in New Mexico, my father chose to be an individual, and my parents decided they wanted their kids to be mainstream Americans, passing down an implicit appreciation of social climbing *along with* and *in conflict with* the realization that our people are excluded, ironically, from the central mythologies of the American identity.

I want to say ours is *the* iconic American story, but that would insult our non-Native allies, the decent folk for whom the consequences of broken treaties and forced assimilation are already a burden, and for whom oppression may also be an inheritance. I don't tell this story to create a divide. I tell it because there are too many dark corners in America that can be relieved of persistent shadows by shining a little light. I tell it because our story belongs to all Americans, some of whom may be surprised by our history. I tell it to celebrate our survival as a culture, as well as the hope, strength, and grace of my family.

This story is as common as dirt. Thousands of Native Americans in California, Arizona, and New Mexico could tell it. Anyone with a grandpa who was haunted by Indian boarding school, who stung his family like a dust devil when he drank. Anyone with a grandma who washed laundry until her fingernails cracked and bled, who went without eating when there weren't enough groceries because she wanted her ten kids to have a few extra bites. Anyone with a mother who kept secrets so her kids wouldn't find out about their father's jailbird past. Anyone with a father who chose the violence of industrial labor over the violence of reservation life because he wanted his kids to get through private school and make better lives for themselves.

So many people could tell this story, it is shocking how rarely it has been told. Too many mothers have watched their kids thrown into cop cars without protest. Too many aunties have put ice on black eyes without saying a word. Too many grandmothers have watched their grandchildren, their hope for the future, head out to a party and never come home. Too many girls have pretended nothing happened after experiencing sexual harassment, only to redirect the hate toward the innocent face staring back at them in the mirror.

Native memoirs are rare because there are rules on Indian reservations. We fear appropriation and fight about who has the right to speak. Talking to outsiders is taboo. And our belief systems often go against this kind of preservation and self-telling. So why divulge my story? Because I want Native kids to feel more connected and less lonely. Because I hate the portrayal of my people as dependents unable to better their own circumstances and tell their own stories. Because I need to understand what aspects of my personality were seeded in that New Mexican town all those years ago.

My inheritance stretches back to the so-called Anasazi, over a thousand years in the cacti, sage, and sandstone lands, in the desert canyons, adobe homes, and turquoise stone Southwest. America runs like a river through my veins, yet throughout my childhood, Native representation gathered dust in museums. On television, in books, I saw costumes and mascots— never a portrayal of a mixed-tribe Native girl listening to music on her Walkman. Without a contemporary likeness of myself in the media, there was no confirmation that anything I experienced in my childhood was real.

My father was born in 1941 and he taught me never to confuse pity with comprehension. His Quechan (Yuma) grandfather was born in a time when California's Indian population had plummeted 90 percent because of foreign diseases, Catholic slave-labor, and the government's hiring of private militia to bring in Indian scalps. California's first governor, Peter Hardeman Burnett, openly promoted genocide, calling for "a war of extermination" in his 1851 second state address. With the help of the U.S. Army, the California legislature distributed weapons to vigilantes, who raided Native homes and killed 100,000 of my ancestors in the first two years of the gold rush alone. The legislature paid $1.1 million to these murderers, and when it was done, the U.S. Congress agreed to reimburse the state.

When I was younger, I avoided writing about these atrocities. I told myself it sounded conceited. To have survived that much violence, my ancestors must have been powerful. It was like I was claiming to have super genes. Today I know my hesitation was shame: the silence that follows an apocalypse. To talk about what we suffered, to concede that we were victims, was not something we did in my family. And yet to write about the culture that was taken via the government's assimilation policies, I must acknowledge the pain and remember the beauty in the middle-class life my parents jerry-rigged for me and my siblings in the high-desert arroyos and sun-scorched histories of the American Southwest.

I was raised to believe in the reciprocity of the land, and I know that, if I went back now, I would see that our favorite camping spot near Purgatory has aged just as much as me. During my childhood in the 1980s, my family and I were fishing on the shores of change. The Animas was the last free-flowing water in Colorado before it was dammed at the start of the twenty-first century; a bald eagle refuge not yet injured by the wastewater that bled from the Gold King Mine in 2015. Dad said the river's full name was the Río de las Ánimas Perdidas, or the River of Lost Souls. He said if we got up early, we might get lucky and see them: the spirits of our ancestors floating downstream in the early morning fog.

I remember waking up and calling Dad to bring me my basketball shoes while I was still in my sleeping bag. Warm from their place near the fire, the shoes' canvas made my toes cozy. I ran down to the water, where the grass was stiff with frost, and there was the smell of smoky pine in every breath. I squatted to wash my face, squinting at the outline of what I imagined to be the spirits of our ancestors on the other shore. If only I knew their names, I thought, maybe I could help them get home.

Today, they are the ones bringing me home. Reflecting on my visit to the Animas River when I was twelve, I hold my ancestors close to my heart, knowing I too will be an ancestor someday, adding to the chain of lives that came before.

With death as my guide, I remember what's important, and listen for the river even now. "Do not participate in the erasure of your own people," the voices murmur. "Do not be a silent witness as we fade."

ALMOST YUMAN

(1972)

✦

We sisters were broken girls. We twisted our ankles sailing off playground swings, toppled out of tamarisk trees, plucked yellow jacket stingers and broken glass out of our skin. We slammed our fingers in car doors, burned our feet in campfires, and then sat in the waiting room at the Yuma Indian Hospital, ice pressed to injuries.

Joan broke her wrist. I broke my collarbone. Lori had a two-inch scar down the center of her chest. Monica slipped through the handrails of a tall metal slide and landed twenty feet below. The reservation was rowdy in the 1970s. By the time I was three, scars were a main source of pride.

Put a little whiskey in Dad's beer, and he got to talking about his friends. Crushed under a fast-moving train. Stabbed in the chest during an alley fight. Propped against a tree at a public park with a hot needle sticking out of an arm. Killed in a land mine explosion in Vietnam. Mom tried to shush Dad when he told us his stories. But he said we needed to know the truth if we were going to survive, to hear how tough the world could be.

Swagger was a sure way for us kids to get praise. Despondency hung over the reservation, and when toddlers and children acted rebellious, adults saw hope and verve. A sassy girl was a girl who might make it, even against the odds. My sisters and I did what we could to impress.

We rejected all things girly. We painted our dolls' faces with markers, tattooing their chins in the style of our female ancestors. We chopped off their hair, and when they grew grotesque, threw their heads in the trash can, and danced their bodies around, calling out like barkers selling tickets to see Geronimo at the World's Fair: "Come and see the Amazing Headless Wonders!" We were unruly Indian girls, not the friendly Thanksgiving Day types who knew how to cook and behave. Our mother said it was too late to teach us any manners.

Dad always said, "Broken bones grow back stronger," raising us the same way his older brother, Gene, raised him. A father's job was to control the pace of the world's wounding, to dole out the pain in slightly bigger doses over time so that his kids would learn not to break under pressure. This is what I think of when I think of my sisters and me growing up: we didn't get anything for free and we blossomed because of it, blood flowering into bruises, skin thick and ripened under the Sonoran Desert sun.

We rarely cried, knowing tears were a sign of weakness, knowing we'd never catch our father or his brothers wet-eyed. I remember seeing one man cry though—our neighbor, weeping the day his dog, Rocco, died.

You never saw a dog as spastic as Rocco. He made a play for freedom every time his owner opened his front door. "Rocco, you shit!" we'd hear him yell. Then the screen door would slam, and the chase would begin.

Rocco would never heel, and our neighbor, who had a bad leg, could never catch him. It was dodge-and-go for thirty minutes every time, an entertaining show that my sisters and I watched with glee. We scrambled on top of the swamp cooler and cheered Rocco on, loving the way he sidled in and ducked away at the last second.

The downside to our afternoon pleasure was the finish. The longer it took the neighbor to catch poor Rocco, the harder he would kick him once he got him leashed. "You fat old bastard!" we yelled at him when he did this.

Rocco's owner lived alone. He passed us Popsicles through the rip in his front screen door, but only if we would stay with him for a while after eating. Cold and sticky and sweet, the Popsicles were a treat we never had in our own refrigerator, stocked only with its week-old refried beans, lard-hardened cheese enchiladas, and Bud Light beer. When we finished, he'd come out and wash our hands with the hose. Then he would gather us around his lawn chair, take one of us on his lap, and crack stupid jokes. We could not leave because that would mean abandoning whoever he had on his lap. The rest of us gnawed nervously on the Popsicle sticks until he let the unlucky one go.

"Next time I ain't taking one of those Popsicles," we would swear. Then his jalopy would crunch up the driveway and we would see him carrying sacks emblazoned with the words Del Sol Grocery to the carport door. Our mud cakes would fall to the ground. We risked plenty for those Popsicles.

"Don't go near that guy." Our parents gave us strict instructions to stay away from him.

Everyone said the only reason he lived in Yuma was because his ex-wife died and left him her house. They said never to trust an Indian who doesn't want to go back to his own reservation. Their mean comments were rooted in jealousy. He wasn't an enrolled Quechan (Yuma) tribal citizen, yet he had inherited a house on our reservation.

Property ownership on our ancestral lands became complicated in 1893, when the Colorado Irrigation Company started lobbying the U.S. government to build a diversion dam on our reservation. Suddenly, engineers and Indian agents were advocating for the government to "give" tribal members five acres each and sell the "excess land" to white farmers. Before this era in history, our home at the confluence of the Colorado and Gila Rivers had been mostly ignored by whites, many of whom had assumed southeastern California was sterile. But it had been an oasis in the desert, beneficial for planting melon, squash, beans, and corn.

By the time I was born in 1969, it was hard to imagine the sheer size of the Colorado River before it was dammed. For eons it had burst its banks in spring, carrying sediment carved off the walls of the Grand Canyon. There was always snow in the mountains, which meant an annual flood was guaranteed, and every year our ancestors went to higher ground until the water receded. When they came down, they planted in the nitrogen-rich silt deposited by the river. They rebuilt the previous year's swales and dams for irrigation, adjusting annually to the new contours of their farmland.

My inheritance should have been a house with abundant crops grown in some of America's most fertile soil, but despite petitioning Congress, Dad's great-grandparents lost their battle and their land to the U.S. government via termination policies involved in the Dawes Act. In 1911, purportedly to pay for canal construction and the tribe's new irrigation costs, the government sold our best farmland for pennies on the dollar. Concrete canals were built for white farmers, cheap wooden ones for us. Maintenance fees resulted in the concrete canals being patrolled and kept in good condition, whereas ours leaked and destroyed the soil with alkalinity.

The 1912 flood was the last time Dad's great-grandparents planted in the traditional way. By 1914, our family members, Dad's Quechan grandfather included, received ten acres each (a number higher than the originally proposed five, but one that paled in comparison to the average hundred-acre allotments on other western Indian reservations). In 1915, the government adopted a rule that Indian agents could lease Quechan land for ten years at a time if it was not being used to their liking, and from that point forward white farmers took over 80 percent of our reservation.

Only three houses had been built by Dad's family. The family had more acreage, but banks would not accept reservation plots as collateral for housing materials—even the houses we did have were gained when my grandpa, dad, and the family drove out to San Diego in 1956 to dismantle and transport prefabricated plywood houses that had been built for shipyard workers during the war. Dad was the fifth child, and by the time I was born, his mother and two brothers called the houses home. Because of this reservation housing scarcity, the rest of the family lived in duplexes, apartments, and run-down stucco houses, rental properties on both sides of the river. Renting was a common circumstance for many big Quechan families, and therefore many people resented Grandma's neighbor for his house on the reservation. Grandma herself was Laguna Pueblo, which meant they might have resented her too.

When the rattler got Rocco, our neighbor's scream ripped the desert. I was hiding behind clothesline sheets in a game of hide-and-seek when I heard him yell the dog's name. I came out of white cotton to see his shovel moving like a jackhammer as he chopped the rattler in two.

He threw the shovel down and limped over to Rocco. His good leg buckled. We inched closer. Rocco was bleeding out of two puncture wounds, and his forehead was starting to swell. "What're you staring at?" our neighbor yelled.

The rock wasn't big, and he only threw one. It struck the back of my hand, and my sisters took off running. Stunned by the pain, I lost them. The memory gets lost too, at this point, but I always say I ran down to the canal. I wouldn't have gone home while I was crying. It wasn't like I was afraid Dad would whoop me. He wasn't as hot-tempered as he used to be. I'd once seen him knock a guy off his feet with one punch, but he was straightening his life out now and calming down. If I didn't go home, it was to avoid his disappointment, and to hide from my sisters, who would have never let me live it down.

Dad had a secret. I began seeing it in his body and sensing it in the way Mom sometimes told us to leave him alone. I felt it in the air like static when he grew angry at the park, restraining himself, barely, in exchanges with leathery men in gallon hats, men who refused to let us play with their daughters. Dad belonged to the desert like a naturally rooted cedar, and the incongruent way he started shrinking small in town was scary. His new docility embarrassed me.

During my early years in Yuma, he sometimes had night terrors, jumping to his feet with his fists raised like he didn't recognize Mom. When life grew stressful, and he had trouble sleeping, he always retreated to the land. I don't know how many times he drove us out to go hiking near Picacho Peak, insisting that it was his job to help us grow strong. Mom always stayed back at the dirt parking lot, at the base of the desert peak, cracking sunflower seeds and reading. I would see her when the trail switched back, shielding her eyes with her book, fidgeting as she watched us climb higher.

The loose gravel was slippery, but Dad refused to carry us and didn't like it when we asked to rest. When we tried to sit and scoot down a slippery slope, he barked for us to stand. We would gain elevation gradually until we ran into rock walls. He would say, "wait," then climb up, and call for us to come closer. He would grab us by our wrists and pull us up the face. Once we were together, we would walk farther until we were on top of the world.

Looking down at our Chevy Nova on the dirt road below, the vein in my neck would pulse, and my head would spin dizzily. The car looked like a toy, and Mom like a small doll waving her arms helplessly, worried to see us so high. The desert reduced Mom, like town did Dad. Out here he was towering, standing at the edge of the cliff, his hair whipping around in his face.

I usually shied away from the precipices, but Dad always came over. Squatting low to look us in the eye, he gave instructions: "If anyone moves from where I put you, you're going to get a spanking." Then he would take my older sisters, Joan and Lori, to sit on the edge of the cliff. Monica and I would huddle together, hoping to stay where we were, but he always returned for us as well.

He would arrange us, two on his right and two on his left, with his arms extended across our laps like a safety bar. My legs would dangle heavy, and the wind would blow across the sweat at my lower back. Whenever I shivered, feeling frightened, Dad would scoff and roll his eyes. "You're not going to fall," he would say, and trusting him, I would manage to relax and see.

The desert stretched on forever, and a green body of water snaked through the mauves and tans. "That's the Colorado," Dad told us, using his chin to point at the river in the distance. Our ancestral homeland stretched on as far as the eye could see.

Then Dad would grow quiet. He was always capable of keeping still for long periods of time. Sometimes we complained and pestered him to go home, sometimes he sucked us into the silence, and I would lean up against his body and feel the weight of his wounding, as well as the difficulty of my knowledge that not everything was getting told.

On the evening Rocco got bitten by the snake, we went to the drive-in theater. It was a favorite outing for our family, along with visiting the cousins or going on hikes with Dad. A central stomping ground, it felt rare to pull in there without seeing some relative or other.

It was the only place Mom and Dad expressed anything but joy at running into family. When we saw a crowd of cousins sitting outside the fence, trying to watch the movie from the sidewalk across the street from the entrance without being able to hear the sound, my parents argued.

Dad would say we should try to squeeze them into the Nova. Mom would say if we took one, we had to take them all, and there was no way they could fit. Then Dad would talk about how his big brother, Gene, used to make him and his younger brothers hide in the trunk of the car when they couldn't afford to buy tickets.

"We know, we know," Mom always said. "Bill farted and everyone started yelling and you got caught."

"It was right when Gene was trying to pay!"

"Don't get crazy," she responded. "No one's riding in our trunk."

Sometimes one of our cousins would scale the fence and run to lift a couple of speakers off the stands in the back row. Turning the volume all the way up, they would stretch the speakers toward the fence as far as they'd reach on their cords before setting them down in the dirt.

"Those speakers aren't loud enough to carry that far," Dad said. He said it sucked that we didn't have the money to get everyone in.

After parking the car, Mom opened a couple of lawn chairs. We always sat outside the car, and usually I loved climbing up on the hood to recline against the windshield while the engine was still warm, but that night I wanted to join my sisters on the swings at the foot of the screen.

Joan, Lori, Monica, and I ran toward the playground, weaving among cars and families as the sun sunk low in the sky. We never had long before the dark arrived and the snack bar commercials popped up to signal the impending start of the show. We pumped our legs and swung as fast as we could until the field of cars started flashing their lights and Joan and Lori pulled our swings to a halt.

On the return, as we were looking for Dad's Morse-code flicker—he did three long, three short, three long because one time we'd gotten lost and it embarrassed him when he saw us crying—Dad's big brother, Gene, stepped in our path.

Like all my sisters and cousins, I admired Uncle Gene. He was six foot two, funny, and vicious as sin, the object of our uncritical hero worship. He'd stagger into our house with one swollen eye, my younger uncles pale and shaking beside him because they'd been his passengers while he raced the train on his way to us, crossing the tracks just in front of it.

I knew that Gene was the undisputed badass in Dad's family, though I didn't fully understand the relationship between him and Dad. I knew that Dad was the second-oldest brother out of ten kids, and that Uncle Gene was five years his senior. I knew that Gene was the last in their family to go to Indian boarding school (for a brief time), where he met his wife, Babe, an Arapaho from Oklahoma, and that they lived with their kids on the family allotment.

What I didn't know then eclipsed what I did. I didn't know that Gene had raised Dad and his younger brothers during their father's alcoholic years in the early 1950s, an era when vendettas between various Yuma clans had been going on for more than a century. It would be years before Dad told me that their paternal uncle had been murdered by some full-blood Yuma guys who were arrested but never convicted, guys who hated their uncle for being effeminate, light-skinned, and a "breed," which meant full-blood but mixed tribe. It didn't seem like a big deal to me that Dad's paternal grandmother was a fair Shoshone-Paiute, or his mother was Laguna Pueblo, but he and Gene grew up in a different era, a time when pure bloodlines meant more than they do now. The fact that Gene was always stirring up problems and fanning the flames of generations-old discord, and that his instinct threatened Dad's safety in my earliest childhood, was something I didn't understand even when they finally told us these stories.

In the Yuma tradition there are two kinds of war parties. *Axwé hayáig* means to seek a major battle, while *axwé omán* means to rekindle hostilities when they start to fade. Dad had grown up watching Gene take on other tribal members, constantly, to prove his power and strength, because their grandfather hadn't allowed his sons and grandsons to learn the Yuma language, and none of the men in their family felt like they fit in.

Gene wouldn't let any of his six younger brothers show weakness, especially not Dad, who was the next-eldest son. He was always leading them into a fight, and when there wasn't a fight, they picked teams and fought with each other for practice. Like the 1950s greaser, Gene lived for war councils and their agreed-upon weapons: knives instead of chains, bats instead of dirt-filled hoses. Like the kamikaze pilots, the men in Dad's family thought a willingness to die for one's family proved loyalty, restored honor, and sat at the heart of moral integrity. Violence was a tradition on our reservation, warfare to the Yuma people was mystical, a visible expression of spiritual power, and that submitting oneself to possible death was an honor meant to enhance and demonstrate your life force.

One time Gene got caught alone on the bridge coming back from town by family enemies from another clan who caught up with him and stabbed him in the side—afterward, their father took Gene to the Indian Hospital, where he refused an anesthetic for his stitches. Another time, Gene forced Dad to fight one of Dad's very best friends when they were both ten years old. When the friend went down, and Dad wanted to stop, Gene threatened to beat Dad to a pulp unless he kept kicking. The longer Dad kicked, the angrier he got, until the anger took over, and the kicking felt good, and he cracked two of his best friend's ribs.

Here is what I could see at that early age: Dad bristled when my uncle Gene came around, especially if he had been drinking, and as I smelled alcohol on Uncle Gene's breath at the drive-in, Dad suddenly appeared at my side. "Come on, kids," he said, holding a bag of popcorn in his hand.

Uncle Gene took a step back and lifted his chin. "Gonna hang out with me and the guys tonight?" A couple of Indians I'd never seen called to Gene from the tailgate of an old truck, but Dad didn't look in their direction.

"Nah, man," Dad answered.

"Who are you, Mister Rogers?" Gene asked.

Dad snickered. He handed the popcorn to Joan, picked up Monica, and took me by the hand. We sidestepped his brother, who slapped Dad on the shoulder as we headed back to our car to watch the show.

I still remember Uncle Gene's thin goatee, combed sharply to a point as we walked away. I always wanted to grab it, but he was scary as he was tall, and even when he picked me up, I was too afraid to touch it.

When we got back to the Nova, I took my place on the blanket on the grass and stared up at the sky. The stars were always visible in the desert, and I didn't feel like watching the show. If Dad had a secret it was here, lodged between him and his brother, and the longer he kept it hidden, the more it began to smell.

That night, Dad pulled out his whiskey when we got home from the drive-in. Always watchful when he drank, I felt relieved when he took only a few swigs before falling asleep on the couch.

It was hotter than usual that summer, our entire world covered in dust. The Colorado River ran low, and not only because of the dams; though it was monsoon season, the monsoons hadn't come.

It was late and I was sleeping on the carpet in the living room when Dad suddenly kicked over a lamp. He leaped to his feet as it crashed on the ground. I sat up and saw him as he rushed out the front door, a weird shriek coming out of his throat like he was imitating the Apache cicadas in the mesquite tree outside. Mom appeared in an instant, rushing outside to try and tug him back in by the arm. I could see his dim outline in the dark, jerking and shuddering like he was crying.

As they stood in the entryway, I heard him say, "I killed a man." He repeated it in a startled voice like it had just happened. Mom hushed him. She led him toward their bedroom in the dark, only the top halves of their bodies appearing above the couch. They floated along like ghosts hacked in two, the horror of my discovery making their appearance grisly.

A crack in Dad's mask had busted open, and a little light was shining in. It would be years before I would learn the full story, but witnessing his night terror was a major foray into understanding the river of traumatic events he held in his body.

What did I learn, in those years after he finally deemed me and my sisters old enough to hear the story? One night when my father was sixteen and doing math homework at home, trying to get to bed early because he had a big football game the next night, Uncle Gene called from downtown Yuma and said he needed to be picked up. Dad was sent to fetch him in the family car, and a gang of Gene's friends piled in when he arrived.

The guys had been drinking, and they wanted more liquor, so Dad drove them to Winterhaven on the California side of the river. Afterward they drove up to the reservation, to Indian Hill, where the hospital, church, and tribal offices sit now. Back then it was a hangout with only one access road, and the higher vantage point made it easy to watch for anyone coming.

A group of Gene's friends were already there messing around, and two of their friends got into a fight soon after Dad and his carload arrived. The police showed up at the bottom of Indian Hill, and everyone ran. Dad, Gene, and five other guys hopped into the family car, and as Dad drove by the cops on the way down Indian Hill, they saw one of their buddies getting arrested.

"Follow the cops to Winterhaven," Gene told Dad.

They went to the station, where they idled outside, watching the cops manhandle their friend. He was handcuffed, and Gene rolled down the window to cuss at the police, even though he must have known they would chase them for it. But they all knew if they could get out of town and onto the reservation the game of chase would be over. The county cops lost their jurisdiction there and could make an arrest only if the crime was

serious. Dad raced along the train tracks away from the following cops
with the pedal to the floor.

They had reached a dirt road, not far from the Hill and St. Thomas
Indian Mission—downtown Yuma and the old Territorial Prison were less
than a mile away on the other side of the Colorado River. They were almost there, about to cross the finish line, but just as they were rounding
the bend into the clear, they hit a section of gravel road that had been
washed out and flooded by a recent rain, and Dad lost control of the car.

Dad said he could see the headlights shining up into the sky before
the car came down on its side. The impact knocked the breath out of
him. The windows were busted, but the car quickly righted itself, then
began to slide nose first into the water. The river flooded in, and the car
started to sink. Doors popped open and everyone crawled out, swimming
for the far shore in a panic. They emerged on the California side of the
river and started running through wheatfields in the dark. Dad ran about a
half mile before remembering the way one of their friends, a close friend,
had been drunk and stumbling when he had picked them up at the bar.

His heart turned to ice. He called out to Gene and the others. "Does
anyone have Smith?" But no one answered or stopped. The fields grew
quiet as their footsteps faded into the night. There was only thing to do—
Dad walked back to the wreck. His head ached, but when he arrived and
saw the police milling around his friend's drowned body, he forgot all
about his concussion. He fell on his knees, remembering all the times
they'd swum together in this very water. When the police saw him, they
cuffed him and took him away, charging him with a major crime on his
home reservation.

Dad was tried as an adult, even though he was only sixteen, then
charged with manslaughter and given a tough sentence for the death of
one of his boyhood friends.

In 1885, fifty-six years before Dad's birth and following some of the blood-
iest Indian wars in history, Congress passed the Major Crimes Act, broad-
ening federal jurisdiction in Native territory and stripping Indigenous

communities of traditional methods of justice. The law gave the government the right to mete out punishments for manslaughter and other serious crimes without consulting tribes.

The American government's first major legal step toward stripping Native jurisdiction occurred in 1871. American settlers had long begrudged Native people their land, but apart from Andrew Jackson, who defied the Supreme Court to remove the Cherokee in 1832, the government had always stuck to the Founding Fathers' beliefs that tribes were autonomous nations. During the 1860s, however, dissidents in the House of Representatives had begun complaining that too much land was being given to Native people. They pushed to promote the dissolution of tribal land ownership through allotments via the Dawes Act and worked to legitimize government policies that forced cultural assimilation.

The Indian Appropriations Act of 1871, in which Congress declared that tribes were no longer independent nations, passed without a vote late in the congressional session—likely because many senators were still against it, fearing it would infringe on presidential authority and an honorable expansion policy. One prescient senator from Colorado named Eugene Casserly said it would be "the first step in a great scheme of spoliation, in which the Indians will be plundered, corporations and individuals enriched, and the American name dishonored in history."

The pushback from Native people was swift, with many tribes opting for rebellion over compliance in giving up land they had occupied for centuries. Timber and mineral rights were incentives for the government to act mercilessly—the Lakota, Cheyenne, and other tribes were massacred by U.S. soldiers in bloody wars—and they used the public's fear of Indian violence to chip away at Native rights, including traditional methods of justice.

The Major Crimes Act that played into Dad's harsh sentencing was put in place in 1885, after a Brûlé Lakota named Crow Dog murdered a fellow tribal leader, Spotted Tail, in South Dakota. Some historians say the killing took place because Spotted Tail was a traitor who sold white ranchers grazing rights on Native land. Spotted Tail had been named head chief by General Crook when Crow Dog and other tribal members were still fighting the U.S. government over their sacred mountains, Paha Sapa, or the Black Hills, where gold had been found. It's likely that Spotted Tail's assimilationist views irritated Crow Dog, a traditionalist who had stayed by Crazy Horse's side through every battle.

The Brûlé people handled Spotted Tail's death as they had for centuries. The elders convened a reconciliation meeting. They sent peacemakers to both families with orders to end the conflict. Both families respected Brûlé traditions. Crow Dog paid $600, eight horses, and one blanket, and Spotted Tail's family accepted. The conflict was over, but despite knowing the tribe had resolved the dispute, federal agents refused to let it go. They had been petitioning for criminal jurisdiction in Indian country for years. Congress had rejected their attempts more than once, leaving crimes between Natives on their own lands to be settled by tribal elders. The federal agents prevailed now. For the first time in history, a Native would be put on trial for the murder of another Native in Indian country.

Crow Dog arrived in court and listened to the prosecution argue that his lenient punishment was a sign of savagery. The opposition argued that peace had been restored, but justice hadn't been served. Civilization required revenge for Spotted Tail's death, even if other tribal members claimed that the killing had happened in self-defense. The court agreed and sentenced Crow Dog to death on the gallows.

Crow Dog's lawyers petitioned the U.S. Supreme Court for a writ of habeas corpus, asking that his jailer show proof of his authority. The Supreme Court ultimately gave Crow Dog a victory, but Congress reacted by creating the Major Crimes Act. The law made the feds the primary investigator of crimes on all reservations through much of Dad's childhood. Then in 1953, when Dad turned twelve years old, a second piece of legislation, Public Law 280, transferred criminal jurisdiction from the feds to six states without consulting our tribal leaders.

Our tribal council, of which my grandpa Ed Jr. was a member, believed close relations with state leaders would only mean a greater loss of control and decided to challenge PL 280 and state jurisdiction by fighting for a piece of river bottomland that had been exposed when the river changed course at the hands of a white farmer's dynamite. Grandpa and the other council members appointed their own judge, police chief, and thirty deputies to man tribal roadblocks with rifles, and delivered a statement asserting that the bottomlands belonged to the tribe, and that they would be evicting squatters. In response, Imperial County's district attorney said his department could take no action because, in his mind, the jurisdiction remained unclear. The state of California had not consented to the new arrangement, and their police force resented the additional responsibility, since it did not come with extra funding from the federal government. The blockade ended with the federal government offering to return the disputed territory—though in the end, they never did.

The bad blood between tribal cops and state police was still new when my sixteen-year-old father was arrested—and racial bias is far harsher when you are perceived as an enemy. When my father appeared in court, he was tried as an adult and, in 1958, sentenced to eighteen months in the California prison system, more than a year away from his family and friends.

Haunted by Dad's harsh sentencing, my grandpa Ed Jr. again sought to pressure an amendment to Public Law 280 in 1965 just before he died, at a congressional hearing on the Constitutional Rights of the American Indian. In his address, he asked that the tribe be given the right to consent to any legislation affecting members of the tribe in the future, since they had not been given that right when the law was passed. But Grandpa's political activism failed.

Dad was angry by the time he returned home from prison, and before long he was in trouble again. He was nineteen when some marines called him and his boys "a bunch of desert niggers." The men were in uniform and looked to have been day drinking. Dad said they were big but moved like they were trapped in quicksand when the boys moved toward them. Two of the marines ran to their motorcycles to escape. Dad took out a guy, left him on the ground, and got back in the car with his friends to give chase. His buddy swung a chain out the car window but failed to knock them off their bikes. When the cops picked him up, they were pissed that he'd put a military man in the hospital, and they gave him a good ass-kicking. Afterward, he sat in the county jail in El Centro, California, with plenty of time before his trial to dwell on what he'd done. This time he was a legal adult, and a repeat offender.

When the cops transported Dad to Chino State Prison after being sentenced the second time, they shackled his neck and ankles with chains. He told me being restrained with such force felt shocking, that it was the moment he knew things were getting serious, that he truly wasn't a kid anymore. He shuffled along in the line, knowing his shot at normal was over, his dreams of graduating with the class of 1960 gone.

After Chino, he went to San Quentin followed by Soledad. Young offenders were separated from the mainline prisoners during yard time at Soledad, but every time they walked the painted line the older inmates catcalled and threatened. Dad said the guards might have put the older inmates up to it, but he was still relieved when, finally, after two months, they sent him back to Chino.

All the teenagers Dad met in prison told the same story. They ran with older brothers and cousins because they wanted to belong. They couldn't let go of their anger. They didn't know how to walk away. Dad remembered Gene teaching him that they had to stick together, how other tribal members, rival clans, even the people in town would be afraid of them if they had each other's backs.

One day Dad was thrown into solitary for a fight. He'd always had a bad temper. Now he fought the guards when they stripped him down and cussed when they threw him in his cell. They said his bad behavior would find him in there even longer, and they kept him inside until he felt completely disorientated and distressed.

Once they let him out, he went to the bathroom, looked in the mirror, and told himself, You don't ever want to do this shit again.

I'd be a teenager by the time Dad told me this story. But even as a

preschooler witnessing his night terror for the first time, I sensed his grief
and felt his certainty that he'd done something terrible. The years of night
terrors marked the final throes of the long spiritual crisis my dad and many
Native men go through to defeat their anger and create an identity they
can live with in peace. If he dwelled on the wrongs committed against our
ancestors, he didn't talk about it. Playing the victim was stupid. Crybaby-
ing around was dangerous. "Poor me" was anathema to his work ethic and
his hope that America would prove to be a meritocracy for his kids.

The following morning, I stood outside and watched Joan and Lori march
into the chaparral with their fists full of dandelions. They were determined
to find where Rocco had been buried and kept blabbering on about the
snake, and poor Rocco, and how sad it was that he was gone. They praised
him now more than ever, and I saw that death had transformed him from
a scoundrel who bit our ankles and snatched our bologna sandwiches into
a saint.

   I'd intended to go with them. I even crossed the street to the neighbor's sticker patch to help pick the bouquets. It was a tiny yard with more
dandelions than grass, and I hurried to get the biggest ones. But the
bruise that bloomed on the back of my hand was ugly. The sun illuminated the spot where the neighbor's rock had struck, and the purple mark
made me ashamed.

   After they left, I went to knock on our neighbor's door, but he'd disappeared permanently into his house, just like Uncle Gene disappeared into
drinking and violence, and the way Dad disappeared into his long work
hours and silence. I tried to peek in our neighbor's window but saw only
my brown face staring back at me. I felt sad, remembering how he had lost
his only companion. Today, I feel guilty knowing how lonely it must have
been for him not to fit in, even on the reservation, even with other Indians.

In the fantasy version of this story, the one where my people were allowed
to keep their land, their culture, their traditional councils, and their methods of reconciliation, Dad didn't go to prison. Uncle Gene didn't fret

about traitors, and our neighbor wasn't deemed a "bad Indian" simply for marrying into the tribe and choosing to live on our land. In the dream reality I craved as a child, the desert was an oasis of peace.

As it happened, I would sit outside the neighbor's house after Rocco's death, watching for any sort of life. Days passed and the neighbor's carport started to stink because no one pulled his trash to the curb. The house's silence echoed with the sound of Rocco's bark, but it was the disappearance of the man more than the dog that haunted me.

"Maybe we never see him because he went home," Monica said. She occasionally came outside and caught me sitting on the curb, staring at the neighbor's empty house. Then she would crouch beside me on the ground and hold my hand, and in our fantasy, we'd imagine him pulling up a rocky drive to be greeted by family and friends.

It was hotter than usual that summer and the dust storms blew inside my head, pushing away that picture, bringing back the images that hurt: our neighbor crying, our father screaming like a cicada in the mesquite. The dust devils twisted my guts, making me wonder why our neighbor kicked Rocco when what he really needed was someone to love. I buried my face against the stinging sand, frustrated by my inability to understand, or cry, or communicate my fear. My eyes were dry, and the desert was dusty. The monsoons still hadn't come, and all I could do was wait.

THE PRICE IS RIGHT

(1973)

✠

The year I turned four, Mom was sometimes happy. Dad had found a side hustle, hauling mail late at night, and the six of us had moved into a new apartment in Yuma. We had always been nocturnal in summer when the days were so hot all anyone could do was curl up and sleep. But this year our midnights were especially fun, because Mom had gotten into the habit of playing her Temptations album on an old turntable to teach us how to do the twist.

"Bend your knees!" she'd shout from the couch, after twisting with us for a while. But we never danced long after she quit, because when Mom was smiling, everyone wanted to stay close to her. After she sat down, Lori and Joan would lounge on the armrests, while Monica and I wedged our bodies between the back of the love seat and the wall.

"Tell us a story," Joan would beg, knowing Mom's mood wouldn't last, and we had to take advantage of the positive vibe while we could. When things were good, Mom loved to talk almost as much as we kids liked to listen.

"You mean how I was a wallflower at my own wedding because your stupid uncles kept buying your father whiskey?"

When my parents left their wedding reception, Mom was sober. Dad, of course, drove. He sped toward Fourth Avenue, the main thoroughfare in Yuma, cutting into the opposite lane on corners, fishtailing with a groom's finesse. Mom grew scared. She hiked up her wedding dress, reached her long leg over his thigh, and stomped the brake with her high heel shoe.

The tires locked up. The car swung wide to the right, before spinning them all the way around to the left, showing them the surprised expressions of people in other cars. "It was like we were riding on the Tilt-A-Whirl at the Yuma County Fair," Mom said.

The car slammed into the side of a busy downtown bar. The Plymouth's front end was mangled. Steam poured out of the radiator. It was a Sunday afternoon in April 1963, and the day was still light. Afternoon drinkers came flowing out of the bar's smoky interior like rice throwers out of a cathedral in a haze of incense and prayer. Being the eldest of fifteen kids had made Mom conspicuous in this small town, and the bar was her father Juan's favorite, so some of the regulars and barflies realized she was a Herrera girl and wanted to know if she was okay.

Sirens started up in the distance. A couple of biker chicks helped Mom out of the car, and she stood with them on the sidewalk in front, staring at the damaged headlight and hood. In her hurry to get out, she'd caught the train of her wedding dress in the door, and it had ripped. When she saw the torn fabric, she started crying. She told us, "I could see your dad through the window of the car, with his forehead rested on the wheel, and I knew exactly what he was thinking."

Dad was from the Yuma Reservation, across the train tracks and river, and he was worried the town cops were going to book him again. But when the cops pulled up at the accident scene and looked at Mom—plopped on the curb in a puff of white satin, mascara running down her cheeks—they decided to be merciful and let Dad go. Mom said they felt sorry for her because she was a good local Catholic girl who'd married a crazy Indian.

When Dad walked in the front door and heard her telling us the story, he laughed and said she was wrong. He said the cops let him go, not because they pitied her, but because Mom was beautiful, and pretty people got away with shit. He pulled off his black boots and lifted his holey socks onto the coffee table. He put his arm around her and said getting away scot-free on their wedding day was the first sign Mom's charm would work magic in his life like a lucky rabbit's foot or a powerful tattoo.

He reminded Mom how romantic he'd been at their wedding, how he'd refused to let her sisters decorate the car with Do-It-Yourself flowers because the phony tissue paper looked too common for a woman of her caliber. Instead, he and his brothers had performed a top-secret midnight operation, sneaking into St. Thomas Indian Mission's garden on the reservation where they cut a bunch of roses to string over the roof of the car.

Mom groaned—"Don't brag about stealing from the church!"—but the two of them laughed, and Dad went in the kitchen to grab a snack.

Mom's protestations never fooled me. She loved the memory of the stolen roses, as well as Dad's claim that her beauty swayed the cops, but what made her light up especially was the way he called her his lucky charm.

This is how my parents twisted bad things around, seeing the appearances of events in fun house mirrors, stretching memories tall and pretty when they were really goofy and squat. They knew a story could be told in various ways, and this is how they chose to shape theirs—and how they would teach me to shape mine as well—by molding their wedding day car accident into their first blessing as a couple.

My parents met in 1962. At the age of twenty, Dad was home again from prison. Mom was a high school dropout. She was sick of sneaking into bars to beg chump change off her father, and figured once she had a job, she'd be free of changing diapers for her mother—a strict Catholic lady who hung sketches of a crucified Jesus on all her walls and believed birth control was a mortal sin.

High school, in mom's mind, was an obstacle to making money. Even when her English teacher stopped by the house to say that she had promise, she stuck to her guns and quit. She wanted to stroll into stores with a wad of cash and buy clothes that fit better than flour bag rags, so she took a job as a seamstress at Hicks-Ponder, a clothing manufacturer in downtown Yuma. Dad and his brother Gene had been hired to haul boxes on the loading dock for the same employer, and when they saw Mom walking to work one day, they turned around to give her a ride.

Mom said all the girls at Hicks-Ponder giggled when Dad swaggered into the sewing room. It was the era of James Dean, and his brooding manner was stylish. Mom's life was so incredibly small—confined to mass, school, and a bedroom shared with toddlers—she considered Dad worldly. By the time he introduced her to pizza at Brownie's Pit in Yuma, she was a goner.

She was stretching a cheese slice onto her plate when Dad first teased her. He said he felt like he was in a fairy tale. "Which one?" she asked, thinking she already knew. Both sides of her family—Herrera and Lopez—praised her porcelain beauty. The nuns called her Snow White when she walked her army of younger brothers—dwarflike—to school.

"The old lady who lived in the shoe," Dad said, loving it when she smacked him.

The same month my parents met, a riot broke out at Ole Miss because a Black air force veteran tried to go to class on the all-white campus. The country was changing, but the change was slow, and knowing the challenges of their generation, I've often imagined how scary it must have been for them to pass the newspaper vending machine as they left Brownie's Pit, the headlines blaring coverage about the evils of integration. Dad said they grew accustomed to catcalls from angry white men who followed them menacingly on the street, not liking the look of them together.

To the outside world, my parents didn't fit. Mom's complexion was too light for a guy like Dad, but beneath the surface they had more in common than it seemed. Both their parents made them speak English, rather than Spanish or Indian. Their fathers were sometimes negligent, yet their mothers refused to divorce. They came from musicians, had a ton of siblings, and knew what it meant to be poor. Mom told stories about the tin roof blowing off her childhood home one night to reveal the stars above her bed. Dad told stories about his grandfather's generation hiding a pair of community coveralls under the bridge near the river so the Quechan men who crossed into town could hide their nakedness and the fact that they didn't own clothes. Mom prized Dad's brawn, but only because she figured she had the beauty and brains to break him. Better a fiery and spirited workhorse than a perpetually laid-off one like her own father.

On their first date, they discovered they had New Mexico in common. Dad's mom came from Laguna Pueblo, a Keres-speaking village next to Acoma. Mom's parents came from Socorro, a town one hundred miles south of Laguna. This meant their families were both shaped by the trauma and violence inflicted by Juan de Oñate, a rich silver baron from Zacatecas, Mexico, who stumbled into present-day Socorro in 1598. With two priests and four hundred colonists—some of whom must have been Mom's Spanish forebears—Oñate was saved by a group of Piro Indians after nearly dying in the Jornada del Muerto desert. In a nod to their miraculous rescue, the colonists named the region's first Catholic mission Our Lady of Perpetual Help, though their gratitude wasn't showing when they went on to decimate the Piro Indians who saved them.

Like many European explorers, Juan de Oñate had arrived in Pueblo country under the guise of advancing Christianity. Of course, he'd really been looking to amass more wealth, and when he realized he'd discovered the biggest group of peaceful Indians north of Mexico City, he knew he'd hit the jackpot. He left the priests in charge of a silver mine he established in Socorro and rode into Pueblo country, where he mutilated the feet of all Acoma men over twenty-five, then enslaved all Acoma children over twelve, delivering them as gifts to Spanish colonists.

An era of rampant slavery began. The region's Spanish governors issued *vales*, documents that gave the bearer the right to seize whatever Indian kid they wanted. A single slave was worth more than a governor's annual salary, yet even the poorest colonists owned a bunch of them. By 1650, the Spanish colonists switched to enslaving Apache and Utes because it was getting uncomfortable to kidnap the kin of people who took care of their houses. By 1670, the slave trade had grown so large, the Catholic church launched an investigation into declining revenues. They were accustomed to receiving 10 percent on the colonists' husbandry, but

Spanish subjects had reduced their herds by swapping animals for Indian slaves.

The Pueblo Revolt—an uprising of various Pueblo tribes against their Spanish oppressors—happened in 1680. Priests were killed. Churches burned down. Spanish colonists fled. The town of Laguna Pueblo was created in the aftermath of the chaos, with refugees from Santo Domingo, Cochiti, and Zia Pueblos coming together. Twelve years later, the Spanish colonists returned to retake the colonial towns, and the slave trade continued for two more centuries.

During those two centuries, an Indigenous class of slave dealers emerged, as did an enslaved population known as *genízaros*: kidnapped Natives who spoke Spanish, took Spanish surnames, served in Spanish homes, and gave birth to "Spanish" kids. By the time the west was flooded with gold seekers, a third of New Mexicans were being held in bondage as *genízaros*. Luckily, the forty-niners were accompanied by officials like James Calhoun, Indian agent for the southwest territories, who came west right before the 1853 Gadsden Purchase, and wrote reports about witnessing hundreds of slaves captured, thereby convincing the government to pass the Peonage Act of 1876. Finally, thirteen years after the Emancipation Proclamation, Indian slaves were set free.

Once liberated, *genízaros* built houses outside Spanish communities, in the borderlands between town and desert. They created strongholds in Socorro, Abiquiú, Belén, and Chimayó. After centuries of slavery and rape—pretty girls on the auction block had always fetched the highest prices—many *genízaros* were afraid to acknowledge their Indigenous roots. They sought to forget their cultural losses, focusing instead on making a life beyond old debts. Mixed bloods were, after all, common. Even Juan de Oñate's wife belonged to the borderland. Her grandfather was the conquistador Hernán Cortés; her great-grandfather, Moctezuma II, the Aztec emperor whom Cortés defeated.

Garcia, Montoya, Herrera, Lopez—many Hispanic people in northern New Mexico think of themselves as *sangre pura* Spanish. Mom's parents wanted us to believe the same. They spoke as if their immigration from the Iberian Peninsula was recent. But even as Mom's family bragged about being descendants of the conquistadors, their features told a different story. Some of Mom's siblings were chocolate brown, some were porcelain white, but their melanin didn't stop their sharp noses and high cheekbones from providing a Rorschach test to strangers. On reservations across the Southwest, Native people often spoke to Mom in their Native tongue. They expected her to be a fluent descendant of their tribe despite her light complexion.

Mom carried the privilege of her light-skinned beauty—gawked at by strangers, catcalled by bigmouthed men, sweet-talked into a photo shoot by a reporter from the *Yuma Daily Sun*—never once confessing her family's *genízaro* past. Maybe she never knew. Maybe her mother Mary's quiet racism never riled her to the point of attack, and she never coerced a confession from her mother the way I did as an adult. Or maybe she understood internalized bigotry, lateral violence, and the dangers of our homeland better than I did and knew it was important to pass. Maybe during her childhood in Socorro she'd seen old women spit on for being brujas with their herbs and spells, and brown neighborhood men pistol-whipped for shouting "Viva Diaz!" Dad's family told stories about the region's violence. His paternal grand-uncle had been shot in the forehead after a card game, after which his great-grandfather had dreamed where to find his son's body and walked across the desert to bring him home. Mom's family hadn't the courage to talk about their history, pretended to be above it, and hightailed it out of Socorro, running from the ghosts of their past.

After leaving Socorro, their first stop was Kingman, Arizona, where Grandpa Juan worked on the Hoover Dam. Traumatized by the number of men crushed by rocks, drowned in the river, or killed by a fall into the canyon below, he looked farther afield. Yuma was Hollywood famous at the time, an elopement destination for the stars. Charlie Chaplin, Bette Davis, and John Barrymore were among the A-listers who got married there. Newlyweds Tom Daniels and Elinor Fair were arrested after returning to Los Angeles from Yuma, because the plane they'd rented for their wedding was paid for with a hot check. All the gossip mags said Yuma was a land of sunshine and crops. Maybe my grandparents imagined a place where the roof could blow off your house and you wouldn't freeze.

Against a backdrop of political change and the emergence of the Native and Latino Civil Rights Movements, my parents fell in love. They left Brownie's Pit after their first date, both hopeful and worried about the future, cradling all that they had in common. Even so, it's their differences I'm thinking of now: Dad never lived a day when he wasn't cracking open, his secrets wiggling toward the outer world in acts of humility and pain; his willingness to divulge information was so important for a child with a mother who held her silence for a lifetime.

The day before Joan and Lori's school started, I wept. I was a nervous child and hated the idea of my sisters climbing onto the school bus without me. I imagined them cookied-and-milked in their classes while Monica and I sat in our dirt backyard. By dinnertime, Mom had given up trying to console me. She'd grown impatient with my tears, which only confirmed my fears about her mercurial nature. According to her, I was acting silly. People had survived much worse.

After eating dinner, we went outside and sat on the porch. It was dark and Mom switched on the outdoor light, attracting an eclipse of moths over our heads. She said it was almost time for bed, and then started talking about Dad's time in welding school.

She said one night, about six months after they'd started dating, Dad had told her he was moving away to Phoenix and wanted her to come. The federal government had sent a BIA, or Bureau of Indian Affairs, officer to the Yuma reservation with information about a program designed to relocate young Natives to big cities. The program was called the Indian Relocation Act, or Public Law 959, and it had been around since 1956. At the time, Dad's father was the tribe's business manager and president of the Arizona Intertribal Council, and he was adamant that Dad and his siblings take advantage of the government's willingness to pay for them to go to trade school.

"I told him I couldn't move with him unless we got married," Mom said. "He wanted to go to Lute's Chapel where the Hollywood stars eloped, but I told him he was crazy. I had to get married by a priest."

Mom said she'd started crying because she didn't want to leave Yuma, but Dad said it was his chance to learn a skill and get a decent job. Mom looked at me directly, emphasizing that Dad wasn't scared to go to trade school. He was *excited* about learning. The BIA officer had played a promotional video that showed a Native chef in Chicago boiling lobsters, and a Native hairdresser in Los Angeles opening her own salon. His brothers had chosen to study heating and cooling, but Dad liked the idea of welding.

Dad said he wanted to stay out of trouble, but it was hard. No one made a living wage on his side of the river, and he was surrounded by rowdy brothers and clan wars on the reservation. Didn't she want to get ahead like everyone else?

"After our wedding, the program helped pay for our move to Phoenix," Mom said. "And the government worker there was so nice—just like your teachers will be nice."

They were met by a woman in high heels who took them to JCPenney in Phoenix, and Mom said the only funny thing about her was the way she exaggerated her enunciation like they couldn't understand her. "Here is where you buy things like u-ten-sils and tow-els."

The way Mom said it made us laugh. But I didn't like her story because it showed how she misunderstood me. I hadn't been crying because I was afraid of school. I was afraid of staying home with her when she grew depressed.

Mom explained that once Dad finished welding school, they moved back to Yuma because the fancy foreman job the BIA officials had promised failed to emerge, and Dad refused to stay off reservation for anything less. Mom didn't admit that Dad was still struggling to find a decent job in Phoenix, or that many employers in Arizona were prejudiced.

And there was more Mom didn't tell us: the feds wanted to move us to cities so they could dismantle our tribal governments, which would allow them to develop reservation land and make it taxable. The Relocation Act was part of the government's Termination Policy, designed to disappear Natives into mainstream America. A federal report associated with the law promoted blood quantum guidelines as a means of disappearing us even further. Relocation would encourage intermarriage with non-Natives, and once a kid was less than one-quarter Native, they would no longer be allowed to enroll in their tribes. If Blackness had historically been defined as "one drop" to entrap more slaves, *not* identifying people as Native meant more land for the taking. By the end of the century, the number of Native people living in cities rose by 64 percent, with many of them homeless.

By and large, the Relocation Program failed to spin reservation lives from rural poverty to city gold, but it succeeded in isolating many people from their families and culture. Yet Mom talked about the program like it was a positive experience.

"Anyway, it was good that Dad didn't find a job in Phoenix," Mom said, "because right after we returned home to Yuma, I got pregnant with Joan."

My oldest sister, Joan, arrived smack dab on my parents' second wedding anniversary. To celebrate their second anniversary, Mom and Dad had caught a ride to the Yuma County Fair with one of my uncles. Mom's due date wasn't for another couple of weeks but having to walk six miles to get home after her skirt-chasing brother ditched them on the midway, she went into labor, and that's how Joan came into the world. Mom said the doctor was surprised when he saw that Joan was born with a tooth "just like a little vampire."

My parents' second try produced another sister. She was given my mother's name, Lorraine (though everyone I knew called Mom "Rainy"), because she was fair-skinned and took after the Herrera side of the family. In all her baby photos, Lori's head looks flat and square as Frankenstein's monster. A lump grew on Lori's chest when she was just a tiny thing, and the doctor had to remove the cyst to be sure she wasn't dying.

Their third child, the sibling born right before me, was a boy who they named Edmond after my father. And he did die. An old Yuma Indian nurse everyone called Bulldog was on duty the night he was born. Bulldog got her nickname for the way she guarded the babies like they were her own. She wouldn't even trust Mom to hold him because the delivery had been so long and hard. Mom said she begged, but Bulldog only agreed to hold my brother up in the doorway for a quick glimpse before taking him away to the nursery.

Dad and his six brothers had gone out to celebrate the birth, so no one was in the nursery to see how pale the new baby was getting. Hours later, he chirped a small cry and Bulldog went over. Taking a closer look, she realized not even Mom was that fair and called the doctor. The old Indian Hospital wasn't equipped for surgery, and my brother was sent to Yuma Regional Medical Center in town. When Mom heard, she grew hysterical, and they had to sedate her.

My brother had a congenital abnormality, a hole in his diaphragm, no separation between his heart and his guts, meaning his internal organs were all jumbled up. When the doctor came out of surgery to tell Dad it was over, his son had died, Dad went into the parking lot and punched a dent in the car door. A few days later, Dad walked to the car again. He opened the dented door with a white cast over his broken fist, Mom at his side with bandaged breasts, funeral finished, and the little casket buried.

They stopped delivering babies at the Indian Hospital after my brother died, and this is how I came to be the first member of my family born off the reservation. I was named Deborah, after the girl on the Little Debbie logo because when I was born, my family was living behind the Dolly Madison Cakes and Wonder Bread Store and my two older sisters loved the discounted cupcakes they sold. My parents had been hoping for another boy, but when they realized the name they'd selected couldn't be given to a daughter, the button-nose, blue-eyed girl on the cupcake box popped into Joan's head. She said I looked *exactly* like the little Debbie girl at the Dolly Madison Store. I obviously didn't, but she was persuasive with her argument, and that is how I got my name.

Still wanting a boy, they tried again not long after I was born, and Monica arrived thirteen months later. That was when Dad told Mom if she had another girl-baby he'd throw her out the window.

Here, Mom stopped telling the story to give a wry chuckle that my sisters seemed to interpret as "your father is so clever with his jokes," but which I always read as "one of you will *definitely* get thrown out the window and it will probably be Deedee because she's the one who never behaves." Deedee was the nickname they gave me as a kid.

"Time for bed," Mom said, slapping her thigh for emphasis. "You two want to be at your best for school."

We went into our bedroom, said our night prayers, and climbed into bed. When she left, I stared at the ceiling, thinking about how lonely it would be without Lori and Joan to take care of me. Being the eldest of fifteen kids had been a *job*, and Mom was exhausted. She was always kicking us outside during the hottest part of the day when there was nothing to do but sit in the shade and stare at the Imperial Sand Dunes. The desert's expanse felt limitless, and it invited my imagination, but there was pain in the isolation as well, because I wanted more attention from my mother.

Sometimes her impatience with us was founded. Once, we forgot our crayons in Dad's car, a green Chevy Nova with hiked-up wheels, and panicked when the crayons melted on the floorboard in a puddle of black goo. We sopped it up with our hands, and not knowing where to wipe them, spread the mess across the roof of the interior. Our fingers left little bird-hopping prints that faded to asterisks over time, petroglyphs preserving the memory of us as kids.

But sometimes she cried for no apparent reason at all. Then she would go into her bedroom and lock herself inside.

I lay awake listening to my sister's soft snores. Unable to sleep, I finally got up and sat by the window where I could hear the wind blowing. I imagined the Imperial Sand Dunes shifting into unrecognizable forms overnight. It felt terrifying how fast the world could morph into something new. Mom's mood was always changing, and now Lori and Joan were leaving me for school.

By October, Mom had grown short-tempered again. I didn't realize it at the time, but she had been patient with Dad's long work hours and multiple jobs, delivering mail, fixing his brothers' cars, working at the gas station, and sanitation department, because she thought it was temporary. There was a job fair at the civic center that month, and she'd been counting on Dad finally getting the welding position that paid what the BIA officials said he deserved. When he failed to get any offers, Mom told him maybe he should widen his search to include other cities and towns. Dad said, "And leave Yuma?"

A storm was brewing between my parents about mobility and money. Even as a preschooler, I could feel it like I felt the shift in humidity before it thundered and rained.

After the failure at the job fair, whenever Dad left for work, Mom's world grew darker. She was depressed, and with Joan and Lori gone, it meant Monica and I were always sitting outside waiting for Dad to come home and eat lunch. The hum of the swamp cooler, the sight of an over-flowing laundry basket in the hall, the sound of *The Price Is Right* playing on the television behind her closed door—I remember how overwhelmed she was, and how scary it felt to climb through the rip in the locked screen door to get inside after being sent outside, because when she caught me, she got mad.

As a result, my strongest memories from that year feature Dad in sweaty clothes and work boots, carrying his metal lunch box at his side. He'd al-ways yelled, "Hey, you little brownies!" after he parked the car. The soles of our feet were tough as leather, and we'd race to meet him without putting on our shoes. Dad never seemed to mind that we were sweaty and dirty. His clothes were a mess too.

He would grab us in turn and toss us in the air like rag dolls before setting us back on the ground. His arms were strong from lifting and low-ering trash cans on his morning rounds, from throwing smelly garbage into the back of the truck before returning the can to the homeowner's drive for the hundredth time.

Dad's arms were deep brown and muscly with small, do-it-yourself tattoos on his fist and left forearm. He had a home-pricked *J* for "Jackson" just above his left thumb and a four-direction symbol pricked in the skin alongside it. A variety of wounds on his left arm included a long scar where he burned off the name of an old girlfriend before marrying Mom. He squeezed my rib cage too hard as he grabbed me, then threw me up in the air. I remember looking down into his eyes as I flew upward, knowing he wouldn't drop me.

One day Dad came home excited and laughing. He said he was with his partner when they both spotted a flash of green paper rolling around in the rotting apple cores, hot dog packages, banana peels, flattened cereal boxes, and potato skins they had just finished throwing into the press at the back of the truck. The compactor was coming down fast, ready to mash everything to bits, and Dad's partner froze but not Dad. He darted in, arm stretching for Ben Franklin's face. Nearly catching the pinch, he grabbed the hundred-dollar bill and came home waving it in Mom's face.

Mom convinced Dad to call in sick to his second job at the mechanic's garage. His nightshift job was part-time, only four nights a week, and this way he'd have the rest of the day off. Mom told us we were going to the Silver Spur Drive-In Theater, but only if we could behave. She gave us our bath while Dad took his nap, and we put on sundresses and shoes and sat stock-still in the living room, waiting for the celebration.

When Dad woke up it was still too early for the Silver Spur, but he and Mom said we should walk to the corner store to buy snacks for the movie.

"You guys can pick anything you want," Dad said.

He and Mom held hands and teased each other as we went down the street. My sisters and I skipped along behind them. I don't remember what I bought, but I remember Joan was carrying Dad's bottle of wine on the walk home, and I remember she dropped it. There was the pop of cracking glass, and the wine ran off the sidewalk into the gutter, a red artery of near enjoyment mingling with cigarette butts and an old Tastee-Freez cup.

Monica started crying. Her shoes and socks were splashed with burgundy, and Mom thought she might have been cut. Dad started yelling at Joan, his angry words flocking around like rabid birds wanting to peck her eyes out. I got in trouble too, for bending over in the gutter and reaching for the glass like I could grab all the pieces and put the holiday back together.

There were slapped thighs and tearstained cheeks. Dad wanted to go back and buy another. Mom said "money doesn't grow on trees," and their argument grew louder once we got home. Somehow, their shouting turned into a fight about Dad's failed attempt to find a better job, and when Mom started blaming him about money, he got so mad he slapped a bright red mark on her cheek. Our family was clumsy at the American Dream, fumbling even when it came to celebrating small wins.

We never made it to the Silver Spur, and the next day Mom was sad. Dad said we should take care of her, but she wouldn't talk to us. Even when she came outside with her laundry basket on the way to hang sheets, she didn't want anyone's consolation or love. She wanted to watch *The Price Is Right* in the bedroom by herself. She wanted to dream of winning a clothes dryer. She wanted to sit on the bed cracking sunflower seeds and spitting shells into a plastic cup.

Indigenous belief systems hold that a child doesn't become human until she learns who she is through her mother's culture and lineage. This meant Dad always pushed us to identify with Mom. He always said, "Your mother is your best friend," but holding on to Mom was like holding on to water. She had Catholicism but no quinceañera, American holidays but no Pueblo feast days. She had only the game show host, Bob Barker, and even him she wouldn't share. With mute ancestors and a loud TV, she found happiness in a future no one else could see.

Joan's ninth birthday, and Mom and Dad's eleventh anniversary, rolled around in April, and the family had a party at Grandma Mary's house. There were lawn chairs in the yard, and people sitting on the hoods of cars. Three of Mom's brothers married Indian girls from the reservation; another three married Mexican girls who were sisters.

It was a sleepy neighborhood, and we kids were playing kick the can in the street when Mom's brother Andy came flying down the road in a friend's jalopy. In an instant, the adults were dragging us out of the street and into the yard. Andy waved out as he went by, then did some donuts at the end of the block.

We stood there staring as he returned. The car came to a screeching halt in front of the house, one tire landing on the sidewalk near my cousin's empty stroller. He stumbled out of the car—drunk and laughing about how he'd almost killed us—and didn't even have time to say hi before Dad came out of nowhere toward him. He broke a ceramic flowerpot on Andy's shoulder, driving him across the hood of the car. They toppled on the ground in a cloud of dust, their arms and legs flailing. The sound of Dad's fist on Andy's jaw made a sickening pop, and Andy took a bite out of Dad's hand. There was blood and grunting and then Mom got a disgusted look on her face and told me and my sisters to get in the car.

We were pulling away when Dad saw us and disentangled himself from the fight. Mom had to slow down to make a left turn at the corner, and I could see Dad through the back window, gaining. He leaped onto the trunk, and I slid down onto the floorboards to get away from his scary face. His arms were outstretched as he tried to hold on, and his right hand was bleeding where Andy had bit him. Mom hit the gas and Dad finally let go, rolling off the car as we sped away.

When we got home, Mom went to her bedroom and locked the door. I could hear people shouting dollar amounts as she turned on the TV. She cranked up the volume, and soon my knuckles grew sore from knocking. Joan said to leave her alone, that she would get mad if she saw me sitting in the hallway. She brought me a baby bottle of apple juice and said she, Lori, and Monica were going outside to play. I was the child born when Mom and Dad were still mourning another baby, so I was the child who didn't get nursed, the child who was, instead, regularly quieted with a bottle of cola or juice or Kool-Aid. The sugar had been bad for my two front teeth, and they ended up rotting.

My sisters left, but I sat on the floor, still longing for attention from Mom. I hated her game show, and I hated Bob Barker. Dad didn't like him either. He once told me that Bob Barker was Lakota and that Uncle Gene called him an apple—red on the outside but white on the inside—because all he seemed to care about was money. Lots of guys in Dad's generation thought poverty was an expression of Indianness itself, and they tried to out-Indian each other by resisting regular jobs. Like many kids on our reservation, I bought into their attitudes, believing resistance showed loyalty, and poverty was a necessary claim. I laughed at their jokes about reservation trash and commodity cheese, and couldn't see how my older relatives, like Dad's mom, ironed their clothes, beaded their regalia, and scrubbed at their hard water stains with the pride of people who know right living and effort is possible even for those who are poor.

Mom took her ancestral loss and turned it into a desire for more— more from Dad, more from us, more from the life I was happy enough living. Dad took his ancestral loss and sprinkled it with nostalgia, his reactions historically complex and hard to understand. After the Gadsen Purchase, Native people were considered enemies of capitalism and placed on reservations by the United States government. Men like Merrill E. Gates, the president of Amherst College and the Friends of the Indian, reviled communal sharing, saying Indians needed to be more "intelligently selfish." But the more you try to suppress a culture's belief systems, the stronger they hang on.

I was falling asleep in the hallway when Mom finally answered the door. Her game show was over, and her eyes looked all puffy. She asked where my sisters were. "They went outside to play," I told her.

She took me by the hand, and we went to find them. As we walked she told me she was sorry Dad and Uncle Andy got in a fight, and I heard her voice break when she said it.

I asked if she thought Dad was okay.

"Your father is always okay," she said.

Mom was confident in her wanting. I guess that's *why* she was Dad's lucky charm. When he felt pressured and confused by tribal loyalties— and tentative about his desire to be an individual—she let him know it was okay. To her, the future meant sacrifice, whether we liked it or not. Dad was the worker with the tools, while Mom was the one who studied the price tags and knew exactly what it would cost to get us out.

NOT YOUR INDIAN OUTLAW

(1974)

✤

It was well past sunrise when my sisters and I bounced out of bed. Joan and Lori were on fall break, so we slept late, and Joan fed us Twinkies for breakfast. Afterward, we played a game of sardines. The rules were easy—three of us packed into one hiding place while the fourth closed her eyes and sang "I'm a Little Teapot" ten times in a row before hunting.

Joan, Monica, and I burrowed a hole in the garage sale fodder under the bed, a mess of toys, clothes, hated dolls, and plastic junk no one had missed in months. We could hear Lori's footsteps running down the hall to check the coat closet. Soon she would enter the bedroom and creep toward our hiding place, electrifying the air like a serial killer escaped from prison.

We had just started stifling laughs, Monica's toes crawling around my ankles, when the phone rang. We heard Lori say, "Hello?" then she called for our mother, Rainy. It was Dad's boss from his afternoon job at the gas station.

"What do you mean he didn't show up for work?" Mom asked.

We crawled out from our hiding place and found Mom stretching the phone cord to the window. She was wearing a gigantic YUMA HIGH CRIMINALS jersey, her hair still in curlers, saying she didn't know where he was.

She shooed us outside, but we left the front door ajar so we could listen as she dialed Dad's nine siblings, one after the next:

"Mona? This is Rainy. Do you know if Mick has seen Looney?"

"Johnny? Rainy here. Has Looney stopped by?"

"Bill. Listen. I need to find Looney."

After calling everyone in Dad's family, we sat and worried for a while until Mom called one of her brothers, who drove us around to have a look at all of Dad's old haunts—pool halls and poker bars, baseball diamonds, Senator Wash, and Swastika Dam—but there was no sign of Dad anywhere. The sun was setting by the time Mom told her brother to take the shortcut out to Uncle Gene's house, kicking up dust as we snaked through the squatters' trailer park on the other side of the reservation. We passed a string of mobile homes in various stages of demise: empty with boarded-up windows, still occupied with broken glass and beat-up cars.

Suddenly a toddler appeared out of nowhere, his diaper flashing white in the headlights. At the sound of squealing tires, the little guy changed course, veering back in the direction of his yard. Shaking, Mom rolled down the window and yelled at his older siblings, "It's after dark! Your brother is going to get hit by a car." His sister flipped us off.

Welcome to the world of Indian reservations, where nearly everyone knows someone who has gone missing. We arrived at Uncle Gene's house, and Mom banged on the door. Uncle Gene's Arapaho wife, Aunt Babe, answered. She said, no, she hadn't seen Looney.

It was getting late, and we had nowhere else to look, so we went home. While my sisters ran to our bedroom, prepared to pick up where we'd left off with our game, I lingered by the door near the kitchen to listen as Mom called up some of the same family members she'd spoken to earlier, recruiting them to go out and look for Dad the next day. "He never skips work," Mom said. "It's not like him to disappear."

That night I stayed up late, listening for the sound of Dad's car, but I wasn't exactly sick with worry. Dad was tough as titanium in my eyes, which made it hard to believe that anything bad could happen to him. Plus, Joan said Mom was overreacting. It'd been an unusual day, but eventually the adrenaline waned, my eyes grew heavy, and I fell asleep.

After checking around the reservation the following morning, Dad's brothers stopped by to see if Mom had any news. They brought their wives and kids, and we crowded into the living room, everyone talking at the top of our lungs. It was the Case of the Disappearing Dad, a bunch of Indian detectives looking for their man. The noise was reaching decibels high enough to crack glass when Mom lost it.

"That's it. I can hardly hear myself think," she yelled. "All of you kids get outside and don't come back in until I say so!" She had woken up in a foul mood, and now she seemed seconds away from bruising our behinds along with our cousins'.

It was a Friday morning, but because of fall break, the neighborhood was teeming with kids, and having a small gang with us was actually a nice reprieve from the worry. My sister Lori yelled, "Let's go!" and Joan said we should take our cousins to see where we'd hidden Dad's belt. She liked watching war movies with Dad, and she called the belt "enemy contraband." We'd named a secret spot in the chaparral our "army fort." It was a place we knew he'd never look to find it.

"Follow us to our headquarters," Joan said, leading everyone toward Dad's belt in the army fort.

We'd only recently made enemies with the Underwear Boy down the street, a kid whose mother let him wear boxers as shorts. He didn't have any siblings and wasn't allowed to celebrate birthdays, Halloween, Christmas, or any other holiday because he and his parents were Jehovah's Witnesses.

The Underwear Boy was fast, and he was always challenging us to races. We fashioned finish lines at different distances in the hope of a better outcome. Joan would yell "Go!" then yank at his underwear to give Lori, our fastest runner, a head start, but even with him hiking up his pants he would leave Lori in the dust.

A week before Dad disappeared, the Underwear Boy had gotten us into trouble with our parents. The argument started when some of Mom's family came over for a barbecue. There wasn't enough room for everyone inside, so we partied in the yard, where the Underwear Boy watched us from across the street.

The next day, he told us parties were wicked, and our family was going to hell. Joan and Lori knocked him off his feet and dragged him through the sand. When he got up, the skin on his back looked like he'd been dipped in a vat of melted redbrick crayons. He ran home screaming bloody murder.

His mother came banging on the door a short time later. She was pissed and yelling, and her voice woke Dad. He had driven his delivery route all night, and his eyes were bloodshot and disoriented when he came rushing into the living room. Later, he told us he thought one of us had fallen into the canal or been bitten by a scorpion. When he discovered what the commotion was really about, he was pissed and snapped us each on the thigh with his belt.

Joan said the whooping wasn't fair. She said we *had* to beat the kid up for calling our family wicked. She was so mad at Dad that she called a meeting and vowed vengeance. She sent Lori on a reconnaissance mission that made my heart do a hot-footed skip. Sneaking into our parents' bedroom after they fell asleep, Lori stole the belt off Dad's jeans.

The following day, when Dad left for his trash rounds, we took the belt out to our backyard headquarters, a circle of dirt surrounded by a ring of chaparral. The belt's leather was surprisingly soft. Lori snapped it in the air, and she and Joan laughed at the way Monica and I flinched. Then Joan coiled Dad's belt like a snake and hid it in one of Mom's old slippers at the base of the largest bush.

That night we heard Dad asking Mom if she'd seen his belt. She said it was probably on a pair of his dirty jeans. After the laundry was done the next day, he came into the living room where we were reading Little Bear picture books. He called to Mom, folding clothes down the hall—"Did you find my belt yet?"—and then stood watching for our reaction.

"I told you," she yelled back. "It disappeared."

He stood staring at us after she replied, then walked down the hall shaking his head. Joan huddled us close and made us promise that we would never ever narc or give in. Even if we were tortured, we wouldn't tell. Dad went to work with his shirt hanging out of his Dickies all week long, trying to hide the rope he wore in place of his belt.

I thought it was a neat trick at the time. But now Dad was lost, and the longer he was missing, the more my anxiety rose. Telling the Underwear Boy story to our cousins when we showed them the belt, I saw their expressions. The older ones looked worried about Dad, and even after Joan explained that he'd given us a whooping, their faces didn't change. In fact, showing them the belt sucked all the fun out of their visit. Dad was out there, somewhere, wearing a rope around his waist, and his disappearance was starting to feel scary.

I wandered back over to the front yard to spy on the adults who had come out of the apartment. Mom was cajoling Dad's brothers, saying one of them needed to drive her down to the police station and corroborate her story while she reported Dad missing.

Uncle Gene snorted. "The cops ain't going to help."

"They'd probably kick the shit out of him for fun," Uncle Johnny added.

Mom said if a cop hurt Dad, the cop would get fired, and Dad's brothers laughed. "Stop it," Mom said, spotting me in the yard. "There are kids around."

Mom thought the cops would treat Dad right because in her mind cops, priests, and presidents were *always* heroes. She'd memorized the Catholic Church's list of venial and mortal sins as a girl and still took them to heart. To her, the world was built on timeless values and the simplest definitions, and any man, woman, or child who was having trouble could get out of it simply by believing in Jesus and repenting of their evil ways.

But there was another reason Mom thought the cops would help Dad. He'd signed on with them for some contractual labor that year. It happened when his boss at the trash dump—who knew he was always looking for more money—gave him a hot tip. He said he'd stopped by city hall to talk to the sanitation department supervisor, and while he was there, he'd seen a job listing for a welder. It was a temporary, independent contractor arrangement like the kind Dad sometimes did for irrigation systems and farmers, and Dad got excited and swung by the station to pick up an application the same day.

The cops hired Dad on the spot, and he spent all his free time, on weekends and after work, altering the cruisers in their fleet. It was his job to install metal screens that would separate the front and back seats in their cop cars. The crazy thing was Uncle Gene had been picked up by the cops a couple of months before Dad went missing, and when the arresting officer threw Gene into the back of the car and went inside to the bathroom, Gene had kicked the metal screen Dad had welded into place repeatedly until it popped off on one side and he could escape out the front door. When Uncle Gene told Dad what he had done, Dad was a little bruised that his brother had found it so easy to break one of his welds, but in the end they'd laughed about the way Dad had inadvertently helped with Gene's escape.

"Just wait one more night before you call the cops," Dad's brothers told Mom. "We'll take a drive up north and have a talk with some old friends."

Mom shook her head like she couldn't believe what they were saying, but by the time my aunts had called for their kids to go home she agreed to wait another day. My cousins came running, and we dawdled around their cars as they piled inside. The sun was sinking low in the sky, yet there was still no sign of Dad.

As soon as the adults started saying goodbye, my worries came in hard and fast. I heard my cousin Tater tell my other cousin Peanut, "We went by Pipa Market and my dad asked Trixie if she saw Uncle Looney. She said maybe he finally got what was coming."

Peanut smacked Tater on the back of his head even before he could finish telling his stupid story. "She better keep her fat mouth shut," Peanut whispered.

After everyone left, Mom refused to get up from her lawn chair in front of the house. At first we sat with her, staring at the oil puddles left behind by the dusty cars. The street felt like a graveyard following the day's buzz and excitement. When we told her we were hungry she said to leave her alone. Normally, Dad would be home on a Saturday night and Mom would be sashaying around the kitchen, frying sunny-side-up eggs to put on top of his enchiladas. Instead, that night, we ate our fingernails, chewing them down to the quick.

The next morning, Dad's mom and sister arrived as soon as the sun rose. Apparently, the Yuma police had pulled the body of an Indian guy out of the river overnight. He was described as a fit thirty-year-old with tattoos. Grandma Esther's eyes were full of sadness when she told Mom, but Aunt Vi said it was just a precaution. She said that they had been asked to head over to the morgue and confirm that it wasn't Dad.

I knew none of this at the time. When I woke up, I could have sworn I heard Mom's voice in the kitchen, but when I stumbled down the hall, I found Aunt Vi instead. She said Mom and Grandma Esther had gone on an errand. I asked if they were looking for Dad, and she said not to worry about him. He was like Wile E. Coyote, even when there was trouble, he always got away.

She said when they were little Dad always wanted to skip school to hang out with the hoboes on the railroad tracks. The hoboes would be sitting there, waiting to catch the Zipper to Los Angeles, and he'd want to sit with them and share his beans because all they had was dog food. Vi and the rest of their siblings would hurry to school and leave him behind, thinking he was going to get in trouble. Instead, he'd show up late and tell the nuns he gave his lunch away. They would feel sorry for him and give him free food from the cafeteria.

"We'd be sitting there eating cold beans while your dad ate a hot plate," Aunt Vi said. "Even when he was disobedient, he always ended up on top!"

Aunt Vi attracted me, my sisters, and cousins like bees to a hive, and only in part because of her stories. She had a moon-eyed smile and a funny sense of humor. Dad liked to tease her because she'd never been married, but it didn't seem to bother her, and I liked the way she laughed it off and punched him in the arm when he called her an old maid. In her late thirties, she dressed stylishly, wore a beehive on top of her head with long hair in back, and was easily the prettiest of Dad's three sisters.

"Want some eggs?" Aunt Vi asked, digging in a paper sack on the counter.

I spread my jacks on the ground. They were small metal stars, and Mom hated them because they stabbed the soles of her feet when she carried her laundry basket through the living room on her return from the clothesline. My stomach grumbled, and I nodded yes.

"Looney was always a rascal," Aunt Vi said, once she started cracking and stirring the eggs. "This one time I made hot chocolate for him and our brothers and he threw a fit because he said I poured him less as a punishment, which I probably did, after the stunt he pulled with Mom's good sheet."

I knew the stunt she referred to. When he was seven years old, Dad took Grandma Esther's best sheet to a big cottonwood, where he climbed to the highest limb, and tried to parachute. Everyone said he was lucky it got tangled in the branches, or he would've broken his neck.

"He got so mad about the hot chocolate—geez, he was crazy—he started tackling everyone, and we had to lock him outside. He was banging on the door, but then all of a sudden it got real quiet. I got nervous, wondering what he was up to. I half expected him to pop out of the stovepipe."

She laughed. This was the best part of Aunt Vi's stories, the way she laughed, like she was hearing them for the first time.

"I was just about to go outside and check on him when the blade of Dad's axe came through the front door. Your father was so scrawny, it took him a minute to pull it out, and I was screaming—'Looney, you're going to be in so much trouble'—but thwack! He kept right on chopping. The boys got so scared they went running out the back door."

"Weren't you afraid?" I asked her.

She nodded. "But I stood my ground until I could see his face through the hole he made."

Joan came into the kitchen, rubbing her sleepy eyes. "You telling her about the time Dad chopped down the front door and drank all the hot chocolate? When's he getting home, anyway?"

Aunt Vi ignored her. "When he stuck his arm through to unlock the door, that's when I ran too. The boys had climbed an old salt cedar and I hid in some brush nearby. After a while I saw Looney come out the back door. I yelled that Mom was going to kill him and he took off running toward Picacho Peak. We went inside, and all the cups were empty, that little turd."

Aunt Vi's laughing was infectious. Soon Joan, Lori, Monica, and I were shoveling eggs into our mouths, listening to her stories. With these childhood escapades, she convinced us not to worry. Dad was indeed the consummate trickster, the rascal who always escaped.

She said one time a Presbyterian minister came out to the Yuma Reservation on a do-good mission, recruiting young boys for a trip to a Cub Scout camp in the San Diego Mountains. Grandma Esther had jumped at the chance to send the boys away for a week. They were wary, but she convinced them it was going to be fun, not stiff and regimented as they imagined. There would be archery and canoe competitions.

"I remember piling them into the car with their knapsacks," she said. "The minister told Mom he would try not to brag when his Indian boys paddled the competition into a tidal wave. Instead, they went around in circles in their canoes and got so mad they started a fight with the winners."

By the second day, Dad was curious about the lighter fluid the minister used to start his campfire. He watched to see where it was stored, and when the minister went to the outhouse, he got the container out of the box and crept up to the fire ring where he squeezed a steady stream into the flames.

"Bad idea," Aunt Vi said.

The flame sped up the arc of fluid toward the canister. Not wanting to get burned, Dad quickly launched it over his shoulder. It landed square on the minister's tent, setting it on fire, and collapsing it in seconds.

"Poor Mom, she was so disappointed when they came home early."
Aunt Vi laughed so hard, she dabbed at her tears with a kitchen towel so
she wouldn't smear her mascara.

She shook her head no when we begged for another story but finally
relented saying, "Only one more." Then she told us about a time when
she and Grandma Esther caught Dad downtown, shooting pool with
some rough men when he was only nine. She said they were walking by
the pool hall window when they saw his bony elbow drawing back for a
shot.

She had just started describing how Grandma Esther had gone in to
drag him out when all of a sudden we heard his voice chime in from the
living room. "I left money on the table that day!"

"Dad!" we yelled. Lori knocked over a chair trying to get to him. Joan
stepped on jacks. Monica and I hopped around him like rabbits.

"What's all this?" He detached us from his legs, hitched up his beltless
waist, and then he put up his dukes to shadowbox. "I was only gone for a
couple of nights!"

It was like Lazarus had risen from the dead.

We quickly learned that Grandma Mary and Mom had freed Dad that
morning. His luck struck when they were trying to park at city hall, in a
car lot that was adjacent to both the jail and the morgue. Suddenly, Mom
spotted Dad in a chain gang of other prisoners, heading over to the court-
house for his arraignment.

At twenty-eight, Dad didn't wear baggy chinos, carry a knife, or drag
race anymore. He hustled between jobs instead: working as a garbage man
in the morning, a mechanic in the afternoon, and a mail delivery guy at
night. He drove four and a half hours to Barstow, California, four times
a week, where he dropped off his delivery and turned back, pulling into
Yuma as the desert glowed pink with the sunrise.

He was doing his best to be a family man, but trouble came to find him
no matter how hard he worked, usually in a combination of siblings and
cops. On this particular occasion, his trouble arrived via Mom's teenage

brother Andy, who had lumbered into the dump while Dad was washing his truck. It was an hour before the end of Dad's shift; an hour and a half before he was due to clock in at his afternoon job.

"Come on, Looney, let me borrow your car," Uncle Andy had begged. He was late and needed the Nova to pick up a friend.

Dad tossed him the keys, saying, "You better be back in time for me to get to my afternoon shift at the gas station."

Uncle Andy showed up twenty minutes behind schedule. Dad came over to the driver's seat. Andy said, "You ride shotgun," but Dad could smell his breath and saw a brown paper sack in the shape of a whiskey bottle nestled between Andy's legs. He pulled open the door and told Andy to get out and let him drive.

Sliding into the car, Dad told Andy he could walk home from the mechanic's garage because there wasn't time to drop him off. He hated being late for work and took off toward his second job, but he made it less than a mile before a cop pulled him over.

The cop who stopped him made them get out of the car for no apparent reason. When he smelled Andy's breath, he asked to see his identification. Seeing that Andy was only eighteen, he accused Dad of buying alcohol for a minor. Dad said no, he'd loaned Andy his car. He demonstrated his dirty shirt and beltless Dickies and said the cop could call his boss at the sanitation department to verify his story. Hell, they could both go there together, since it was only a few blocks away.

By then Dad was sitting on the curb with handcuffs on and the cop smacked him on the head for talking back. He zipped his lips quick, knowing how common it was for Native guys like him to be beaten, or even killed, by the police.

It wasn't the first time Dad had been profiled by a police officer for something he didn't do. The first time he was fifteen years old, driving home from town with his little brother Dino and Dino's friend, both of whom were too young to have driver's licenses. They were in the friend's father's car when a cop hit his sirens and started coming up on them fast. Dad's fear of policemen kicked in, and he stepped on the gas. Even knowing he hadn't done anything wrong, his panic overpowered his common sense, and he fled.

Unknown to Dad, the make and model of the car he was driving matched the description of a bank robber's vehicle. In a scene that feels like it came straight out of the Wild West, the cops fired their guns at Dad and his twelve-year-old brother and thirteen-year-old friend, riddling the trunk with bullets.

Once across the river, Dad drove into a row of cantaloupes, jumped out of the car, and ran into a neighboring field of corn for cover. He was a fast runner, high on adrenaline, and he didn't think twice about abandoning his little brother Dino and the friend. The cops were shocked when they opened the door and found two middle schoolers crouched on the floorboards of a shot-up car. Dad's father was called to pick up Dino and his friend, and he told everyone it was the first time he had ever been apologized to by a white cop. He said even the superior officers at the station seemed terrified. The following day, a bunch of adults went over to Dino's friend's house to check out the bullet holes in the car, dad said.

Another time, before Mom and Dad had any kids and were living in Phoenix for him to attend ABC Welding School, the FBI stopped Dad as he was walking to the bus station to get to his training program. When he showed them his baloney sandwich in his metal lunch box and told them he was just cutting through the alley to make some time, they asked for his address and said they'd be checking up on him. Later that week they stopped by and knocked on the door to ask Mom if it was true that he lived there.

Gangster. Outlaw. Juvenile delinquent. As a teenager, Dad had always been a "criminal," even in those years when he wasn't in prison, and he'd managed to attend high school. The moniker was embedded in the city of Yuma's history: when its high school burned to the ground, the town leaders decided to house the new campus in the old Yuma Territorial Prison until a new one could be built. From 1910 to 1913, students sat in cells to learn, and during this period, the Yuma High School football team beat Phoenix Union High School in a game they were expected to lose. Widely regarded as the underdogs, they were accused of stealing the game like a bunch of criminals. The coaches and team decided to celebrate the insult, and the school approved "The Criminal" as its mascot in 1917.

Everyone I knew wore YUMA CRIMINAL jerseys like the one Mom wore for her pajamas, and everyone had a cousin or brother, father or uncle, who had done time. No wonder a lot of town folk held an unconscious belief that tough-looking kids around town were dangerous—they were literally labeled. Dad forbade Mom from wearing her jersey in public, even though she liked it. He said it was already too easy to buy into the roles that the man doled out. In his mind, dressing up like cops and robbers was a stupid game to play.

When Dad got pulled over that day in 1974, Uncle Andy had begged the cops to let Dad go to his afternoon job at the gas station. He swore that he had found a bum to buy him booze in exchange for a couple of swigs. But the cop told him to sit down and shut up until backup arrived. They stuck Dad in the patrol car and took him down to the station. Dad tried to call Mom and Grandma Esther, only to find their phone lines ringing or busy.

When Mom and Grandma Esther spotted Dad headed to the court-house alive rather than dead at the morgue, Mom had initially been ecstatic. But by the time they got home she was furious. She followed Dad in from the car, not even pausing to hold the door open for Grandma Esther, then stomped down the hall to the bathroom and slammed the door.

We could hear her banging things around, but she didn't come out and start yelling until after Grandma Esther and Aunt Vi went home. She said she was going to kill her brother Andy, and then she yelled about the cop refusing to call Dad's boss to verify that he had been at work instead of out drinking with her brother. When Dad shrugged his shoulders and told her to calm down, she turned her anger on him.

"I'm so sick of you putting everyone else first," she said. She ran through the old litany about their brothers, his stupid loyalties, how she was sick of him lending money to his family and hers. "Why did you trust Andy with the Nova?" she asked angrily. "You know how he drinks!"

Dad leaned back on the couch and sighed. "At least you aren't planning my funeral," he said.

With one jab, he deflated her like a balloon. She sat next to him and took his face in her hands. She kissed him sweetly and started crying. When she calmed down, she said, "You probably lost your job at the gas station. We're never going to get out of this dump!"

"Is that what you're worried about?" Dad asked. He picked up the phone. His boss said no problem, he could come straight to work if he wanted.

Mom did the sign of the cross and went in the kitchen to throw some hot dogs in boiling water. She filled a thermos with milk and started packing Dad's metal lunch box. My sisters and I circled around, happy that their fight was over.

Dad went to take a shower and change his clothes. He called for Joan, and she skipped down the hall to see what he wanted. A few minutes later, they walked through the kitchen, her face bright red, and went out the back door together. She had promised that she would never tell where it was hidden, but when they came back inside, she had two shiny quarters, and he had his belt.

Dad's eyes shone as he snaked the leather through his pant loops. He tugged at our braids and winked, saying, "You guys have got guts," then kissed Mom on the cheek and headed off to change brakes at the station.

THE PHANTOM LIMB

(1975)

✠

Mom set up our artificial Christmas tree earlier than usual that year. "The Little Drummer Boy" played on the television set, and my sisters dragged chairs in from the kitchen to hang ornaments. Tinsel from the branches drooped to the floor, but without Dad telling stories it wasn't fun. I missed hearing him talk about how his grandfather used to play "Silent Night" on his trumpet from St. Thomas Indian Mission's belfry tower. Or how, if we went to Laguna Pueblo, where Grandma Esther grew up, we'd see the Eagle clan do their Eagle dance after midnight mass.

Dad had drifted away from us that winter, unmoored by his mother's refusal to accept chemo for her cancer. When he was home, he paced like a caged lion, his eyes all swollen and red. He even started going out with his brothers to drink and cause trouble again, which he hadn't done for years. When I slept on the couch, I'd see him come in late at night—slurring his words, bruised by fighting—and watch Mom scold him through clenched teeth about how his brothers were "bad influences" and he was supposed to "stick to the plan."

Before Grandma Esther got sick, Dad had been traveling a lot, taking welding tests all over the Southwest with the hope of finding work that paid better than the assortment of odd jobs he was currently holding down. Ten years had passed since he'd attended welding school with the Indian Relocation Program, and he'd finally conceded that we would have to cast a wider net—beyond the Yuma region—if he wanted to put his education to good use.

But when he found out about Grandma Esther's illness, Dad's job search slowed down. He told Mom he couldn't be going out of state all the time—that there was no way he could abandon his mother when she had cancer.

If Mom was upset, her disappointment was nothing compared to Grandma Esther's. We drove out to the reservation, turned onto Jackson Road, and entered her house with the sagging eaves and turquoise trim. We sat on her old brown couches and watched her grow angry as Dad told her he wasn't sure he could leave. All her life, she said, she'd seen good people waste away on the reservation. Yuma was the land that time forgot, and if Dad was going to get what he wanted, he had to go out and fight for it.

"Don't you dare give up!" she said. "Get your harvest. Don't die in the rocks."

Her reaction came as something of a surprise to me and my sisters. But it shouldn't have.

The idea that Native migration started with federal relocation policies was always a myth. Grandma's people at Laguna were proactive about leaving home for employment long before the government stepped in. In 1880, the Atlantic and Pacific Railroad entered New Mexico to build a locomotive line from Albuquerque to the California border. Laguna lay right on the path, and when the people spotted railroad workers approaching the pueblo without permission, they called a meeting. After centuries of surviving—slave traders, squatters, and drought—the tribe was determined to face this new challenge by making demands.

Jimmy Hiuwec, secretary of the tribal council, led a group out to meet with the railroad crews and tell them that they didn't have permission to build tracks across Laguna land. Blocking the railroad extension earned the tribe a visit from A&P executives who negotiated an agreement. In exchange for allowing the railroad to pass through, A&P would forever employ Laguna people if they wished to work, so long as the Laguna governor granted the workers his approval.

The relationship was tested after World War I, when white labor unions decided to strike in Richmond, California, and the new railroad owners, Atchison, Topeka, and Santa Fe, called upon the governor of Laguna to send men to California. Still unable to fulfill the numbers, the governor called on Acoma Pueblo to send men too. Laguna railroad communities sprouted in Winslow, Arizona; Gallup, New Mexico; Barstow and Richmond, California. They grew so big, the people there gained official status as Laguna Colonies from their homeland. They held feast days, deer dinners, traditional dances, meetings in their Native language, and elections for colony governors in conjunction with the tribe as a way of preserving their cultural traditions.

Aside from believing it was possible to leave the reservation while still maintaining one's culture, there were other reasons Grandma Esther supported relocation: she feared that the violence and alcoholism on the reservation would get Dad and his brothers killed. And like her husband, my grandpa Ed, she believed that the feds would eventually terminate tribal governments, dismantle reservations, eliminate the Bureau of Indian Affairs, and settle land claims in favor of corporations. In her view, what wasn't taken from Natives now would be taken later. The future held wars over water, according to tribal prophecies, and this meant her kids had to be prepared.

All of Dad's siblings had been advised by their parents to attend training with the Relocation Program, though each of them had ended up returning home to look for jobs. Most of them found work in Yuma— but Dad's training as a high-pressure welder was specialized and hadn't paid off yet. He had been working as a city employee, gas station guy, and mail hauler for nearly a decade now, and could only find easy welding jobs (like the one he had done for the cops). He was frustrated, but he continued to say that being with Grandma as her health waned—and as he tried to convince her to receive cancer treatments—was more important than work.

Grandma Esther had a different idea. Among her people, death was considered natural and necessary, an honoring of new lives waiting to be born. Relinquishing your place in the material world would ensure that there would be room for another. Dad's father, Grandpa Ed, had died several years before, and Grandma said he was ready to take her home. The sicker she became, the more she suffered the intermittent twitch of his presence, like the pain of a phantom limb. He visited her in waking dreams—boiling water at the stove, rubbing her feet at the foot of the bed. So, despite being told that she had a rare type of cancer that had spread through her sinus cavity, Grandma had decided to refuse surgery. She wouldn't accept treatment of any kind, refusing even painkillers. Instead, she ordered Dad to forget about her illness and stick to his plan. Even as she prepared to die, she insisted he move on.

The canyons of Grandma Esther's homeland in New Mexico contain Pueblo healing plants—alongside toxic waste. The village where she grew up, Paguate in Laguna Pueblo, sits along the Grants mineral belt, where a Navajo man named Patricio Martinez was hired by the railroad and the Anaconda Mining Company as a uranium scout in the late 1940s. He discovered high-grade ore in 1950, after which a yellowcake mining boom took place in western New Mexico that lasted thirty years and led to 60 percent of U.S. uranium being taken from the region.

In 1952, Anaconda Mining Company opened the Jackpile Mine ten miles south of our family's village. There, three open-pit uranium mines, some of the largest in the world, remained operable until 1982—yet when Grandma contracted cancer, no one talked about the possibility of environmental causes for her illness. No one mentioned the poison that bled into the mountain runoff, gathering in the groundwater of wells in the region, affecting Navajo, Hopi, and Laguna Pueblo alike. No one noted how roads and houses were sometimes built with ore and rock from the mines. And no one brought up the atomic bomb that Grandma Esther saw tested when she was at Laguna Pueblo in 1945.

The story she told about her life leading up to the war and the atomic bomb went like this: she and Grandpa Ed, who was half-Quechan (Yuma) and half–Shoshone Paiute, met at an Indian boarding school in Phoenix. Soon after, they married, and the agreement between Grandma's people and the railroad led Grandpa to take a job at the Laguna Colony in Winslow, Arizona. By the late 1930s, hundreds of Laguna people were living there in boxcars converted into housing. The jobsite was close enough to Laguna that families from the colony could go home for holidays, feast days, and weekends. It was a happy time. Many of Grandma's relatives lived at the colony, and babies born there were affectionately called "boxcar babies."

Dad wasn't due to be born until January 1942, but when Grandma Esther heard that Pearl Harbor had been attacked, she went into premature labor. Trying to stave off his early arrival, she hurried home to the boxcar colony, where a medicine woman from Acoma gave her brown foot tea to stop the contractions. It looked like she might be in the clear, but in the following days, the men in her railroad camp began pounding war drums. They polished rifles and put on war paint, and Grandpa Ed came home expressing a desire to enlist. Many Natives across the United States had already signed up for the war—even before Pearl Harbor—but now the desire to fight had hit home, and her labor pains started again.

If anyone understood the dangers of fascism—and the fight between notions of racial superiority versus racial equality—it was Native Americans. My grandparents and great-grandparents understood the war as a life-or-death struggle for the very freedoms they had been hoping to attain for many generations: the right to local democracy, cultural independence, and Native religions. Their generation had something to prove, and across America, Natives stood in line at draft offices ready to fight against the totalitarian idea of a super race, even though they would serve for a country that treated them as "lesser" at home.

Speaking to the U.S. vice president, leaders of the Iroquois Nation said, "We represent the oldest, though smallest, democracy in the world today. . . . It is the unanimous sentiment among the Indian people that the atrocities of the Axis nations are violently repulsive to all sense of righteousness of our people." The Navajo Nation's council pledged their loyalty "to the system which recognizes minority rights." Pueblo dancers went on tour to raise money for war bonds. The Blackfeet contributed to the nation's food supply by building "victory gardens." One million dollars was donated to the government by the Quapaw Nation. In every region, Natives bought war bonds at a rate equal to that of other Americans, even though they were considerably poorer.

Animated by colonial oppression—and aflame with a desire to protect Mother Earth and their ancestral homelands—my grandfather and his relatives wanted to assert their manhood in a new era, to protect their families with the same courage their grandfathers had during the Indian wars. By the time Pearl Harbor was attacked, one out of ten Indian men had already enlisted. In 1942, the *Saturday Evening Post* asserted that the United States wouldn't have needed the draft "if all volunteered like Indians."

Hitler declared war against the United States on December 11, 1941, the same day my father was born. When his head crowned, Grandma took a deep breath and pushed. Dad was tiny and colicky, and his voice combined with the war cries and drums echoing off the sandstone cliffs outside the boxcar. Grandma named him after her father-in-law, Edmond Senior, and her husband, Edmond Junior, whose sense of peace was to be erupted by the war. Like many Natives, Dad's father wanted to fight. He wanted to continue the strong warrior traditions of his tribe and prove his courage in battle.

But he had a wife and a new baby, in addition to four older children, and Grandma had an argument about why he should stay. Unlike other Native people who were achingly poor after the Great Depression, he had a job. While most Quechan (Yuma) people were making less than one hundred dollars a year, he had the railroad and was able to feed his family. He didn't need to go to war. She took the side of the Hopi, Ute, and Tohono O'odham people, who resisted the draft, refusing to trust the U.S. government.

In the end, Grandma talked Grandpa out of going to war, though over time she was forced to concede that the victory was mixed. Grandpa Ed's brother Joe headed off to fight for the navy, and Grandma saw her husband listening to radio broadcasts about his brother's squadron claiming victory at the Battle of the Midway. Grandpa's unmarried sisters joined the war effort as plate welders in machine shops, and suddenly the work he was doing felt like the work of women.

Staying home to provide for his wife and kids made Grandpa Ed feel like a coward. Military men had uniforms, swagger, and pride, and their tales of valor wounded Grandpa's self-worth, destabilizing all he had created for his family. He grew depressed, started tipping the bottle, and ultimately left his job with the railroad. His father was tribal president of the Quechan (Yuma) Nation, and he thought he would take his family home and join his father in making a difference in politics. Instead, the move back to his reservation would end in tragedy.

Everyone feuded during the holidays that year when Grandma was sick, and I couldn't understand why our aunts thought Grandma's nixing of medicine was praiseworthy when Dad and his brothers didn't. The men insisted Grandma Esther was too young to die. She had always been strong, and she wasn't even sixty. What if the doctors could buy her time? Didn't she want to live long enough to see her grandbabies grow? They kept talking until Aunt Vi exploded. She said to leave Grandma Esther alone, that she wasn't going to change her mind. She had a right to her own body, even if they thought it was selfish.

Selfish. That was certainly not a word Dad had ever used, or heard used, to describe Grandma Esther. All his life, Grandma Esther had aimed to please. She was sacrificial to a fault, long-suffering when it came to her sons' violence and drinking. She had been patient with Grandpa during the war, stepping up when he failed, encouraging him back on his feet. Dad said no matter how late he and his brothers stumbled home, they would find her mumbling prayers over a candle of our Lady of Guadalupe for their safety. She even stuck to the company line about Indian boarding school, letting Dad's brother Gene go when he was curious about it, claiming the years she had spent there weren't that bad.

Dad's response to her cancer frightened me. He rattled and raged, but Grandma was unfaltering: her death wasn't up for discussion. And in this way, she used her final days as a shaping force, saying Dad should honor her memory by finding a better job and moving us on.

All week long, a dust storm blew. And then Christmas arrived with packages, ribbons, and bows. Dad welded a seesaw-like rocker with a metal base and recycled wood for two facing seats. He gave me a music box that played "Raindrops Keep Fallin' on My Head" and said it was a gift from Grandma Esther, who was too sick to celebrate or cook red chile stew.

I played the song repeatedly, but the storms didn't pass. We couldn't play outside without the sand stinging our legs, and after a while the toys grew dull. We hid the blood-sucking Raggedy Ann doll we received from Grandma Mary in the closet. We played in the living room, using record sheaths as stepping-stones across imaginary worlds of hot sand. I longed for clear skies and a visit to Grandma Esther's, but instead Aunt Vi came over on New Year's and sat with Dad. She said Grandma's health was declining. She said she was still lucid and moving around, but that Grandpa Ed's traditions were showing up in her. She had started to have fever dreams, or what the Quechan (Yuma) people called the *icama*.

Grandpa's people had once shaped their entire culture using the *icama*. To become a leader, a man or woman had to relay their *icama* dream journeys to a group of medicine people who verified that it was real. In this way, the leaders of the Quechan (Yuma) literally dreamed their way into their civic positions. But it wasn't only for civic responsibility that one sought the *icama*. All types of goals could be manifested with the power found in the world of dreams.

In the 1970s, it was still common for the Quechan people to believe in the old tradition of dreaming. Even Grandma, who held a mixture of Christian and tribal practices, knew that our existence was layered, and the world revealed itself in more than the physical dimension. The universe was seen and unseen—just as I'd heard my parents recite when they said the Nicene Creed at St. Thomas Mission. Grandma was being graced with power. The *icama* was giving her strength. She was talking to Grandpa on the other side and gaining the courage to die.

When Aunt Vi left, I asked Dad about the *icama*, and he told me there were lots of things that science couldn't explain. Take the geoglyphs in the desert just north of our reservation, he said. There were four-legged and two-legged figures etched into the earth there, big as football fields and visible only from up high. Archaeologists said they had been built by our ancestors in a time that none of us remembered, and they had been rediscovered by some white guy who saw them from his plane. How did our people know how to cut those shapes into the rocks at such large scale? Had they hovered over the earth in their dream bodies, bringing designs from their sleep into their working day?

If Mom had been home, she would have said it was normal for people to see their dead family members when they were preparing to die. Mom talked about angels in heaven, and while she and Dad had different stories, I loved listening to them talk about the unseen world. To me, it was an animating force that gave life to the rocks and trees. I could smell it in the rain and feel it in the sun on my skin. It was a pleasure, I remember thinking as a child, to feel it humming in the simplest things. In this way, I never doubted. My only question was why Grandma longed to meet Grandpa again. I'd never met him, but the stories they told me about him always scared me.

After Dad's father brought Grandma Esther and the family back to Yuma from the Laguna Colony, he grew short-tempered and brutish. World War II was a sad time for tribal leaders, and as Grandpa Ed witnessed his father's woes as head of the Quechan tribal council, he followed him into a world of frustration and pain.

Most homes on the Yuma reservation were single rooms with dried mud for floors. Cooking was done outdoors with irrigation water. Faulty canals had ruined the reservation's farmland, yet the people were surrounded and mocked by money-making orange groves owned by white farmers. Dad's father, grandfather, and other tribal members gradually lost the fantasy of governmental support, and many of them turned to drinking. People died in the brush after imbibing in the "squeeze," an alcoholic drink created by straining Sterno, or canned heat.

Just before the end of the war, Dad's father got into a drinking accident with his friends. His buddy was driving across the bridge beneath Indian Hill when he sideswiped a flatbed truck carrying steel rods. Grandpa's right arm was resting on the windowsill and the rods chopped his elbow off. He walked up to the Indian Hospital, a tenth of a mile away, but passed out before he could tell the doctors he had the elbow in his pocket.

As a fullback on the Phoenix Indian boarding school football team, Grandpa Ed had been named MVP several seasons in a row. Dad said he and his brothers used to hang off his biceps when he flexed, but when he came home from the hospital, he was skinny and scary with one empty sleeve. After his wound healed, he sank even deeper into his drinking, and Dad and his family had to move into an army tent behind my great-grandparents' house.

Grandpa Ed didn't work for two years after that, and sometimes the family only had one can of soup, so Grandma would pretend like she had already eaten. To make matters worse, Dad's grandfather was embarrassed by his son's disability, especially when strangers asked if he'd lost his arm in the war. Great-grandpa was proud of his newspaper job and his position as a leader of the tribe. He was one of the only tribal members with a car, and he harassed my grandfather for being depressed about his disability, instigating arguments that resulted in brawls.

It happened every time they had a few drinks together, usually in the middle of the night. Dad said he and his siblings would wake up to the clamor and run out into the fields with Grandma to hide. They slept between rows of cantaloupe until things got quiet and she said it was safe to go back to their tent. But if Grandma was patient with her husband's bad years, she drew the line when it came to her kids. When he came home drunk and went after her son, she stepped in the way. And after he hit her once, and Uncle Gene had to knock him out with an iron skillet, she called her uncle to take them home to New Mexico.

My great-grandpa Ed Sr. had been elected to lead our tribe in 1938, during a time of great hope and change. Roosevelt had appointed a new commissioner of the Bureau of Indian Affairs in 1933, a man named John Collier, who respected Native people and had longstanding ties with the northern Pueblos via the Taos Art Colony. Collier criticized the government's assimilation policies. He thought preserving Native culture would benefit all Americans, who had much to learn from the socialist tendencies he had witnessed in Taos. He wanted Indian boarding schools to protect Native ways and advocated for an end to prohibitions on our languages and religions. He saw that Native culture depended on a relationship with the earth and halted the Dawes allotment system, which had reduced tribal land holdings.

Nazi propagandists had also been painting the U.S. government as fascist in international radio campaigns, using centuries of colonial oppression to argue the moral high ground. Germany sent spies to Indian country to document the poverty and try to learn Native languages being used in the war. Collier and Roosevelt worried that the propaganda would destabilize Latin America with its thirty million Indians—and Mexican oil and Brazilian rubber were at stake.

My great-grandfather was overjoyed when Collier persuaded Congress to pass the Indian Reorganization Act or the "Indian New Deal" in 1934. The IRA pledged medical care, welfare, and agricultural assistance on reservations. It established a revolving credit fund from which Natives could borrow capital for economic ventures. Most importantly, the act aimed to return surplus land and help tribes buy new acreage.

Collier insisted on mutual consent. Each tribe had to accept or reject the IRA deal by popular vote. U.S. policymakers had always denied the legitimacy of Indian land tenure, as it involved communal ownership, and Flora Seymour, a BIA official, attacked the IRA as "the most extreme gesture yet made by the administration in this country toward a Communistic experiment." William Pelley, a presidential candidate in 1936, said Roosevelt was instilling "communism among Indian tribes." His organization, the Silver Shirts of American Christian Patriots, formed an alliance with the American Indian Federation, a group formed by Joseph Bruner, a Muscogee Native, and Alice Lee Jemison, from the Seneca Nation, to fight the Indian New Deal, abolish the BIA, and unseat Collier. Bruner and Jemison testified before the House Committee saying Collier's IRA was trying to make Natives "un-American."

In addition to being tribal president, my great-grandfather was a lino-typist at the *Yuma Daily Sun*. He was always reading the news, and in the lead-up to World War II, he grew bitter with the IRA debate. He couldn't believe Natives were campaigning against it, that Bruner and Jemison were sowing doubt on reservations. It took him years to convince the Quechan to vote yes on the IRA, after which the people disagreed about whether to make the tribe's government a corporation, which they needed to do if they wanted to borrow government funds.

Ed and his council secretary, Patrick Miguel, were finally able to complete a proposal for a tribal farm in 1940. They presented the report to Collier's office, but by then the anti-IRA sentiment had grown in Congress. Representative Melville Kelly of Pennsylvania said a reservation was "a prison pen," and Wisconsin Representative John Schaefer called for an end to Indian "concentration camps." To stop investments in Native America, politicians were mocking our sacred homelands.

My great-grandfather never did get a response to his proposal, and like many Native activists, he wasn't fooled by the respite that the IRA deal provided and suspected that assimilation policies would return in full after the war. Even as Natives served in battle, Collier was starting to reverse his pledge. A million acres of tribal land were taken during the war, for bomb testing, aerial gun ranges, and Japanese internment camps. The Laguna and other tribes fought Collier and the BIA, saying they didn't want their land used for violent purposes, but they wouldn't listen. The Lakota lost 300,000 acres during the war, yet when they won a multimillion-dollar treaty violation claim against the government, they generously responded: "When our country is at war, we feel payment of these claims should be deferred. If it will help the country, a few more years of waiting will be accepted."

It was the summer of 1945, and Grandma Esther hadn't been back to Laguna in almost two years. If she had known that the government was gearing up for their first test of the atomic bomb south of town in the Jornada del Muerto desert, she might have gone home to Yuma sooner than planned.

It was the early morning of July 16, and no one knew what the bright light, loud blast, and rattling windows meant. Even before sunrise, the people of Laguna came outside to look at the sky and ask what had happened. Grandma Esther stood in the road, brushing the fallen ash off her clothes, never guessing it was radioactive. That afternoon it rained, but the government didn't warn them to beware of the water in their cisterns.

The Trinity test was seen by people in Las Cruces, Santa Fe, Albuquerque, and El Paso. A government agency called the Office of Censorship—"Loose lips sink ships"—tried to keep the news local. The government lied, claiming it was an accidental explosion at a munitions dump in Alamogordo, New Mexico. But the fabricated tale didn't stop the speculation. The *Socorro Chieftain* reported that the flash was so bright, even a blind university student being driven to Albuquerque by her brother-in-law saw it.

As in all scenes of tremendous violence, people at the scene of the blast reported incongruous beauty in its aftermath. Brigadier General Farrell described the explosion as "magnificent, stupendous, and terrifying." He wrote, "It lighted every peak, crevasse, and ridge of the nearby mountain range with a clarity and beauty that cannot be described but must be seen to be imagined. It was that beauty the great poets dream about but describe most poorly and inadequately."

William Laurence of the *New York Times* jotted down a description of the VIPs in the moments after the detonation, "The little groups that hitherto had stood rooted to the earth like desert plants broke into dance, the rhythm of primitive man dancing at one of his fire festivals at the coming of Spring."

How oddly fitting that the journalist on the scene likened the scientists to earliest man. In the wake of America's biggest scientific experiment, one that would end World War II, Laurence saw our common trait: the joy of men who have learned to use fire, the joy of men who know they will win their battle, the joy of men receiving a sign that their god is stronger than their enemy's. Craters blasted in the desert, craters now growing in the soft tissue of Grandma Esther's face.

It was February, only two months after the doctor's official diagnosis, when Grandma Esther's untreated sinus cancer became visible, and she started wearing bandages on her face. They stretched across her cheeks and joined at the bridge of her nose. Joan said Grandma smelled like a mummy. She laughed nervously when she said it, but it didn't strike me as funny. I used to love to go to Grandma Esther's house for visits. Now I was frightened by her weeping cheeks.

One day, Mom needed a babysitter and Aunt Vi said we could come over if we stayed quiet. Grandma was sleeping on the couch when we entered, and it felt weird not to run over, climb on her lap, and feel the soft pads of her hands on my face. All my life she'd been the embodiment of warmth, but now she was out of reach. Mom told us to behave and left, and then Aunt Vi scooped Grandma up like a child and took her to the bedroom to rest. Like many Laguna people, Grandma had always been small, but now she was even smaller. She trilled in pain as Aunt Vi carried her down the hall, the sound lonely and sad as a canary in the coal mine.

A few minutes later, Father Paul showed up from St. Thomas Indian Mission. He had brought communion for Grandma and said he knew she wanted to give her confession. Aunt Vi offered him coffee, but he was in a hurry, and so they went down the hall to wake her. While they were gone, Grandma's Shoshone-Paiute mother-in-law—my great-granny Ethel— came to the door. Like Grandma Esther, she was a foreigner on the Yuma reservation. Unlike Grandma Esther, she was an ironclad traditionalist who lectured about the old ways: herbs, seasonal practices, prayers in her Native tongue. When she saw me on the couch, she got right to the point: "You're cute until you smile." She was all plain talk and hard truths, and it stung. But Dad said to get used to her because the mean ones lived forever.

Granny Ethel disliked Father Paul, and she gave him the stink eye when he came out of the bedroom. When he left, she went down the hall with her sage and sweetgrass. First, she would smoke the sage out an open window to dispel pain from the air, then she would close the windows and call good spirits to Grandma's bedside by burning the sweetgrass.

As soon as Great-Granny went into Grandma's room, Aunt Vi picked up the phone to call Uncle Gene's wife, Babe. They lived next door, and when Aunt Babe walked over, the two of them raised their eyebrows at Ethel's sickbed visits. They sat at the table and whispered about how Grandma and Granny's husbands had remained father-son rivals after the war, thinking maybe it contributed to the way Ethel and Esther had never gotten along. Or maybe their being at odds had been inevitable, what with Granny Ethel's disdain for the papacy set against Grandma Esther's unabashed love for the Mission Church of San José near her childhood home in Laguna.

All my life, I'd seen how much Grandma Esther loved the rituals of the mass. She used to describe the animal skins adorning the altar and the sanctuary ceiling painted with Laguna symbols back at her childhood church in a voice that revealed the same reverence she used to describe the beauty of her homeland: the smell of pine resin, the sound of turtle shells clacking on the legs of dancers, the taste of the season's first sweet corn.

I sat near the kitchen, listening to Aunt Babe and Aunt Vi try to make sense of Grandma Esther. Aunt Vi told Aunt Babe about Grandma's recent *icama* experience, and Aunt Babe asked about her decision to adopt Quechan funerary practices, even though Father Paul didn't like it. The *keruk* had been prohibited by the pope until 1963 because the ceremony ended in cremation. Father Paul still frowned on the practice, reminding Grandma Esther that European pagans had also burned their bodies as a rejection of the Christian afterlife.

Aunt Vi hated that Grandma Esther was being scolded by the priest for engaging with her husband's Quechan traditions in tandem with her last rites. She remembered how Grandma's people had been persecuted by white Protestants who came to Laguna in the early railroad days. A couple of them took Laguna wives, after which they rose to power as governors and destroyed the pueblo's kivas, calling the fusion of Laguna ceremony and Catholicism witchcraft.

If Grandma Esther had been afraid of the Kachina dancers as a little

girl, it was because of generations of religious persecution. Yet now Aunt
Vi was realizing Grandma Esther had held a deep appreciation for the old
ways all along, and she said it wasn't Granny Ethel's job to call Grandma's
fear of Christian judgment drivel, just as it wasn't the priest's job to govern
her beliefs. It was her business how she went about living and dying. Aunt
Vi sounded upset, and when I thought about Grandma being afraid of the
Kachina dancers as a child, I felt a deep sadness myself.

In April, Aunt Vi called and said Grandma wouldn't survive the night, and
we should come home right away. We were at an All-Indian baseball tour-
nament on the Mohave reservation in Parker, Arizona, about two hours
north of Yuma. Mom had been trying to stop Dad from playing all day
because his thumb was broken. But after his team fell into the loser's
bracket, he took off his dressing and splint, jammed his baseball mitt on,
and headed out to catch behind the plate. Mom said he was an idiot. Dad
looked down at me, attached like a leech to his leg, and said she was a
worrywart; it was a well-padded glove.

Uncle Mick pitched, Dad caught, and their brothers and cousins
played the field. They'd battled their way back into the running, and the
championship game was just about to start when we got the call. The
other team refused to take the trophy, gracefully handing it over when
they learned the reason the Yuma boys were forfeiting. Dad peeled off
his DUST DEVILS jersey and shook hands with the other team. He and his
brothers gathered prayer promises and loaded the cars with their gear.

Mom, my sisters, and I piled into Dad's Nova, and we hit the highway for Grandma Esther's. The road between Parker and Yuma goes up
and down over hills. Dad was driving fast, and the rise and fall made my
stomach tickle. Our car was in the lead, and I got up on my knees and
turned around backward in my seat, watching my uncles, their wives, and
children in the caravan of cars following us back to our reservation.

We slowed down when we left pavement for dirt and turned onto
Jackson Road. We got out of the car and entered Grandma's house, her
big-bulb Christmas lights still hanging after the holidays. We sat on the

rug and crammed onto the couch with our cousins, while our mothers huddled around the coffeepot in the kitchen, and our fathers went back to the bedroom to talk to Aunt Vi and see what was happening. I felt like a baby bird in a crowded nest with my cousins, all of us chirping at once, our voices a confused chorus of "whys."

Grandma Esther's sister, Helen, had caught the bus to Yuma from Laguna the week before. She was a nurse's assistant, and when Dad came back to the living room, he said she was at Grandma Esther's side with a hand to the artery in her upper thigh so she could tell us when she was gone. He squeezed Monica's thigh to demonstrate where the pulse should be. His eyes were red, but he seemed resolute. He said Aunt Vi was rubbing ice on Grandma's lips, and that she was still aware, but barely talking. His Aunt Helen said that she would stop swallowing soon, then her throat would start making a rattling noise when she breathed.

Dad seemed comforted by Aunt Helen's presence. He told us that she was translating for Aunt Vi. This was good news because Aunt Vi had told us that the sicker Grandma had grown that month, the more she'd started speaking Keres—the language of her childhood, and a language no one else in the family could understand. At first, she only reverted to the language when she was feverish and falling asleep, but then she started speaking it even while awake.

I felt sad for Grandma. She was far away from the family she had grown up with in Laguna, yet I could feel her ties to that era becoming stronger. She was fading into an older world, one the rest of us couldn't remember or see. *Shipap* was the only Keres word Aunt Vi said she could understand. Aunt Helen described it as a world of white, the place where babies came from, and where people traveled to when they died. It was cared for by *Iyatiku*, the Corn Mother, who planted her heart in the soil to give us crops. *Iyatiku* lived with us in the beginning, but when some of the people forgot their rituals and right living, their misbehavior created a famine. Then *Iyatiku* grew upset and left for *Shipap*, and the peaceful people decided to escape the troublemakers as well, using a vine to climb into our current home on earth.

Hearing this, I thought I finally understood why Grandma Esther had declined treatment for her cancer. She was ready to climb away from the troublemakers. She was tired of all the violence she had encountered in her lifetime: the powerful men who started wars and built bombs, and the poor ones who drank and fought with their families. Maybe she had always felt out of place on Grandpa's reservation. Maybe she even felt out of place in mine.

Aunt Helen said Corn Mother left instructions for us to share the fruit of her heart, to be at peace with our neighbors so the right kind of rain would come, and the earth would be healthy and strong. In my childlike way, I came to understand Grandma Esther's rosary, her soft Laguna murmurings as she hung laundry, and even the way she called Granny Ethel to her bedside for natural healing over surgery as an expression of nonviolence. Healing the aggression in our lives was central to healing the world.

Only Grandma's sister, Granny Ethel, and Aunt Vi stayed by her all evening. Dad and his brothers took turns in the bedroom, going back in with their full families when Aunt Vi said it was their turn. Uncle Gene's family stayed with Grandma for a long time, and Dad said it was because he was stubborn and wouldn't promise that he would leave the reservation for a better life.

While we waited for our family's turn, I looked out the window at the mulberry tree, remembering Grandma Esther before she got cancer. Her cheeks had been smooth. In my memory, she was like a polished stone rubbed against the world until all the irregularities disappeared and the skin on her face shone. The house felt claustrophobic, and I begged Dad to let me wait outside. He said no. He said Grandma Esther didn't want me to be afraid for her, and that death was a part of life.

When we went to go back to the bedroom the walk down the hall felt surreal. But entering the room was not as frightening as I had feared. Aunt Vi smiled at me from her chair alongside the bed. She stroked Grandma's hair and spoke to her in whispers. The adult faces in the room were strong and impenetrable, but when Dad picked me up and put me on the bed near Grandma Esther's side I felt at home. The creases in her hands looked like the cracks that formed in drying mud after a hard rain. If anything scared me, it wasn't my fear of death. It was that she'd refused painkillers and therefore had to be in pain.

When it was time to leave, I didn't want to go. Every single one of us kids felt like Grandma's favorite. It was like the sun was shining just for you when she sat and held you in her gaze. She was the only one who'd made me feel pretty, even when I smiled. Dad said God made mothers so that every child had a best friend, and I was jealous that he had her his whole life when she was leaving mine. They led me away from the bedroom with my legs trembling. I looked at my older sisters, especially Joan. She was dry-eyed and sturdy. I felt like a weakling, too emotional, a scaredy-cat in comparison to her and Lori.

Mom went to say the rosary on the couch. Dad took us outside. He lifted me and Monica into our beloved mulberry tree, setting us on a branch where we could see him eye to eye. He said we had roots just like the tree. They were our bloodlines, these roots, and they stretched down into our legs and rushed through our veins. Our roots reached into Grandma Esther's life. I imagined myself just like the tree, knotted and gnarled at the base, reaching into the soil in ways that were hidden, standing in a history that stretched to the horizon.

When Grandma Esther's soul slipped free of her body, Aunt Vi came out of the bedroom to tell us, but she didn't have to. A breeze had entered the room. Even before she said it, we felt Grandma Esther dancing around the house. I heard Mom whisper: "It's beautiful." But saying it only detracted from the feeling. Her passing created contradictory emotions in everyone. The family alternately cried and smiled, sad to lose her but happy that her suffering was done.

The day was a gift that brought us together—a chance for stillness and honesty. Still, losing her devastated us by striking at the roots of our family's traditional knowledge. She was the last Keres speaker in our immediate family, a holder of wisdom gone. How lonely it must have been, living on a reservation where no one spoke her language. How sad she must have felt knowing her grandchildren belonged to a future that disregarded her past.

Maybe she died lamenting what she hadn't expressed. Maybe love was a consolation in the isolation, but it didn't change the fact that Laguna was miles away, and her memories of it had remained largely personal.

In the years to come her loss would break us apart like a tree under an axe. Her kids respected her, and in the end, they honored her dying wishes. Dad resumed his job search, and four of his siblings moved west to take work in Los Angeles. Only Uncle Gene and Uncle Johnny would stay on the Yuma reservation.

The following week, early in the morning, my mother cornered me in my outdoor play. She bathed me all by myself, wrestled my chubby arms and legs into a Sunday jumpsuit, and then announced that a new dental trailer had been opened by Indian Health services. I longed to stay in the desert with my sisters, but I went along. It was rare to have alone time with my mother.

My aunt Kathy had been called to babysit, and I watched her with my sisters out the window of the car, stretching a hose across the side yard to make a mud puddle in the dirt. As we drove across the bridge, the river shimmered in the afternoon light, and a flock of terns swooped and dived, making my stomach tickle.

Perhaps I'll never know if it's true, though it felt true then and it feels true sometimes now, that the nitrous oxide they administered to me that day in the dental chair brought my grandma Esther back to me. I stared up into the yellow dental light and its heat spread through my chest. I heard the dentist saying baby teeth had no roots and it wouldn't be bad. I was frightened but my crying ceased when I felt Grandma Esther's warm palm flatten against my cheek.

"Shush," she said. I felt the dentist pulling and pulling. I felt the old Indian women assistants holding my arms and shoulders down. I heard my moans from a distance, as if I were someone else. I heard the cicadas singing in their otherworldly drone, and I heard my grandma Esther saying, "The fever dreams won't hurt you."

BICENTENNIAL GIRL

(1976)

✠

In a reversal of our usual dance celebrations, Dad was boogeying around the living room like he was auditioning for *Soul Train* while Mom, my sisters, and I sat stunned, watching from the couch. He was dancing to KC and the Sunshine Band, and his moves were amazing, a combination of "Shake Your Booty" and powwow flamboyance.

He came for Mom at the refrain, spinning her around like a doll, laughing and shouting, "We did it!" with beads of sweat glistening on his forehead. He closed his eyes at the end of the song, pointing his turquoise-ringed finger at us on the couch like the dance had been choreographed and he'd been trained to freeze on the last beat.

It was March 1976, and after years of searching for an out-of-state job, Dad had finally been hired as a welder at the Four Corners Power Plant on the Navajo reservation in northern New Mexico. According to him, we owed it to the Navajo tribal council for opening the Navajo Coal Mine, as well as for insisting on "Indian hiring preferences" when they signed their deal with the electric company that built the coal-fired power plant and offered him his new job.

He plunked down near us on the couch and pulled out a Rand Mc-Nally pocket atlas that he'd picked up at the gas station where he worked. Everything felt patriotic that year, with Bicentennial celebrations and the Montreal Summer Olympics planned for the summer, and the 1976 edition of the atlas had a red, white, and blue cover. I lingered over the map legend with its green highway lines and dots to mark the mileage before Dad showed me our new town: Farmington, New Mexico. It was over six hundred miles away, an unfathomable distance for a kid like me who'd never gone farther than San Diego.

"Who can do the math?" he asked, when I wanted to know how long it would take to get there. Joan ran for a piece of paper, but Lori did it in her head. "If you drive fifty-five miles per hour, it will take us eleven hours."

According to Dad, we were "moving on up" like George Jefferson, Archie Bunker's old neighbor, and he couldn't contain his glee.

Mom was upset, surprisingly, though not about leaving, just about the immediacy of the move. It was Friday and the company wanted Dad to start on Monday. How could they expect him to relocate his entire family in the middle of the school year? Couldn't they give us time to finish and say goodbye? Dad said the plant was in Waterflow, an outpost in the middle of nowhere. The guys who worked there lived in Kirtland or Shiprock or Farmington because there was no housing nearby. There were no buses, and he couldn't walk to work. If he went alone, he'd have to take the family's Chevy Nova. Mom furrowed her brow with worry. For a second, I thought she might cry.

At the time, neither of my parents knew car rental companies existed, and until Dad started getting his new pay, they couldn't afford a second vehicle. We heard them whispering all night about what to do, even after they thought we were sleeping. Mom said there was no way she was pulling us out of school in the middle of the year, and Dad said there was no way he could risk losing the job. Finally, Dad called a guy he'd met at his welding test, who lived nearby the new plant, and the guy agreed that Dad could sleep on his couch and bum rides.

We drove Dad to the bus station the next day. He bought his ticket, told us to be good girls while he was gone, and promised he would be back for us when school was over in May. Then he climbed up the steps of the bus to his seat. We could see him through the window, giving us a thumbs-up, and grinning like he'd won the lottery. He was off on his solo

adventure, and we stood on the sidewalk blowing kisses until the driver
pulled away.

Three weeks later, he was back. It turned out he loved the job, but not sleeping on a couch. And it turned out Mom didn't appreciate single parent-
ing. Though it was only April, and school didn't let out until June, our
parents went to disenroll us. I had to clean out my desk and pack all my
fat crayons in my backpack for the last time that year. I was a first-grade
dropout, and Joan and Lori would be leaving their fourth- and fifth-grade
classrooms behind as well.

On the day we left the reservation for northern New Mexico, a mob
of cousins milled around the moving truck to say goodbye. Dad was
planning to hitch the Nova to the back of the U-Haul, and Mom had
filled every square inch of the car with stuff. The windows were blocked
with bags and boxes, and even our cat, Inky, was shoved into the maze.

Dad and his brother Johnny finished loading the U-Haul with our
Big Wheels, beds, the brown flower couch, a black-and-white TV, and
our kitchen table and chairs with the vinyl seats that stuck to the back
of my thighs on hot summer days. When they were done, Dad jumped
on the truck's bumper and pulled the rolling door shut. He and Johnny
locked arms.

"Thanks, bro."

Uncle Johnny shrugged. "No problem."

"You guys get in the truck," Dad told us. Then he pulled a ball of
crumpled bills out of his pocket and handed it to Johnny. "Take Anita
and Tonia to dinner."

Uncle Johnny got stiff. "Why you gotta tell me what to do with it?
You think I'm going to waste it on booze?"

But Dad knew how to handle his little brother. "Shut up," he said,
grinning. "It's my day, not yours." He punched Johnny's arm, and they
laughed, then Dad hitched the Nova to the bumper of the U-Haul and
climbed into the cab.

As we pulled away from our old house in Yuma, the neighborhood dogs shot out from their resting place under the porch to bark and chase us down the road. I looked out the side window until the dust settled, we hit pavement, and I couldn't see them anymore.

As we drove, Dad lectured us. "You gotta work harder than other people," he said. "No one can say you've failed unless you've given up." He was wide awake and full of energy and wouldn't stop talking. "Remember that our tribe got chopped in half when the U.S. and Mexican border was created. Imagine if you were in Algodones trying to get by." We were rising toward the Kachina mountains and Flagstaff by the time he finally settled down. Around the same time, Mom stopped sniffling and dabbing at her eyes, then the truck grew quiet, and I realized we were entering a place of water and pine.

Seven hours into our drive, when Dad pulled into a gas station in Kayenta, Arizona, we ran to check on our cat, Inky, but we couldn't see her in the Nova. We worried that she was dead, and begged Mom to open the doors, but before we could poke our heads in and grab her, she shot through our legs and darted around the side of the station. Dad was pumping gas, and when we couldn't find her, he said we weren't going to waste daylight chasing a cat. Monica cried, but we never saw our furry friend again.

The idea of relocation reemerged in 1948, after Collier had been ousted, and an epic blizzard hit Navajo and Hopi lands. The disaster occurred just as the Truman administration was trying to pass a foreign aid program known as the Marshall Plan to gain allies in the Cold War. Under review in Congress, the plan stirred controversy with Native veterans and activists who were frustrated that the government was espousing democracy abroad while oppressing them at home. Rather than fulfilling promises to Natives who shed blood for America, the Truman administration was bestowing money on former enemies.

Napoleon Johnson, a state supreme court justice from Oklahoma who was also a Cherokee citizen, reminded Congress that Native people had sent more than thirty thousand "to fight for our institutions and American way of life." Lily J. Neil, Navajo council member, complained to federal officials, saying they were "making all these big loans to foreign countries, and bragging about what they are doing so fine and noble, for the countries who tried to ruin us," while ignoring "their obligations to us North American Indians."

Feeling indebted to Navajo and Hopi code talkers who had just ensured Japan's defeat—and perhaps frightened by Soviet politicians who were using the poverty of Indian reservations to attack America's democratic ideals—the Truman administration airlifted food into the two snowbound reservations to fend off starvation. A year later, the Navajo Hopi Rehabilitation Act was passed to avert more catastrophes and create better infrastructures. But some politicians said the money was ill spent, that the two tribes would never be able to support all their citizens, and so Congress enacted their first relocation program (without job training) to reduce their populations.

Native activists argued "the Indian problem" would never be solved by relocation. Instead, Native America needed development. They referenced the Marshall Plan, saying tribal lands should be treated and funded in the same way the United States did with other underdeveloped nations. They proposed the "American Indian Four-Point Plan," asking that money for scientific, technical, medical, and industrial progress be made available to them as well, and presented it to Congress in 1957, but by then termination policies like the Relocation Act had been invested in instead.

Before dying in 1965, Dad's father insisted there would come a day when the government would "let all their treaty obligations go." He watched Dad get married and worried about how he would provide for his family. Yet even as I'd seen my father struggle to find a job on our reservation, I was too young to understand the history. I'd never met my grandpa Ed. I didn't know that he spent his final years ranting and raving about the rich man's insatiable greed. If Grandma Esther's religiosity made her fear the violence in Yuma, Grandpa Ed's pragmatism made him distressed about the poverty.

While most people trained by the Indian Relocation Act went to big cities, we had landed in a border town at the edge of the Navajo Nation. Built around the San Juan Gas Pipeline, the Four Corners region boomed in the 1960s after the U.S. government teamed up with El Paso Electric to detonate an underground nuclear bomb east of town, fracturing the earth's bedrock to free natural gas. A bunch of card-carrying Republicans from Texas took over Farmington, even as hundreds of Navajos supported the town's economy by shopping there on weekends. In our new town, we were still Indians, but we were the good kind of Indians, the kind you would not mind having as your neighbors. We rented a small house, kept our yard tidy, and went to mass with strangers on Sundays. Dad's work buddy sold him a yellow Thunderbird that we drove down the hill for Chinese food.

Joan and Lori hated their new classrooms at Sacred Heart Catholic School. I couldn't call it *my* school. I only saw it when we dropped them off, or when we went to church, because Mom refused to enroll me. "She's way ahead of her classmates," she told Dad, convincing him we'd save money if I waited to attend until the following fall.

At first, Joan and Lori made fun of me. "Our new school doesn't take nerds," they said. But after the first couple of weeks, their smiles were gone. They didn't care that attending Catholic school without scholarships meant our family had come up in the world. They hated it. Most days, one or the other of them would feign a fever to miss, and when they got home in the afternoon, they often cried.

Lori said, "The nuns are too strict."

Joan said, "The kids are brats."

Even seeing Joan and Lori struggle in their new school, I missed the classroom and wished I could go. I wanted to keep up with the kids in my grade. It was upsetting to get left behind, and more so to hear my sisters' horror stories about how hard Catholic school was. My imagination twisted the halls of education into a dust devil, and I started to feel homesick for Yuma.

Mom dragged me and Monica to mass every morning so she could watch Joan and Lori file into church with their classes. She studied the other girls, trying to pick out the ones who were giving ours trouble. Joan and Lori stared at me with sad eyes as they walked by, but there was nothing I could do. A priest named Father Ben said mass. He was a fun Franciscan who played the guitar and took the eighth graders to one of the region's Pueblo ruins every year: Salmon, Mesa Verde, or Chaco Canyon. The nuns, however, were Ursulines, the very first order to land in the United States. They were from the Deep South and mean.

"Too bad Father Ben doesn't teach," Dad said.

One day at mass, Mom started crying while we were waiting for the students to come into the church. I tried to hug her, but she wasn't in a cuddly mood. I kept staring at her until she pinched my thigh and told me to leave her alone. She stood and sat on cue, but she kept sniffling and blowing her nose.

In Farmington we were nobody. There was no running into one of Mom's fourteen siblings at Del Sol Grocery. There were no All-Indian baseball tournaments, and even if there had been, Dad didn't have his six brothers and five cousins to enter an all-Jackson team. There were no dinner invites from Dad's older sisters. Here, there were no mulberry trees to climb, no frogs to catch, no septic tanks to serve as base during tag with the cousins. I even missed the old, funny-smelling ladies on the res who raised their eyebrows and said they knew *exactly* who my family was when I told them my last name.

That spring, Mom suggested I come up with a way to compensate for my lost months at school by giving myself little assignments. I thought it was an excellent idea and created a plan to memorize every state in the country. By the time I finished, it was summer, and swept up in the patriotic fervor of America's second-century celebrations, I spent the last free month before school sitting outside with my *U.S. Presidents* book, cracking sunflower seeds until my lips burned from too much salt, trying to memorize all the names. I started with honest George and ended with our peanut man, Jimmy Carter. My plan was to impress everyone on the first day of school by reciting them in chronological order.

I sat beneath our backyard apple tree to study, with a baseball cap over my braids, and my picture book of presidents open on my lap. I practiced into July, enunciating the seventh name, Andrew Jackson, with special emphasis because my father said that a hundred years ago our family had been named after him. "All the oldest families on our reservation were given presidents' names by the government," he said. He said we came from a long line of civic leaders, from Grandpa Ed and leading back to Granny Ethel's great-aunt—but it didn't mean much to me. None of them were famous. None of my teachers talked about them in school.

On the other hand, here was Andrew Jackson, recognizable. The dirt road leading to my grandma Esther's old house, my uncles' houses, and our family land on the Yuma Indian reservation had a sign that read JACKSON ROAD, and I planned to make the most of it in school. He gave me something to brag about in the classroom. I planned to ask my new classmates if *their* families were named after a famous president. I traced his bushy eyebrows and widow's peak with sticky lemonade fingers. Just the sight of the old guy made me feel important, like we were related to American royalty.

One day, after growing bored with my studies, I wandered inside to see if anyone was watching the gymnastic competition at the Olympics. Instead, I found Dad on the couch watching a baseball game.

The Dodgers were at bat when suddenly Vin Scully, the broadcaster, announced a couple of intruders. "Wait a minute," he said, "there's an animal on the field." He said it so calmly, I initially thought he was hallucinating. But then he added, "There are two," and I realized he was using the word *animal* to refer to a long-haired man and a younger boy who looked enough alike to be related.

The protesters had jumped the fence near the third-base line, and we watched as they ran into the outfield. The camera panned in on the pair as they unfurled and poured kerosene on an American flag. Then they knelt before it and fumbled with a book of matches. Dad yelled for Mom,

"Rainy, get in here! You're missing it!" He scootched to the edge of his seat, excited, and I bounced up and down beside him. We both waited for the tongues of fire, for the flag to turn into a scorched black spot.

"Why are they doing that?" I asked. "The Bicentennial," he answered just as Mom came into the room to see what the fuss was.

Suddenly, from the corner of our TV screen, the Cub's center fielder raced in to snatch Old Glory away from the protesters before they could burn it. "Wow," Dad said. He leaned back, deflated, but the crowd instead went crazy. People in the stadium leaped to their feet and cheered as the outfield scoreboard flashed the words RICK MONDAY YOU MADE A GREAT PLAY! Security officers arrived on the field. The Dodgers' coach, Tommy Lasorda, was livid and yelling, his spit flying in the father's face as he and his son got arrested.

After the excitement died down, Dad went into the kitchen for a beer and Mom went down the hallway to finish her sewing. I was left staring at the TV, embarrassed to ask if anyone else noticed that the man and his son looked like our family.

"Don't forget your brother fought in Vietnam," Mom called to Dad as she walked by the kitchen.

"I didn't say nothing," he replied.

My sisters had been free of school since early June, and they'd been calling me Cha-Ka after the Neanderthal in *The Land of the Lost* all summer long. I was desperate for them to stop before the school year began, and my new classmates heard, so I fawned over them in the hope that they might go soft.

We were standing in a record store with Dad, who was buying the new Richard Pryor album, *Bicentennial Nigger*. I told Joan that her new feathered haircut and red softball uniform made her look like a brown-skinned version of Wonder Woman. I told her the way she stretched her softball mitt out for a line drive, then fired down third to first for a double play, was done with such speed it reminded me of the superhero's gold bracelets deflecting bullets in battle.

Lori laughed in my face and told me to shut up. Joan browsed the band sheaths with one hand and flicked the baseball cap off my head with the other.

When we got home, Mom took Monica to run more errands, while Joan and Lori walked to the park to play freeze tag with the only Navajo girls in the neighborhood. They were all older than me, and none of them liked it when I tagged along. My nostalgia for Yuma was growing, and every day I worried more. What if my memorized list of presidents wasn't enough to help me make friends? I went straight outside with my book to study.

After a long time in the backyard, I took a break from the memorization, deciding I needed a snack to concentrate. I went in the back door to the kitchen and overheard Dad listening to his new record. The voice was a black minister, played by the comedian Richard Pryor, and he was talking like he was ancient in the skit.

"We are gathered here today, to celebrate this year of the bicentenniality, in the hope of freedom and dignity. We are celebrating two hundred years of white folk kicking ass!" The audience hooted and laughed. "We offer this prayer, and the prayer is: How long will this bullshit go on?"

I slumped down against the wall and listened to Dad chuckling on the couch. It wasn't the first time I had heard about Richard Pryor (Mom said he had a "potty mouth"), or about Black slaves. Even so, I didn't know what Black history had to do with us.

Throughout my youngest years, there were hints that our political relationship with the United States was complicated. I had heard Dad praise Mohammed Ali for being antiestablishment. He cackled derisively when he clicked past John Wayne on TV. He looked sad when he got off the phone with his Vietnam vet brother who was still trying to recover from all the stressful scouting duties he'd been assigned because his white platoon leader said Indians were "naturally stealthy." There was the expression on his face when Rick Monday ripped the American flag away from the two protesters at Dodger Stadium. And there was Mom, perpetually shushing him, so we kids wouldn't grow up jaded, though I didn't understand that was her mission at the time.

In a second skit, Richard Pryor played a two-hundred-year-old slave with "white stars and stripes on his forehead" and a "lovely white folk expression." He was laughing about death as "The Battle Hymn of the Republic" played quietly in the background. After talking about the disappearance of his wife and kids he said, "Lord, have mercy. Yes, siree. I don't even know where my old mama is now hyuck, hyuck. She up yonder in that big white folks in the sky hyuck, hyuck, and ya'll probably done forgot about it."

Then the music stopped and his voice grew suddenly serious, all semblance of the happy simpleton gone: "But I ain't never gonna forget about it."

My neck felt hot, and a knot swelled in my throat. Pryor's voice sounded as deep as Dad's when he got angry. I thought about Grandma Esther and the "big white folks in the sky." She too had always said "Lord, have mercy," and I didn't understand my complicated emotions remembering it. I just felt a sudden, stabbing sadness.

History takes time to come into focus for a Native child in an assimilated family, but I was intuiting *something*. My mouth felt dry as I listened to Dad laughing. I stared at my reflection in the chrome legs of our kitchen chairs, scared that there were two Americas, two gods, two forms of patriotism. I thought of the crowd at Dodger Stadium yelling like they wanted to kill the long-haired protesters, and I felt suddenly unsure about my recitation plan. While I didn't know exactly *what* I wasn't getting, I thought maybe if Dad knew about the way I'd been fawning over Andrew Jackson's picture, he might not be proud of me.

The next day, I felt sick of studying. I even felt too ill at ease to follow Joan and Lori down the street and ask them to let me play when they went out to find their new friends, Zena and Zelda Benally. Instead, I sat in front of the big box fan, humming into the whirr to hear the distorted sound of my voice.

When they came in for lunch, Joan said I was stupid to worry about school and Lori said I should appreciate the summer, a time when I was free to be me, veg out in front of the television, and use sentences like "you ain't the boss of me" and "I'm gonna get me something to eat" without anyone telling me otherwise.

Joan laughed so hard at Lori's comment that she choked on her Kool-Aid. But then she got serious. "Catholic school is *rough*," she said.

I chewed on my nails all afternoon. When Dad got home, I waited until the sound of the lawn mower cut off, then I went outside to talk to him. Rather than tell him how homesick I was for Yuma, I told him I was worried that I had gotten behind. I'd lost days of school, and Sacred Heart sounded scary.

I said, "Joan and Lori say the nuns are really strict, and Catholic kids have bionic brains. What if I can't catch up?"

"Bionic brains?" He laughed. "Is that what your sisters are telling you?"

I shrugged.

He shook his head. "Everyone has a few bumps when they start something new. That's just normal."

"Did you go to school with nuns?"

"Yeah, but your school won't be like mine."

"Why not?"

"Things were different back then."

"Like how?"

"When I got in trouble, Sister used to rap my knuckles real hard, but one day she gave me the ruler and said from then on, whenever I got in trouble, she was going to hold out her hand and I was going to hit her instead."

"What do you mean?"

He stared past me with vacant eyes. "She put out her hand. She told me to swat her palm with the ruler as hard as I could for my punishment."

"Why?"

He looked at me as if suddenly remembering me there. He shrugged. "I don't know, but I could hear her sucking in her breath when I hit her."

We sat and stared at a line of ants making their way across the patio.

"It must've hurt," he said, before heading to the garage.

I called after him. "Why do we have to go to Sacred Heart instead of public schools?"

"Because the public schools in this town are crappy," he said. "Now get inside for dinner."

All summer long Dad tried to fix the homesick feeling in the house by keeping us busy. He bought us softball gloves and record albums. He took us to restaurants, the roller rink, and movies. But for all his encouragement to stay positive, I was suspicious because he was drinking alone, staying up late with too little sleep, trying to re-create the reservation in small yet obvious ways. He drank his beer in tall singles wrapped in paper bags like his brother Johnny did back home. He looked for beat-up dives with questionable-looking characters to eat Sunday breakfast in. Mom liked going to the fancy side of town, but Dad liked the rough side.

One Sunday after church, he'd found a diner he wanted to try on the rough side of town, and we grabbed a corner booth. Dad ordered Indian tacos all around, but Mom wrinkled her nose and said she wanted enchiladas. We gabbed about Mom's bowling league and the skates Joan wanted to buy. The food was rich and filling, and when we left the restaurant, I felt happy. But as we were walking to the car, we saw a Navajo couple arguing in the parking lot.

"They're drunk," Dad said, watching with calm interest.

I climbed in the backseat with my sisters.

Dad started the motor. He revved the engine, but he didn't pull away. Mom said we should leave. "Let's go," she told Dad, but he sat there with his hand on the gearshift, watching what was happening.

The couple went from yelling to shoving each other. Mom tried to push my head down on the seat, but I fought her to see. The man socked the woman hard in the jaw and she fell, her hair spreading in the air like a fan.

"I can't watch," Mom said, covering her face.

The guy ran to the driver's door and got in his truck. He revved the motor and started backing out. The lady was lying in between the tires, and it seemed the truck would go around her, but at the last minute she lifted her head and looked toward the truck. Then she hugged her arms to her body and rolled right into the path of the oncoming wheels. The two left tires bumped right over her chest.

The Indian guy sped out of the parking lot and disappeared down the street as the lady lay wounded on the dirt and gravel drive. Dad opened his door but decided against it when the manager of the restaurant came running out. I looked away and couldn't look back. Monica couldn't look either, but Joan and Lori had their faces pressed to the window. "She's still moving," Joan said, her voice sounding scratchy. Sirens started up in the distance. He said, "Someone called the cops," and we rolled slowly out of the parking lot.

Dad said, "The tires would have gone around her if she hadn't rolled."

That night in bed I heard my older sisters whispering. Lori said, "That man looked like Dad."

Joan was outraged. "No, he did *not* look like Dad," she said. "He looked like Uncle Johnny. Dad's a welder!"

She said the word *welder* as if it meant "doctor."

They fell asleep, but I felt afraid of the tree outside, the way its long branches cast shadows across the wallpaper like monstrous arms.

We'd seen a terrible thing. We had moved to a foreign town, and we were completely alone. Just like in Yuma, Native people in Farmington drank, but here I didn't have Grandma Esther, my aunts, and cousins to lean on. The cocoon of safety provided by our extended family had broken open, and I was raw and rubbing against a scary new world.

My stomach was queasy. I got out of bed and made my way down the hallway, following the dim glow of the TV. My parents were relaxing on the couch, watching *The Sonny & Cher Comedy Hour.*

"I can't sleep," I said.

"Well, okay," Mom told me. "But don't complain when it's time to get up tomorrow."

I sat cross-legged on the floor in front of them. Dad said that Cher was part Indian, and I stared at her on the TV. She shimmied across the stage in a sequined dress, glamorous as any woman I'd ever seen. I looked hard, wondering if she wore thick makeup because Sonny sometimes socked her and she needed to cover the bruises.

I finally came out and asked, "Why did we have to move away from Yuma?"

Dad turned the volume down and then dragged me next to him and Mom on the couch. Mom asked if I saw what happened in the parking lot. I said yes, and she said that kind of violence mostly happened between family members.

Dad put his hand up to stop Mom from talking. He said he loved the reservation but had to be able to criticize it as well. "Staying would have held me back," he said, "and you and your sisters too. We had to leave to find a better life."

I nodded, and he hugged me to his side.

"But I know you miss it. We lost a lot in leaving. Your school. Our families. Your cousins."

"Our cat," I reminded him, remembering Inky's tail disappearing down the alley in Kayenta.

"Inky too," Dad said. And when I smiled, comforted, he added, "Now go back to bed. It's getting late." But lying in the dark, I found the security Dad's words provided quickly fade.

Yes, we'd lost our homeland to look for something better. But I'd also lost something deeper. My perspective, and a sense of both past and future. If we had stayed in Yuma, my pride in our presidential surname would have died faster. Living on the reservation, somebody would have explained our name's origins to me. Someone would have told me that on the day our reservation was allotted, fraud had already tarnished the treaty signing.

During allotment, the white Indian commissioner had rounded up as many local Natives as he could and told them: "If any of you refuse to obey the orders [to sign], the police will see to it that you do." Those tribal members who hid or refused had their signatures forged with newly assigned names—Jefferson, Washington, and for Dad's great-grandpa, Chappo Jackson. Our family had been rechristened after a man I foolishly spent the summer worshipping because my library book never mentioned that he was dubbed the "Indian Killer" for ordering his soldiers to murder women and children, or that he was the one who signed the Indian Removal Act of 1830, forcing the relocation of sixty thousand Native Americans on the Trail of Tears.

My knowledge of history, over the course of my childhood, came together like a puzzle, one edifying piece at a time. My father's poor education, my mother's shame, the early death of my grandparents, propaganda driven by the church and state—all these circumstances had combined to ensure that no one told me New Mexico's pueblos had been inhabited for a thousand years, making America's two-hundredth-birthday celebration both an omission and a snub. No one told me the father-son duo at Dodger Stadium were protesting the lack of health care in Indian Country.

I was a bucktoothed kid who spent all her Bicentennial quarters playing cowboy games at the arcade, and who worked all summer trying to memorize the list of American presidents—and this ensured that years later I would have to live with the insult of how vague my self-awareness was, and how stupidly it allowed me to behave. I rolled around in bed that night, unable to sleep. And when I finally did dream, I had nightmares that Dad was driving the truck and Grandma Esther was under the wheels.

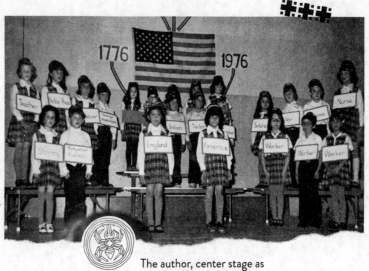

The author, center stage as
England, at Sacred Heart
School in Farmington, New
Mexico, in 1976.

[ ]

I only have the dream once. In it, I'm strapped to a chair. At first, I think it's a dentist's chair, but then I open my eyes and realize I'm on a space shuttle. I am holding hands with a stranger, and together, in a herd of passengers, we disembark down a long tube. We enter a glass hall, where I hear powwow drums. Out the window, I can see a welcoming ceremony: Comanche, Mandinka, Navajo, Hmong, citizens of many nations wearing their regalia. They are joined together in dance. Some of their movements, I know. I wave at the women who jingle. Their lids of chewing tobacco, rolled into cones and sewn to their dresses, dangle and knock. Male fancy dancers jerk their heads, bend their knees low, and spin.

The drumbeats pound in my head like blood, and somehow, I know it's a water drum. I know that a piece of coal from a prayer fire was dropped into the water with a hiss before the drum's buckskin top—soft from being soaked in water—was stretched to make sound. Feeling proud that I know this, I look toward the glass ceiling, wanting to see my earth in the sky, but the moment I lift my face an enormous chunk of the blue-and-green surface explodes.

I yank away from the stranger, who is still holding my hand. "I have to go home," I say. I want to burn in my red rock canyons. I want my bones to be black as oil. But the stranger grips me tighter and pulls me toward the dancers. Struggling against them, pulling to get my hand back, I feel terror, knowing return is a myth, and only airspace is immortal.

I look down and see that my skin is ancient and wrinkled.

CROWNED

(1977)

✤

Though there were twenty-two students in my second-grade class, only three of us were Indians. Cherie was Ute, and I didn't like her. I decided I didn't like her on the very first day, when she asked me what I *was* even before asking me my name. She carried lip gloss in a little purse and presented a porcelain doll for show-and-tell that scared me. Robert, instead, was quiet, and strong, and could hit a softball farther than anyone in our class. He was husky like a grown man, and his thick hair, cut straight across the back of his neck, reminded me of a hedge.

"Robert's Navajo," I had said to my family after we first met at school. The customary quiet between Catholic boys and girls meant we rarely spoke, though I admired his power on the field.

"You're supposed to call him Diné," Dad had corrected me, using their original tribal name for themselves. He worked with Diné at their reservation power plant, so he knew.

On the day my classmate Billy almost died, he was at the blackboard working on one of our first carry-and-borrow problems. He was a skinny redhead with divorced parents and a million freckles, no favorite of our tough teacher. Sister Angelica Anne swatted Billy's palms so often, he flinched whenever she passed by his desk. Now he gripped the chalk with white knuckles and kept looking at the clock, as if willing the minute hand to spin around and announce the end of the day.

"Stay focused on your math problem," Sister Angelica Anne said, smacking the board with her ruler.

The sound of the ruler's rap startled the whole class, and really affected poor Billy. He sucked at the air, his skinny chest heaving, his face turning white. He dropped the chalk and doubled over, struggling to breathe.

"Get him something!" Sister yelled. She shook his shoulders, but it only made him grab his throat and wheeze louder. Looking back at us, she yelled again, "Somebody do something!"

My schoolmates and I sat like boulders in a field. Billy's lips were turning purplish blue. He was hyperventilating, and Sister was panicking too. We already knew she was useless in a crisis. Fire drills made her hands shake.

Our classmate Robert jumped out of his desk and ran down the aisle toward the back of the room. He slipped a little as he rounded the corner at our gerbil's home base, then dug in and started down the final stretch to the cubbies near the front door. He reminded me of a baseball player cutting across center field, an outfielder sprinting to catch a Ruthian blast before it cleared the fence.

When he arrived at the far end of the room, he dove into a Pete Rose and disappeared. I had to kneel on my seat to see him down in the coat closet—jackets, hats, and mittens dangling over him as he rummaged in the lunch boxes. He fastened on somebody's sack lunch and popped up with the bag upside down. A white bread sandwich and Fritos spilled out. Two dimes for milk hit the floor and rolled away.

He took the brown paper bag to the front where Billy was slumped in Sister's arms. He stuck the bag over Billy's mouth and Billy heaved it big and small, big and small, until his bulging eyes shrank back to their normal size. Sister fell back in her desk chair and said thank you over and over, like she was a doll with a broken voice box.

The spring semester had been in session for a while when Robert made his save, so I'd had the better part of the year to consider how I felt about him. On one hand, I wanted to hit a softball the way he did in my Little League.

Even against the big kids at Sacred Heart—the school's fastest windup pitchers—he kept his cool. He just inched back in the box, choked up, and pulled the ball up the first-base line. He was never late on a swing, and the fact that he was a lefty only added to his appeal.

But in the classroom, he embarrassed me. When he read out loud his cadence was off, and his fluency sucked. The smart kids snickered. I hid my hands under my desk and crossed my fingers to give him luck. I imagined having telepathic strength and *willed* him to enunciate his words. I couldn't understand it. He talked smack with such confidence on the softball field. But when we returned to the classroom, he hemmed and hawed.

Sister shamed him for his poor reading skills, and I hated it. I wanted to show her we Indian kids were smart. Dad always said that people like us had to exceed expectations if we wanted to rise above our circumstances. If we wanted to get out of Farmington, find professional careers, and live the kind of life he expected of us, then we had to get straight As. According to Dad, who was always pragmatic, my sisters and I were lucky. We had privileges he never did. We were pretty and light-skinned. We came from a family of intelligent leaders, and if we worked hard, we could make a difference in the world.

If I had struggled to understand my parents' striving in Yuma, in Farmington I thought I saw what they meant. Velvet van Ryan lived in a house with a swimming pool, fancier than anything I'd ever seen. I went to her birthday party, where her skinny mother, who spoke with a Texas twang, said "the picture show" was bad because it filled kids' heads with immoral thoughts. They were a weird family, but I noticed how Sister treated Velvet with kid gloves—way better than she treated me—and it made me want to be even smarter, to impress Sister, and any other teacher in my path. At nearly eight years old, my ambitions were not precise. I just knew I wanted to be what my parents called "a success."

Up until the day Robert saved Billy, my campaign to win Sister's respect had been going well. In the library only one other kid was on the same reading level as me. Sister said it was Becca's job to read thick novels, and it was my job to read nonfiction. Mom had bragged about my interest in the presidents, after which Sister led me to a shelf filled with the lives of Ben Franklin, Patrick Henry, Nathan Hale, George Washington, and other early Americans. From that moment on, she said I wasn't allowed to read fiction, only books that were "full of facts."

Now, as I looked at Robert, who had a herd of classmates pounding his back like a hero, I had to wonder if perhaps I'd miscalculated in my earlier judgments. What if Robert wasn't a friend or an embarrassment? What if he was a threat? Would our teacher have room in her heart for both of us? Or was Robert going to be Sister Angelica Anne's favorite Native student for the rest of the school year?

"Some people react in a crisis, but others freeze," Dad said. His old Chevy Nova was on a jack, and I could only see his legs. He was replacing the back tires with a new designer set that would make the rear of the car higher than the front.

I had just told him about Robert saving Billy in the classroom. "Well, how was I supposed to know that a paper sack would help?" I asked.

"Robert has more street smarts than you," he said. "A lot of full-blood kids are spunky like that."

I didn't appreciate the admiration I heard in his voice. He talked like that about my full-blood cousins too. And it bugged me, because I thought he was right. There was something cool and capable about them.

I went inside and found Mom in the kitchen talking to her new friend, Libby. Libby was half-Navajo, mixed blood like us, and the best baker of pies I had ever met. "When it's Libby's, Libby's, Libby's, on the label, label, label, you will like it, like it, like it, on your table, table, table." I couldn't keep the commercial from popping in my head when I saw her.

"Why the long face?" Mom asked.

I told her what had happened with Robert.

"And why should that make you feel sad?" Libby asked.

If I'd been worried about Robert becoming Sister's favorite, now I also had to deal with Dad calling him "street smart," and so I didn't tell Mom and Libby about my fears. I already felt like their charity case. Every day my sisters got invited to play with the Benally girls down the street. Zena, Zelda, Joan, and Lori were close in age, and Levina was Monica's age. The Benallys lived in a modern two-story house that Dad said was too fancy. Libby whispered about how weird it was that they had purchased it when the previous owner had killed his wife in the house. She said most full-blood Navajos like the Benally family would have been freaked.

That fall Libby had been visiting when I threw a fit about losing our cat, Inky. I missed having a pet, and I called Mom a "liar" because they'd never followed through with their promise to get us a dog. The next day, Libby had come over with a mutt from the dog shelter. She didn't even ask permission. She just dragged him into the yard. He was a hyperactive mongrel with dark brown hair and bad teeth, and I hated him immediately.

I'd become an expert on dogs by that point. Sister had given me permission to check out a nonfiction book on the Westminster Dog Show, and I was obsessed with Grand Champions, Field Champions, and Agility Champions especially. I read about coat colors and sires and pedigrees. I studied the lineages of my favorite winners and admired the care their owners put into keeping their family lines pure. Without realizing how many of them were weakened by inbreeding, I dreamed of owning a pure-bred dog.

When Libby saw how indifferent I was toward the half-breed she'd given me, her face flushed with embarrassment, and she took him away. Mom said I was spoiled, but to me he looked like a poor kid's dog, like a reservation mongrel who would pull at his leash on every walk. Dad said I owed Libby an apology, but he and Mom never really wanted me to have a pet, and they let it drop. After that, Dad got big on dog-sitting for his coworkers, as if he thought other people's animals might make me less moody.

Mom and Libby were still staring at me from the kitchen table, waiting for an answer about my long face. "I'm not sad," I said, shrugging. "*Spunky* rhymes with *flunky* and that means street smart is dumb." Seeing their confused expressions, I tried to act nonchalant, but as I went down the hall to my room, I heard Mom calling me "neurotic."

Looking back, I know the tension I felt was larger than Sister Angelica Anne, our relocation, and my family's new circumstances. I didn't know at the time that the federal Commission on Civil Rights was investigating Farmington the year we moved there, and national newspapers had started referring to it as the Selma, Alabama, of the Southwest.

The rise to notoriety began when three teenagers from Farmington High School (my future alma mater) tortured and killed three Navajo men a few months before we arrived. They drove their victims out to Chokecherry Canyon where they lit firecrackers in their orifices, burned their private parts, and mutilated them while they were still alive. When they grew tired of torturing the men, they searched the sage and sandstone canyons for rocks and bashed the men's heads in. Yet despite the savagery of their crime—they put one of the men's fingers in a jewelry box and brought it to a high school football game to brag—they were tried as minors and sentenced to only a brief stay in reform school.

At first, Navajo protesters had hoped that the boys would be convicted as adults. But when they realized they couldn't expect sentences that rose to the severity of the crime, they marched in protest for seven weekends in a row. Shoppers stayed away from Main Street, frightened by their demands for justice, and business owners grew angry and impatient. They urged the mayor, Antonio Webb, to stop issuing permits for the demonstrations. Webb set up a hotline to quell the panic and downplayed the nature of the violence, telling reporters, "I don't think race had anything to do with [the murders]. Just high school kids rolling drunks, and all the drunks were Navajo."

The day after the judge handed down his lenient sentencing, the city council refused to give the activists another permit. They said it would interfere with the sheriff's posse parade that was celebrated annually and scheduled for that weekend with the theme Reverence for the Old West. The streets were packed for the Sunday parade. Wearing vintage frontier uniforms, the cavalry reenactors rode in on horseback. Navajo protesters tried to block the procession, and police fired teargas. A riot broke out, and Farmington made the national news.

My parents were sick with worry when we arrived, though they decided to keep it a secret. Jimmy Ignacio, the son of one of the victims, worked at the plant with Dad. He was tracking one of the boys who had gotten out of juvenile detention and told Dad he suspected the boy of further murders. A Navajo man was thrown off a bluff and killed behind San Juan Regional Hospital. An insulation worker Dad knew was beat up and run down by a truck one night when he ran out of gas. Dad's supervisor called Dad slurs and threatened him with violence. The supervisor got transferred to another plant, and then, a short time later, Dad heard he'd been convicted of manslaughter in Holbrook, Arizona, for kidnapping an Indian and leaving him on the train tracks to die.

Mom and Dad whispered behind closed doors about the dangerous racism in Farmington. Dad told her he had some good white supervisors, Gene Wood and Ray Sims, who were trying to protect him. He said to have faith that things were changing. She was afraid and cried to go home. But he wanted his job, so she made him promise to hold his tongue and stay silent, no matter the insult or threat. They agreed not to tell me and my sisters because we were little and what was the use? We didn't go out alone or dress in Navajo clothes. We had our light skin for protection.

With the federal Commission in town now, good white people had started speaking up—especially the shop owners whose pocketbooks were being threatened by the unrest. The newspaper reported the government investigation had found rampant racism at all levels of society. Suddenly, the city's election zones were being redrawn to allow Navajos to sit on the County Commission, and the Federal Justice Department filed a lawsuit against San Juan Regional Hospital for refusing to treat Native Americans in its emergency room. The U.S. Equal Opportunity Commission sued the city for employment discrimination. Policy was changing, but it takes so much more to change society's heart.

Despite not being told the whole truth by our parents, those early years in Farmington were haunted. I had nightmares. I was afraid. I sensed how Dad kept us close when we walked around downtown. There were times when Mom grabbed our hands and whisked us away without explaining why we were leaving JCPenney or some other store. I never said a word about the tension in the air, even to my sisters. At the time, I attributed it to the move, pressures at school, and the loss of our family back home.

The day after Robert's save, Sister let him carry the gifts up to the altar during morning mass and asked him to be the line leader on the way to lunch. Among the white and (so-called) Spanish kids in our class, he'd never been picked for these tasks before. His success made me worry I was going down. I got a B on my math test, and an A minus on my cursive homework. It felt like my future was falling apart.

It was therefore a great relief when Sister said it was time to open our language arts books and read out loud. She went down the aisles, critiquing each child's pronunciation and fluency. The girl next to me counted the kids in front of her to figure out what paragraph she would be asked to read, but I wasn't nervous.

When Robert's turn came, he faltered a little. But overall, he did better than usual, and I felt my heart pounding with a mixture of envy and pride. When Sister got to me, I stood up and read. And I read. And I kept reading. She was supposed to tell me to stop, but instead I went on for a page and a half. When she finally told me I could sit back down, she looked around the room and said, "Now *that* is how you read a story."

I'd never been so proud.

Not long after, the bell rang for morning recess, and Sister let all the kids go outside except for Becca and me. She said we could go in a minute, but first she wanted to ask if we would be willing to perform a poem for the events the teachers had planned in April, to commemorate the revolutionary battles at Lexington and Concord in 1775.

"Paul Revere's Ride" was the longest rhyme I had ever seen. Becca would memorize seven stanzas, and I would memorize seven, and once we had the poem down exactly as it should be, we would tour the classrooms, performing Longfellow's words for every student in the school. Sister said it was important to understand that she wouldn't be working on it with us. It was our job to memorize our lines at home.

After agreeing to do it, I headed out to the playground, my heart battering with pride. I sat on the steps in the sun and watched Robert dominate in a game of kickball. I was happy, and when he got a runner out, I cheered.

A girl named Nicole came over and sat on the steps beside me. She was the least popular girl in class, maybe because she was always licking the back of her hands, which made them smell terrible. She rarely spoke, except to meow like a cat, and when she did speak it was about how she wanted to become a veterinarian. I smiled at her, figuring I may as well be nice.

"Look," I said, pulling a paper out of my pocket. I had drawn sketches of all the pure-bred dogs I admired. I loved laboring over the Standard poodle's fluffy balls of hair.

Nicole admired my artwork before asking me to play horse. She said it was my job to corral her, which sounded easier than it was. She pranced and neighed and bobbed her head as I chased her in a flat-footed frenzy. I dangled an invisible carrot, appealing to her imagination, but I never got within fifteen feet of her.

After a while, Nicole got tired of the game, and we sat along the chain-link fence behind the baseball diamond. She whinnied and nudged my shoulder with her nose.

She wanted to show me a Native couple walking along the sidewalk on the other side of the fence. Sacred Heart School sat on a hill above downtown Farmington, and there was a large Indigenous population there. Nicole and I stood up as they approached, and I saw that they were jolly and stumbling, as if they'd had a few beers. They called me "little sister" through the fence.

Nicole whinnied loudly and galloped away. I watched her bolt across the playground before they called me to come closer. I put my hand on the fence and said hi. I wanted to be polite, but they switched to Navajo or Apache or some language I couldn't understand. I was telling them to speak English, when Sister Angelica Anne yanked me by the arm.

I hadn't seen her coming and I was startled. I pulled back, trying to free myself, but her hand was a vise on my wrist. As she dragged me away, her voice sounded angry, and I realized she was genuinely afraid of them. "Don't talk to my students!" she yelled, her body tensing. She acted like they had done something wrong.

I looked at the couple over my shoulder as we retreated across the playground. Sister blew her whistle to make everyone line up. I fell in position behind Nicole, who turned around and wrinkled her nose. "Drunk Indians," she said, before we filed up the stairs toward the lunchroom door. Sister Angelica Anne put her hand on Nicole's shoulder, and I thought I heard her whisper "animals" under her breath.

Before going inside the building, I turned to gawk one last time, and saw the couple walking away. I remember thinking they seemed fine. They looked like my uncles and aunts. But then I saw them through Sister Angelica Anne's eyes, and I realized that she didn't see two young twenty-somethings having fun. To her, they were dangerous, utterly lacking in intelligence or restraint.

My face felt hot as I remembered Vin Scully's insult during the Dodger baseball game. The way he'd called the protesters on the field "animals." I wish I'd known that this slur said more about mainstream society than it did about us, that it was evidence most Americans undervalued the animal world, while I came from a people who valorized it. Grandma said we were from the badger clan, but I didn't think of her, or reclaim the pejorative, that day at school.

Instead, I felt embarrassed and sat in my seat blushing down to my toes. And as we opened our books to study, I thought about how I'd just found out that Dad had gone to prison as a minor because he'd wrecked a car and one of his friends had died. I knew his baggy pants, tattoos, and intense gaze sometimes scared strangers, especially white women. But I also knew that he worked hard and went to church and coached several softball teams as a volunteer for Little League. He was a good father. But I wondered what Sister Angelica Anne saw when he came to Sacred Heart for school events.

I looked at Robert across the room. Sister Angelica Anne was berating him about his lunch box. Slothfulness was sinful. He had forgotten it overnight in the coat closet, and it was stinking to high heaven. A few days before, I'd been jealous that he was the hero. Now I was afraid he could never be the good guy. I thought of Tonto, always the sidekick, always monosyllabic, backward, and dumb.

I watched Sister go through her file cabinet for our next lesson and sat up straight and tall. Despite being upset, I felt a rush of relief that she liked me. I didn't want her to see me like she saw the couple on the other side of the fence. I wanted to be respectable, the anomaly in her mind. I was Indian, but through obedience and silence I could rise. It was in my power to be the exception if I kept my mouth shut, toed the line, and jumped through Sister's hoops without protest or complaint.

That night, Dad came home with a Dalmatian, a real Dalmatian. Purebred. He said, "Don't get excited. We're just dog-sitting for a guy who lives in Shiprock."

This was the dog of my dreams. Sadie was tall and skinny and shaky and afraid. She was sensitive and elegant. If you moved too fast, she jumped like a nervous grandma. My sisters thought she was ugly. Lori said, "She looks funny around the mouth."

"You can almost see her ribs," Joan agreed.

I rolled my eyes at how dumb they were about her lineage and class. When they wouldn't shut up, I grew angry. "At least she's not a mutt like you guys," I told them, bracing myself for their punches.

I played with Sadie all week. I connected the dots on her back with my finger, walked her to the park on a leash, and checked out a book on her breed.

"Did you know Dalmatians were owned by English noblemen?" I asked Mom. "They trotted next to the carriages of rich people."

I imagined Sadie receiving treats from a lady in a fancy dress. I envisioned her guarding the horses of men in three-piece suits and top hats. Mom even let Sadie come inside the house because she was well behaved and special, different from other dogs—especially the ones I'd known on the reservation. "If you and Dad let me keep her, we can get a fancy pillow and put it by the fire for her to sit on," I said.

"She's not yours," Mom told me.

But I couldn't help wishing that she was. Sadie was a great listener who kept all my secrets. I told her about the couple at the fence, and how strict Sister was, and how hard I was working to be the best student at my school. With Sadie around, it didn't matter that my sisters were always busy with the Benally girls, or that Inky was gone.

The following week when I arrived at school, everyone was buzzing. A pile of poster boards sat on Sister's desk. She said, "We're going to have a play."

She held one of the poster boards up as an example. Across the top was written, BLACKSMITH. Beneath it was a drawing of a horse.

"This poster was made by a student a few years back," she said. "See what a nice job he did? Each of you will get a blank poster and an Early American role. You'll draw a picture beneath your job title just like he did."

She dug in her desk for scotch tape. "I'm taping your speaking part on the back of your board. Anyone who comes crying because it's lost is going to get in trouble. Understand?"

She folded her arms and looked around the room, her eyes lingering on Billy.

"Good. Come up when I call your name. Becca, School Mistress!"

Becca rushed eagerly to the front of the room with her chest puffed out. She reminded me of a chicken stretching her head across the henhouse.

"Robert, Indian!" Robert's head hung in a shuffling walk.

"Nicole, Nurse!" Nicole pouted on her way to get her poster board, and I knew it was because she wanted to be the blacksmith. When she got back to her desk she mewed.

"Billy, Sheriff!" Billy giggled nervously as he went to the front of the room.

Sister proceeded down the list of students. I sat perched at the edge of my seat. My palms itched with sweat.

In the end, everyone was assigned a role except for me, and a girl named Julie Maestas. Sister brought us up to the front of the class and said—"You two wait here"—before disappearing down the hall.

Robert said, "Debbie's gonna get the main part!"

Becca said, "No, Julie's going to get it!" (Our Longfellow performance had gone well, but I still couldn't call us friends.)

The class argued about me and Julie until footsteps sounded in the hall, and we all quieted down. Sister Angelica Anne entered, carrying a red, white, and blue headband in one hand and a gold crown in the other.

"I got these out of the storage closet," she said. "We've been using them for years. I hope you girls respect the school's property and take good care of them."

She explained that Julie and I would stand center stage, representing America and England, while our classmates would form a half circle around us. When I heard center stage, my heart pumped with pride.

"Deborah," Sister scolded. "I'm talking to you!"

I snapped back to attention.

"If you're not going to listen, I might have to give the part to someone else."

I looked at her blankly.

She spoke slowly. "You will play England. Here is your crown. Here is your line."

"Julie, you will play America." Sister handed her the red, white, and blue headband.

Julie stared at my crown sadly as she walked back to her seat. Her headband looked faded and floppy in comparison to my stiff, golden crown. I looked across the room at Robert. It was the first time we'd held each other's gaze, and I had no idea why he was frowning with disappointment.

That afternoon, when I arrived home from school, I dropped my book bag in the living room and ran to find Sadie. I wanted to tell her about my lead in the school play, but she was nowhere to be found.

"Mom," I yelled. "Where's Sadie?"

She came out of her bedroom and told me to stop shouting. She said Dad had taken Sadie home to Shiprock because her owner had returned from vacation. "I told you not to get attached," she said. "We can't afford a dog like Sadie."

The following Monday I was sitting at my table, waiting for Robert to come into the lunchroom. The day before he'd been in a fight with an older boy. It was after school, and no teachers had been around, but he had a bruise under one eye now, and the old, hunched posture he used to have before saving Billy's life.

Nicole came and sat with me. "I bet Sister's paddling Robert," she said.

I'd suspected the same thing, but I didn't want it to be true. "Maybe she's just talking to him."

"No, my grandma told Sister about the fight after school. Do you want to play horse when we go outside?"

I hadn't realized Nicole's grandmother was a fourth-grade lay teacher at Sacred Heart. They had different last names, and while I'd heard horror stories about her grandmother from the other kids, I hadn't made the connection. Figuring it out now, I knew why everyone kept their distance from Nicole. If she caught you doing something wrong, she ran to her grandma to tell.

"Why in the world did you tell your grandma?" I asked.

"Why not?" She shrugged.

I grimaced and shook my head before saying I didn't want to play horse.

Nicole got angry. After a moment of silence, she asked, "How come you get to be England?"

I was screwing the lid on my thermos. Mom had sent me cold cream of mushroom soup. It was my favorite, but only when warm.

I shrugged. "Just lucky I guess."

Nicole squinted her eyes, making them look beady and mean. "My grandma said it doesn't make any sense for an Indian to wear that crown."

When I inhaled, I felt a sharp pain in my rib.

A few weeks later, on the night of the big performance, I walked into the Sacred Heart School gym to find it brimming with parents and siblings. Libby and Mom were sitting on the aisle, and I saw them turn around to watch us as we entered, filing in two by two. Flashbulbs went off, but I refused to smile or look around. I focused on Sister Angelica Anne, who was standing onstage flagging us down as if we might forget where to go.

We climbed the steps in pairs and several nuns helped us line up in our spots. Sister Angelica Anne gripped my shoulders hard, adjusting my spot by a quarter of an inch. She fussed with Julie's headband, then turned to face the audience.

"Welcome to our play, *From Colony to Country, America!*"

The stage lights were hot, and I felt itchy under the collar as the play proceeded. Nicole finished her nurse's line with a tiny meow. Billy stuttered and Robert mumbled. A couple of kids messed up their lines. When it was my turn, I remembered everything Sister had told me about talking as loudly as possible.

"England," Sister called out.

I recited, "What started as a colony is now a country! I salute you, America, and wish you prosperity in all that you do."

Afterward we milled around at the back of the gym, waiting for our turn to get juice and cookies. Lori whispered, "You looked like a dork."

Mom messed with my braids and asked, "Why didn't you glance over so I could get a good picture of you?"

Joan added, "Yeah, why didn't you smile at us? And how come you yelled your lines?"

My mom's friend Libby told them to leave me alone. "You did fine, honey," she said, but her eyes looked sorry for me.

Robert walked up, his father's hand on his neck like he was guiding him.

Robert's father shook hands with my father. Then he looked down and gave me a funny-looking smile. "England, huh?"

I felt Dad's body tense up, just like it did at basketball games when his brother's team was losing, and we were sitting too close to the opposing team's fans.

He put his arm around my shoulder. "She was England, all right, and I saw your kid was a farmer."

After Robert and his father walked away, Dad looked at the refreshments set up by the PTO. "Those cookies look cheap," he said. "Let's go get ice cream instead."

I craned my neck to look over my shoulder at Robert and his father as we left. Robert's dad was bent over, telling him something at eye level. He looked angry, and Robert looked sad. I thought maybe he was in trouble for mumbling his lines, and I felt sorry for him. Or maybe I felt sorry for myself. Even though I was way ahead of Robert in our studies, I couldn't shake the feeling that he was wiser. It was like he had been initiated into the adult world with a secret code I still didn't have.

The following Saturday I was sitting on the swing set in our backyard when I heard a familiar bark and saw Sadie standing in the alley outside the gate.

"Sadie!" I screamed.

I ran over to let her in the yard. She licked my face and wriggled around like she wanted to climb up in my arms. "Dad!" I yelled. "Sadie came back!"

He opened the sliding door and stepped out, calling Mom to see. "Rainy, come and look!"

She came to the door too.

"That dog walked thirty miles to see Debbie," he said. "Lester told us she ran away this weekend. He said they drove all over the place looking for her but couldn't find her anywhere. I'm going to call and let them know she's here."

Mom looked at me and said, "You know we can't keep her, right?"

"I know," I answered, hugging Sadie. "I'm just so happy she came back."

To me, Sadie's return felt like a sign that I was as noble as she. I may have been born into a poor reservation world, but Dad said we came from a family of tribal leaders, and I was destined to do great things. I had the beauty and talent to rise above my half-breed status. I was destined for a better life, and Sadie had walked thirty miles to kiss me because she smelled my bright future on my cheeks.

FIRST FUNERAL

(1978)

✛

Sister Benedict said we'd be attending the funeral of a prominent Realtor. That's how she said it, like he was an appendage to his successful
career. The other kids in my third-grade class waved their arms with
questions. We'd never been asked to sing at a funeral mass before, and
many of them were unfamiliar with the rites and rituals. They wanted to
know what it would be like—Would the casket be open or closed? Would
we need to dress in all-black? What would we be expected to say to his
family?

At first, Sister said nothing in response. She just sipped at the warm
Coke she always drank from a thermos when she taught. But after a few
minutes, she told my classmates to put down their hands. Was it true, she
wanted to know, that not one of us had yet attended a funeral?

Around me, I saw heads nodding, but I kept my own head still.

Though diminutive in stature, Sister was a hard woman. Demanding,
suspicious, even cold. She said there was no reason in her mind to keep a
child from a funeral. In fact, when it came time for her sister's service, her
parents had insisted that she go, and she was made the better for it. She
launched into the story about her own first funeral.

Apparently, when Sister was only twelve years old, her sister's pajamas
had caught fire while she was trying to curl her hair using metal tongs
heated with a gas burner. "Suddenly my little sister was on fire," she told

us. "I saw her shoot out the back door into the yard. It was windy and I yelled at her to stop, but she wouldn't, and the flames grew bigger and bigger. I tackled her with a blanket and rolled her around in the grass to smother the flames, but her hair had melted against her head, and she looked unrecognizable."

Behind me, I could hear a few of the girls had started crying. In the front row, one of the biggest boys in the class looked pale.

"We took her to the doctor, of course, but they said there was nothing they could do for her. In the end, it took her a week to finally pass on, and I was sitting right next to her when she saw the angels come. Stop sniffling!"

Suddenly Sister rapped her knuckles against her desk. Her voice rose like it did when she preached the Old Testament. "There is nothing simpler than death, no reason to hide it from children, and you will open your mouths wide when you sing at the funeral. Do you hear me? You will not cry."

To my left, Nicole swiped at her eyes with the back of her hand, while on my other side, a boy blinked back tears. They were trying their best to do as Sister had commanded, but they were struggling. Meanwhile, my own eyes were dry as dust.

Finished with her story now, Sister Benedict sat at her desk, but after a moment she looked up again and noticed me. More than noticing, she scrutinized me like she did when we studied the Bible. I saw her take in my tearless cheeks, and at first, I felt proud to have kept my composure while my classmates fell to pieces all around, but then something shifted in her expression and I had to wonder whether pride was, in fact, what I should have been feeling. Her suspicious eyes seemed to ask what kind of girl didn't cry when faced with her story.

Suddenly, with Nicole still sniffling beside me, I became convinced that I'd made a mistake. I was sure that, by failing to cry, I'd let Sister see the Native side of me, the howling, dry desert I often felt moving inside my chest. I wasn't like the other children, that's what her gaze seemed to recognize. I came from a place that was not unfamiliar with death.

On the day of the funeral, several kids, including Robert, didn't show up to school. Sister Benedict was visibly displeased by their parents' "cowardice" (a few of them had complained about the curling iron story, as well as the plan for our class to sing at the mass), but she remained undeterred about her plan. She made us put on our jackets to march over to the school's church, reminding us that song was the most potent way to pray, and that our attention during the miracle of the Eucharist helped the poor souls in Purgatory who were stuck in a sort of prison waiting to see God. I nodded as she spoke and tried to look serious, so she wouldn't doubt my love of God, or remember that I was different from the other kids with my brown skin and tearless cheeks. When we were dressed and ready to go, she made us stand alongside our desks as she lectured us about the ceremony.

"You'll have to come down from the choir loft to receive communion and I have to warn you, the casket may be open." Most of us had never seen a dead body. "If it is—don't stare—but don't avoid looking either. Give a polite glance as you walk by, his family will be there watching you. Remember, this is an important businessman who was loved by many people."

We lined up at the door single file and walked across the school grounds to the church. It was a windy day and I shivered in my hand-me-down school uniform. We curled up the spiral stairs to the choir loft, genuflected alongside the pews, and scooted our way down the bench until we arrived at our assigned places. My seatmates and I, in unison, pulled the kneelers down to the floor and bent onto their hard wood. We said a prayer before sitting, and I stayed on my knees longer than everyone else so Sister would see I was devoted and trying to conquer the feral side of me. I had been assigned a spot in the front row where I could gaze down over the congregation and easily see everything.

The old brick church had long stained-glass windows that filtered drowsy light. The building always made me calm. There was something about the vaulted ceilings, the buttressed arches, the altar out in front with burning candles and incense. We went to mass every day, early in the morning, and I loved the reprieve from the classroom. Sitting with my schoolmates, it was easy to forget that Sister was behind me, judging and observing. The poetry of the Psalms, the repetition of the rituals, quieted me. Peace flowed through me, and I felt a momentary confidence that the world meant no harm.

That day, I saw the mourners dressed in black. They sat in the front two rows. I imagined their suffering, remembered our catechism's claim that there was an eternal value in pain. I examined the paintings we called the Stations of the Cross: Jesus being crowned with thorns, Jesus being scourged at the pillar, Jesus falling to the ground with the cross on his shoulder in a puddle of blood. The paintings hung along the wall at eye level, closer than usual, since we were upstairs in the loft.

Sister Angela Marie, Sacred Heart School's resident organ player, appeared on my left. She was ancient. She barely lifted her feet when she walked, always moving in a shuffle, but she came to life in front of her keyboard. Mom and Dad had hired her to give me piano lessons for a couple of months, but despite showing musical talent, I'd quit. Sister had made it a habit of hitting my knuckles with a ruler every time I dropped my wrists, and while it hadn't felt malicious, it hurt.

As Sister Angela Marie played, we listened to the readings, followed by the Gospel and the priest's homily. The mourners beneath us stood, sat, and knelt on cue while we punctuated the service with hymns. We opened our mouths wide and sang, "You shall cross the barren desert, but you shall not die of thirst. You shall wander far in safety, though you do not know the way. You shall speak your words to foreign men, and they will understand."

I observed the family of the deceased beneath me: the wife and his adult children who held their grief in like they were afraid. Their suits, from our vantage point, looked perfectly pressed, without wrinkles, and when they cried, they lifted their tissues to their noses in a controlled manner that muffled the sound. When I went down for communion the casket was closed. At first, I was disappointed. But then, relieved of the command to look at the body as we filed by the casket, I seized the chance to observe the oldest woman, the man's wife, up close and personal.

I could see her trembling in her black suit, as if an earthquake wanted to escape her body but she knew how to keep the rumbling deep inside so that only the faintest trace of the shuddering escaped her core. It reminded me of the time I'd seen Mom stifling her tears in church—how scary to see anyone shaking and fighting their own body. How long could we hold in our sadness without getting sick? I stuck my tongue out for communion, hung a left, and crossed in front of her. I faced forward but could hear the Realtor's wife choking on her sobs as I passed.

My clothes felt scratchy. My button-up shirt choked me. The collar was too tight, as were my French braids, and my hair was pulling at my face, making it feel taut as a hardened mask. As I walked to the back of the church, I caught a glimpse of Sister Benedict above me in the choir loft. She stared down at me, her face full of fire, her mouth frowning—and my breath caught in my chest. It was exhausting to be always under her magnifying glass, acting cautious and articulate, reduced to less than my authentic self. The dust devils swirled in my chest, and I fought to keep them down.

When I got back to my pew I knelt and prayed to be worthy, respectable, and clean. When it was time to stand, Father Ben closed the mass with one of my favorite Bible passages. He bent forward over the lectern, blinking behind his spectacles, his booming baritone voice speaking words that resonated in my chest because they felt like a sign from God, meant just for me.

"And whoever speaks a word against the Son of Man will be forgiven," he read. "But he who speaks a word against the Great Spirit will not be forgiven, either in this life or in the age to come."

The Catholic Church, where those in control depicted God as an old white man, felt like a straitjacket during my childhood. The Holy Spirit was mine though, because I could relate to its impermanent forms: a swooping white dove, a jumping tongue of fire, a wind shaping the sand dunes in the desert.

The following week my sisters and I were lounging in front of the TV in that sacred time on Saturday mornings before our parents woke up, when we were free to watch Hanna-Barbera cartoons and eat as many bowls of Lucky Charms as we wanted. A rental car commercial with O. J. Simpson in an airport had just come on when our mother appeared in the middle of our sock-strewn mess.

She had mascara smeared around her eyes like a raccoon. I looked at her mouth as she spoke, the wrinkles around her lips radiating in a pattern that reminded me of an overripe apple. I instinctively knew something bad had happened and reached out to grasp my little sister Monica's hand as she delivered the news. She said, "Your dad's brother Johnny and his wife, Anita, died last night. They flipped off the bridge between the reservation and Yuma and drowned in the car."

I don't know how long the idea sat there, the image of murky river water and inhaled algae, before I thought of our cousin Tonia, Uncle Johnny's only child, a four-year-old girl with glossy eyes and a helmet-like bob. Tonia collected small things from people, the people she liked most. The tinier the better—she kept the collection in an old cigar box under her bed. My sister Joan had given her a fancy bobby pin with a small glass butterfly at the tip. When we saw her during Christmas and summer breaks, I always tried to elicit a request, thinking maybe she'd ask me for something, but she never did.

Mom shut off the TV, saying it wasn't appropriate to watch in a time of mourning. She told us, "I've already started packing, and I don't want to hear a peep from you guys. Your dad was up all night on the phone with his brothers and sisters and he barely fell asleep. When he wakes up, we're taking off."

The car Uncle Johnny had been driving was a long, sporty bullet with electric windows that seized up and stopped working once they went under water. Unable to roll the windows down, they were trapped in the car. When Dad woke up, bloodshot and heavy, he made us help load the van with our bags. We piled inside and drove home to our family with

Dad bug-eyed and staring. We crossed the border from New Mexico into Arizona and started the long journey across the Navajo Reservation.

Every time Dad had a vacation, we went home to the reservation. But this was not like our usual visits. Dad stared out the window and didn't talk. It grew dark, and when my sisters and Mom fell asleep, I moved to my spot on the ice chest between the two captains' seats, like I always did. Finally, once the van quieted, he started talking. He said maybe Johnny could have forced a door open if he had stayed calm and waited for the water inside the car to rise to the ceiling so that the pressure outside matched the pressure inside.

According to Aunt Vi, who Dad had talked to on the phone, the family had initially held hope. When the divers first went down looking for victims or bodies, it was dark, and they came up saying there was no one in the car. A homeless guy who had been walking along the river when the car flew off the bridge told the police he saw two people emerge from the water. But as the sun rose, and the day grew lighter, the divers found Uncle Johnny and Aunt Anita, hugging each other in the backseat of the car. She had a black eye, as if they'd been fighting, or as if she'd been banged up in the wreck. They were locked together, we learned when we got to the family, their long hair floating around them in the water like streamers.

Traditional funerals on our reservation last a full twenty-four hours. Southern California Natives—the Cahuilla, Luiseños, Kumeyaay, and us—perform the *keruk*. The family had burned all Uncle Johnny's stuff before we got to town as the first portion of the ceremony. When we arrived, there was a mass at St. Thomas Indian Mission, after which Father Rusty sent us, our uncles, aunts, and cousins on our way. I saw in his eyes that he knew—of course he knew—that the church part was secondary in significance to the tribal portion. He had been invited to attend the *keruk* with us after mass, but he wouldn't come.

"Go your way now," Father Rusty said grimly as we filed out and headed down to the tribal cemetery, which held the Cry House and cremation grounds.

We piled into the back of the van, moaning because our cousins got to walk down the Hill to the Cry House instead of riding in their parents' cars, and we wanted to walk with them as well, but Mom was being over-protective and wouldn't let us out of her sight.

The cremation grounds sit on a desert lot with tombstones at one end and a simple building with a ramada and kitchen at the other. The ceremonial site is gated, and once everyone arrived, the groundskeeper locked it behind us. We went into the Cry House. It was a big room and had pews like in church. My Uncle Johnny and Aunt Anita were laid out on two old hospital beds in the center of the room, their bodies water-logged and swollen. We sat with them. We talked to them. My cousin Anna brushed Johnny's hair. But we were restless kids, and despite feel-ing sad, the afternoon grew long, so we asked if we could go outside and play.

"Only if you stay away from the graves," Dad said.

Dad and Uncle Bill had often told us a childhood story about playing at the Cry House with some of their elementary school friends. They said an old hospital bed used in the ceremonies had been sitting outside, and one kid decided to lie on it like he was dead. Their other friend, who spoke decent Quechan, started singing a funeral song, and as they were mocking the ceremony, the bed began to violently shake. Terrified, they jumped on their bikes and fled, but when they got to Pipa Market, they saw that Uncle Bill was missing. Sometime later, he came running without his bike and said he had been peddling to get away but despite pumping as hard as he could his wheels just stayed in the same place.

"Don't be disrespectful to your ancestors," Dad said, looking us in the eyes. We all knew what he meant, so when we went outside, we avoided the graveyard and went behind the kitchen instead.

With everyone in town for the funeral, we and our cousins made a big gang. We hunted around for frogs, but they liked water, and we were too far from the canal to find any. We looked for shapes in the clouds, but they were rare in the desert, so we decided to play tag instead. We chose the "chaser" with a game of fists in the center: one person knocked out by the song's final word on their outstretched fist until the last kid standing was "it."

Our favorite singsong went, "My mother and your mother are hanging out clothes. My mother pops your mother right in the nose. What color was the blood?"

"Purple."

"*P-u-r-p-l-e*! And you are not it!"

Then we dodged and ran. We laughed and pushed each other down and fought and made up. We had fun until it grew dark and our parents brought us back inside for the ceremony. We found Mom standing at the back of the room with Aunt Vi, who was gathering newly purchased items to put on the cremation fire the following morning. Dad had bought some beautiful new blankets to send with his brother, but Mom wanted to put our school pictures on the fire instead.

Aunt Vi looked tired, like Mom was trying her patience. "You can't put their pictures on the fire! That's like tempting the next world to take them."

Mom crossed her arms and rolled her eyes, like she didn't believe a word Aunt Vi was saying, and Dad had to step in. Dad always had to step in when Mom didn't agree with his traditions. She hated, for example, the way the women in his family served their kids and husbands their dinners first, before sitting down themselves, and she would often sit at the table with the men. Most of the time, Dad didn't try to stop her, but this time he took her outside for a talk, and when they came back inside, I saw her put our photos away with a huff.

It was time for the gourd rattlers, men from the bird clan, to pick up their instruments. They stood in two long lines at the far end of the bodies, moving their feet and hips slightly but staying rooted to their place. I squeezed into a pew next to Dad, who was sitting with his sister Eve. The men started singing a song in Quechan, and the old language illuminated the room with grief.

Dad leaned toward his sister and whispered, "I can never remember this song's name. What is it?" And she answered quietly in his ear.

They looked at each other—memories I couldn't access bringing them to tears—and then Mom came and squeezed in between them. We listened as the men sang songs I couldn't understand. I asked Dad what the songs meant, and he said some of them were about my uncle's and aunt's lives, but most were guiding them on their three-day trek across the desert to the next world.

All night long, they sang. And all night, the women in my family danced the clothes of my relatives to the gourd rattler's music. Each deceased member of our family had an outfit in their size, measurements, and style tied together in a bundle with a bright scarf. An outfit for Uncle Johnny, Aunt Anita, Grandma, and Grandpa. Grandma's dress had a button-up breast and collar. Her shoes looked like a nurse's pair with rubber soles, while the pantyhose were caramel, lighter than her skin, the type that she preferred.

They swayed side to side, lifting and lowering the clothing bundles with their feet planted in place; from sunset to sunrise, they did this movement, without setting the bundles down. After hours of dancing, the women holding the clothes began to fade, and the people whose clothes they were holding started to come back to us. This was the way Johnny ran pigeon-toed across the court to fake a basketball shot; this is the way Anita's eyes curved into crescent moons when she laughed.

Finally, midnight arrived, that hour when the world is at its darkest, and the other families, the ones not so close to Uncle Johnny and Aunt Anita, began crying, to help Dad and his brothers and sisters with their grief. I had dozed off on the bench when I heard the women, their voices deep and mournful, "Ah-ah, ha!" They started crying in unison, their mouths wide open, their voices rising and melding together in the dimly lit room. Outside the windows, the Sonoran Desert was dark as it could be.

My father's body shook when he heard them cry. I could feel it trembling as I leaned against him, the earthquake inside him gaining power until he could no longer contain it, until he split open, and I could see his grief. He got up and walked to the hospital beds, removed his turquoise ring, and slipped it onto Uncle Johnny's water-swollen pinky. Mom came to get me and my sisters then. She said we were done, that she was putting us to bed in the van.

We followed her into the night, complaining. Why did we have to leave when our cousins got to stay? Didn't Dad need our support? I had no idea, at that point in my childhood, that Mom was *genízaro*, but I could see how challenged she was by Dad's traditions. His ways, to me, felt so much more meaningful than hers, and she seemed to see that I felt this way, and resented the fact I loved his customs more. Or maybe her sadness was personal; maybe Dad's traditions sparked her own ancestral loss.

She tucked us into sleeping bags, where I slept fitfully until a pink hue appeared on the horizon out the window. Then the Cry House doors were thrown open, and men, who had transferred the bodies to simple wooden caskets, came out to walk them slowly across the desert to the cemetery. The gourd song grew louder as sunrise approached, and we jumped out of the van to join the procession. Fifteen steps and stop. Gourds rattling. Twenty steps and stop. Voices rising. The men carried the bodies, starting and stopping, until we arrived at the cemetery grounds, a hundred feet away.

I held tight to Dad's hand and walked beside his trembling body. A pyre of cottonwood stood in the cemetery, directly over where Uncle Johnny's and Aunt Anita's white tombstones would be placed once it all burned away. Their bodies were removed from their caskets and put on top of the cottonwood for their journey home. The caskets were then turned upside down on top of the funeral pyre as well. After that, the women stepped forward one at a time to add the clothes from the dance. When they finished, Dad gave us the gift blankets to place on top. I walked back to him still wearing the ceremonial shawl I had worn for the night, but he made me return and add it as a gift to our ancestors as well. Finally, just as the sun peeked over the horizon, the Cry House groundskeeper lit the fire.

Soon any proof that our loved ones had been there would be gone, but we weren't allowed to stand in the cemetery and watch the fire burn down. Our tribal tradition taught that the longing between those who had passed and those who remained could be a threat to the living, so we walked back to the Cry House for breakfast. And as we sat there, waiting to be served by our aunties in the kitchen, Granny Ethel talked about how my big brother had been born right after Grandpa Ed Jr. passed away, and she said, as she had many times before, that she believed her son had been selfish enough to take my brother to the next world with him. Mom's face tensed up at Granny's comment, and though she had too much respect to argue, I knew she preferred for my brother to be in limbo where the priests said unbaptized babies went.

That evening, we had a party at Uncle Gene's house on Jackson Road. He and Uncle Johnny had never left the reservation, and Aunt Vi said she wished Johnny hadn't stayed, as if she thought leaving might have saved his life. Dad shook his head and said nothing would have stopped his anger. "Look what the bastards did to us," he said, lifting his chin toward the horizon.

By then, I'd learned enough to know that we'd been wronged, though the specifics of our history were still vague. Dad grew quiet, and I couldn't put it into words myself, but it felt like my uncles Johnny and Gene had chosen poverty on the reservation for a reason, that their marginalized existence was self-imposed, and maintained as an act of resistance. And even as Uncle Gene got stumbling drunk that night, I still saw him as the coolest uncle in the world.

When Gene got rowdy, Dad poured his beer on the ground and said it was time to go. My older cousins hugged us goodbye, saying they guessed the funeral pyre had finally burned down and they could return to the cemetery now. They had whitewashed a pile of softball-size rocks before the funeral and planned to carry them out to the cremation site where they would place them around the two graves in the shape of a large white heart.

When I went back to school the following week, Sister Benedict made me stand at the front of the class.

"Tell them where you've been," she said, in one of her moods.

"I was at my uncle's funeral," I said.

"Tell them how he died, tell them who was with him," she said. She dissected me with her judgmental and cruel gaze. But who was she to teach me about the perils of alcohol, and the dangers of giving into feelings of victimhood, anger, and pain?

I spoke to her defiantly, saying, "It was a party and he wrecked the car."

"Tell them who he was with," she repeated.

"It was my aunt," I said, staring into her eyes without blinking. "It was her birthday."

I thought of the gourd rattles and the midnight criers. I thought of how the bodies looked in the dark. I thought of my own small body, already aged, frail and dying itself. I looked at Sister, who was trying to elicit shame, and I refused to cry. I remembered the fiery sun and smoking barren desert we had crossed on our way back inside the Cry House. I could hear the bird clan singing in my mind, and I felt strong.

I turned away from Sister Benedict and felt her talon-hands shoving me back toward my desk. I leaned backward into her push, dragging my feet as she urged me along. I wanted to howl and howl loudly, but I shoved it all down, deep in my body. I felt the rumble and tremor, but I refused to let it rise to the surface. I refused to let it rise because the howling was beautiful. I had seen that it was beautiful, and Sister did not understand— and Sister did not deserve to see.

PANCAKE ALLEY

(1979)

✛

Our favorite diner in Farmington was Pancake Alley, located downtown near the Animas River bridge. Their menu had Indian tacos that Mom always craved. During the summer, we would sometimes park a few blocks away from the diner to stroll past the Totah Theater, a Pueblo Deco building that screened action flicks with Bruce Lee and Clint Eastwood. But when we went to the restaurant in winter, we always parked as close as we could, and then as soon as we got out of the car we ran. The freezing north wind from Colorado felt so different from the Sonoran Desert. Even after four years in Farmington, it was hard to get used to.

One day in March, we went to the restaurant with Dad to wait for Mom, who was at parent-teacher conferences. I normally loved dinner at Pancake Alley. We hung our jackets in the coat closet and took a booth by one of the big street-facing windows. It had the best people-watching views, but that night my stomach hurt, and I couldn't enjoy my gawking. My fourth-grade teacher had accused me of cheating on a test, and for the first time in my life I was worried that I would get a failing grade.

I'd initially been excited to get Mrs. Toronto, even though I didn't like her granddaughter, Nicole, and Joan had told me as a teacher she was tough. At the start of the school year, I had reasoned that a lay teacher wouldn't be so moralizing, so prone to look in my soul and see "heathen." Joan said she was strict, but that didn't stop me from entering her classroom with confidence that fall, thinking I would excel academically. I was still wounded by the way Sister Benedict had judged Uncle Johnny, but I knew I was smart, and I was sure that this year would be different.

As expected, Mrs. Toronto focused less on catechism and more on science and math. If she believed our Catholic school was the best in town, it was for the rigor rather than the presence of religion. She dozed off in mass, and rarely spoke about God. I never felt her watching me as I prayed, not scrutinizing the time I spent in confession. Yet even as I sensed she cared nothing about spiritual colonialism, I began to see that her brand of racism was even worse than the nun's proselytizing suspicions.

No matter how much I focused on my studies, or volunteered for classroom duties, Mrs. Toronto frowned with derision. She scowled every time she handed me back a paper with an A. Her handwriting in the margins of my work looked angry and jagged. At times, she pressed so hard with her red pen, she tore a hole in the page. It felt violent, and it confused me, until finally, the week prior, she'd accused me of cheating on a math test, and I realized she didn't want to help, save, or convert me. She didn't want me to do well at all.

From our booth, I could see all kinds of folks walking by, big-hatted Texans, light-skin Hispanics, Navajo cowboys, and hawkers selling their wares on the street. Navajo grandmas with their grandchildren wandered inside the restaurant to hawk jewelry to diners: juniper berry necklaces, turquoise rings, concho belts, beaded bracelets with geometric patterns, and horse-hair bolo ties. They always talked to us in Diné. "Ya'at'eeh" meant hello— even I knew that—but then Dad always had to say that we couldn't understand what they were saying.

I had my face close to the glass, watching for Mom to pull up and park on the street, when, suddenly, a Navajo grandma stood before our booth, modeling big jewelry on her small-boned wrists and fingers. She reminded me of my grandmas, except that this grandma wore a long velvet dress and a velvet button-up blouse. When Dad said—"We don't speak Diné"—she simply stood her ground and held the jewelry up higher.

I hated disappointing her. Even Dad shrunk up a bit after saying he didn't want to buy any. He opened his palms and shrugged, embarrassed. But when the grandma before our booth refused to give up on the sale and continued to speak in Diné—like she thought the words would return to us, like it hadn't occurred to her that we might be from a different tribe— Dad swapped his embarrassment for impatience. He ignored the grandma and told me and my sisters, "Go wash your hands for supper."

It was clear that he was irritated, and that made me nervous, so I didn't move, and neither did they. I caught a glimpse of our waitress at a nearby table. She had noticed the grandma badgering for a sale and was now waving her hand to catch the attention of her boss at the cash register. When she finally caught the manager's gaze, she looked, pointedly, at our table, and he seemed to understand. Staking a receipt to a metal spike, he moved away from his station to come over.

The Navajo vendors were allowed to sell in the restaurant, but they were supposed to move on when customers didn't want to buy. Now the waitress had tattled on the grandma for breaking the rules, and our involvement made my hands sweat. I had social anxiety. I didn't want people to stare. I didn't want Dad or the Navajo grandma to get in trouble, and Dad's temper in awkward public encounters made me nervous.

During my childhood, I'd often been wary of the way Dad reacted to people in public. He sometimes exchanged words with mouthy cowboys on the street. Other times, at company holiday parties, he grew sheepish with his Navajo coworkers. His assistant softball coach, Mr. Wilson, was Navajo and Mormon, and they got along great. But sometimes, with more traditional Navajos, Dad seemed awkward.

The sheer size of the Navajo reservation was imposing, as were their enrollment numbers, the ubiquity of their language, the liveliness of their traditions, and the wars they fought with the U.S. government. A quarter of Farmington's population was Diné, and that excluded the shoppers who drove in from the reservation on weekends. We were in their territory, and Dad spoke about them with awe. He felt he owed them his job. When uranium ore was discovered in the Colorado Plateau, their tribal council facilitated mining, as they put it, "in the interest of the nation and the Navajo reservation." From uranium ore they had moved to coal mining and coal-fired power plants.

But Dad's relationship with them became more complicated the longer he worked with them. When he told his Navajo friends that New Mexico was also his homeland because his mother was Pueblo, they laughed and said Pueblo wasn't a tribe but a Spanish word for "town." When he explained that his granny was Shoshone Paiute, they said he had too many tribes. And when they asked about his traditions, Dad had to admit the Quechan didn't have many. The Navajos, with their many songs, ceremonies, oral histories, woven rugs, sand paintings, and silversmith work, were a force in the region.

When we lived in Yuma, I used to love to see the old folk on the reservation. A few men still wore their hair in river dreadlocks. Some of the women still tattooed their chins. But other than these remnant traditions, everyone shopped in town and watched TV. In Farmington, some of the Navajo girls on our softball team talked about learning to weave with the wool from their family sheep. Other Navajo girls, like the Benally and Wilson families, were city kids like us. But it was the rural ones with their old ways who inspired my curiosity and comparisons.

I asked Dad why we never learned to do traditional stuff back home. He looked embarrassed and at first said he didn't know. But then he admitted that the Quechan didn't have many crafts, maybe because our traditional hunting was mostly fishing. There were no bone needles for sewing, no hide canvases for painting, and no weaving, since our tribe never owned sheep. Granny Ethel sewed beadwork on her regalia, but those crafts were from elsewhere. Dad said Navajos sometimes looked down on our simpler ways, and he seemed sorry about the Quechan lack of interest in material things. He brought up the *icama*, the second dimension our ancestors believed we could enter through dreaming. He said early diaries by Spanish explorers pointed to the *icama* in their observations of our tribe.

Our ancestors' dream philosophy led to nonmaterialism and a lack of interest in oral histories. Once I grew up, I read the accounts myself—according to the Spanish conquistadors, men who moored their galleons in the Gulf of California and rowed smaller boats up the Colorado River to the Yuma area—that our ancestors were difficult to interview. Even when they found Indians who spoke Spanish, the histories they offered were scanty. They could talk about past wars, past encounters with other tribes and Europeans, but they had no interest in positioning the events on a calendar for their listener. They weren't interested in naming seasons and paid little notice to "time," even after understanding that it was an important practice with other people. The *icama*, journeys taken in their sleep, held their attentions instead.

Navajo criticism threw Dad off more than white criticism. With whites, his interactions felt transactional. With Navajo people, his anxiety ran deeper. It took years, but I eventually came to understand why Dad felt diminished by Navajo culture. He had been incarcerated for four years, which meant he had missed his formative education at home. Yet even if he hadn't been sent away, it would not have alleviated his cultural cringe, since the embarrassment was a direct outgrowth of our unique tribal traditions. Aside from the *keruk*, our cremation funerals, and *nyima'ts xavtca'ts*, or our harvest festivals, rituals and ceremonies were nonexistent. The *icama* made a Quechan person's relationship to the Creator entirely individual; there were no pulpits in Native America, no prescriptive methods or rules for finding your spiritual path.

In the diner, Dad changed his mind. When he saw our waitress alerting the manager, he agreed to buy something from the Navajo grandma. He pointed with his lips at a juniper berry necklace she had on a display board. "We'll buy that one," he said, handing her the money.

The grandma was counting his change when the manager arrived in a huff. He said, "I don't mind you selling here, but I told you not to pressure—"

"She ain't bothering no one," Dad said. He gave the waitress a look as he spoke to the manager, like he didn't appreciate her tattling.

The manager responded, "I thought—"

"You thought wrong," Dad said.

Dad's curt attitude made the manager back away. Joan took the juniper berry necklace, and she and Lori started bickering about who got to wear it. Dad settled the argument by taking it and telling them to be quiet or he was going to get mad.

The manager left and the waitress took our order, blushing. Dad got the usual for Mom, even though she still hadn't arrived, and I noticed that the waitress avoided his eyes, afraid that he was mad. When she left the table, I tried to find a neutral topic. "Sure looks like it might snow, don't you think?"

I watched our waitress clip my family's order to the line cook's carousel. When she waved goodbye to a group of oilfield hands, the flesh on her arm flapped loose as a wattle. Her hunched shoulders and pulled-back chest suggested frailty. Did her hands tremble as she ladled the stew? I looked from her to Dad, who took the juniper berry necklace and shoved it into the front pocket of his flannel shirt.

I sympathized with our waitress. Dad could be scary. I found him scary. He was an acne-scarred Yuma Indian with a thrice-broken nose, crooked and tough. His tattooed arms were burly from weight lifting. His scraped and bruised knuckles looked as if they had landed plenty of punches. Years of manual labor—gripping wrenches and screwdrivers, welding torches and grinders—had stiffened his tendons. To stretch them, he habitually clenched and unclenched his fists.

At first, when I'd heard he wouldn't be going to our parent-teacher conferences, I'd felt relieved. But now, seeing him look out the window for Mom, I considered telling him about my teacher's accusation. If anyone was going to believe me, or take my side against a white teacher, it was him. He may have felt diminished by other Indians, but I'd never seen him suck up to white people in Farmington like Mom.

I started to say something, but just as I opened my mouth to speak, he looked out the window and said, "There she is," and I saw Mom arrive in the family Thunderbird. She parked across the street, jumped out, and ran across to the restaurant. A blast of cold air entered the diner as she burst through the door and marched straight up to our booth without stopping at the coatrack. Her eyes were red and puffy from crying.

"What's wrong?" everyone started asking, but Mom looked straight at me.

"You have some explaining to do," she said. She crowded in next to Dad, leaned forward, and pinched my leg under the table. "What difference does 'smart' mean if you're going to hell, huh?"

When Mom was angry or tired or hungry, her tongue became a blade. Even on good days, she sharpened it with dark humor, mostly against Dad. She loved to argue. She was smart and quick and knew exactly which words would cut.

She told me how ashamed she was of me, how I'd made them look like terrible parents. "Mrs. Toronto treated me like a fool," she hissed. She turned to tell Dad, "I can't believe she'd do this to us."

"What did she do, kill a priest?" Joan asked, before a murderous look from Mom shut her up.

"Maybe if you give her a chance to talk," Dad said, his voice rising like it did when I took a strike without swinging on a perfectly good pitch. The late-afternoon sun was sinking, and the lights in the diner felt suddenly strong and stage-like. I didn't turn my head, but it felt like everyone was staring at me.

Outside the snow was starting to fall in thick chunks, the first accumulation since Christmas. I looked at Dad, hoping he would see through my teacher's prejudice and lies and get angry at Mom for taking her side. Surely, he would know that there were people like Mrs. Toronto, who believed the worst about a person for no good reason.

Morning mass, language arts, long division: the day Mrs. Toronto accused me of cheating started like any other. She prepared us for our math test with a practice sheet, then told us to clear our desks. As soon as she went down the hall to grab copies, everyone started talking. The Italian kid who sat across from me, a boy with big ears named Chuckie, passed a note to a girl he liked at the back of the room.

Our wooden desks each had an open storage space beneath the seat. I chatted with a classmate as we put our stuff away, tucking my math paperwork into a library book before bending to shove it into my storage space. I had a hard time making it fit, and I knew I'd have to organize the space, and throw papers away, if I wanted my desk to look clean for parent-teacher conferences the following week.

Mrs. Toronto returned. She handed out the exam, then walked the aisles, watching us as we took our test. She didn't say anything about the library book sticking out of my storage bin, the top edge of my multiplication facts chart semivisible. But after the test was done, she rose like a giant in front of my desk, attacking me in a voice that stank of coffee, saying I had exposed my multiplication facts on purpose, intending to help both myself and Chuckie.

I hadn't cheated. I hadn't even noticed the facts chart sticking out of my book. And I wasn't trying to help Chuckie. His gangly long arms, big ears, the hint of balding at his temples, everything about him made me cringe. He had a rotation of girls he liked, and when my sisters discovered I was one of them, they started humming Rickie Lee Jones's song "Chuck E's in Love" to humiliate me. Sometimes, when he and I stood next to each other in the lunch line, he puckered up his lips and made kissing noises at me.

Mrs. Toronto grabbed me by the elbow, dragged me to the front of the classroom, and forced me on my knees. Then she circled, her voice crashing over the room in waves, until all I could hear was the classroom's fluorescent hum. Finally, after an excruciating amount of time, she grabbed my hand and turned my palm up to be reddened by her ruler.

The swats she gave me stung, but the physical pain was nothing compared to the shame. I was an excellent student. I worked hard in her class, yet she was determined to see me fail. She didn't like Indians, I realized, and that's all I was to her.

Her granddaughter Nicole, who was a C student, sat in the front row shaking her head, and on top of resenting her for being a tattletale, I suddenly disliked her even more for being white. In my mind, her whiteness meant she would be met with kindness, and be given the benefit of the doubt in ways that I would not.

My hand throbbed and my face felt hot as I stood and walked back to my desk. I watched Mrs. Toronto ask Chuckie if he had "accepted" the help I offered him. Chuckie's ears were inflamed. He said no, like he wouldn't accept a million dollars from the likes of me, even if it came with a lifetime supply of candy. Mrs. Toronto beamed and said his honesty had saved him from a paddling.

I went home with my tongue cemented to the roof of my mouth. I said nothing to my family and returned to school the next day with a sheepish smile frozen on my face. I couldn't fight for fairness because I didn't believe in it anymore. I finally understood, with people like Mrs. Toronto, effort was never enough.

Weirdly, she acted nicer after she accused me. She handed back our math tests with a smile, and the F near my name looked so odd, and made me feel so confused, I didn't know how to position my arms and legs in my desk anymore. She asked us to get out our science books, but I couldn't focus. An F required a mother's or father's signature, and the upcoming parent-teacher conferences loomed.

All week long, my stomach stretched tight, like my innards were wrapped around a heavy piece of lead. Eating dinner at home, my meat loaf was appetizing as a ketchup-laden slug. Mom and Dad were going to be mad at me. They paid tuition so my sisters and I could overcome our circumstances. We were supposed to lift the family to a new level of respectability, to show everyone we were just as good as they were, that we weren't loser Indians.

I didn't eat, but no one asked me why. I had failed them. I couldn't impress or convince my teachers that I was good, and so I would never live up to my parents' expectations. By Sunday night, I had worked my health into a frenzy, and Mom found me moaning in bed. It was past midnight when she came into the room and asked what the matter was. I told her I was sick. She put her lips to my forehead and declared I wasn't hot. I told her my stomach hurt. I didn't cry, but my voice cracked, and she finally understood that something had happened.

She sat next to me on the bottom bunk, slouching forward so that she wouldn't bump her head on the bed above. "Tell me what happened," she said.

And that's when I lied. I was afraid to tell her what I had become in my teacher's eyes. I lied because if I spoke the word *cheater* out loud, the accusation might become truth. Plus, I was embarrassed by the whole Chuckie thing. I told her I was upset because a girl in my class had been swatted, knowing the story would sound true because it was. It had happened the year before, and it was so horrific, and I was so haunted by it, that I had kept it a secret until now.

There had been a sweet Mexican girl in my third-grade class who got caught with a boy in a playground tunnel. Our teacher, Sister Benedict, used the girl to teach us a lesson about sin and kissing. The situation was a nightmare, made worse when the girl knelt for her whacking, because that's when I heard tinkling and the kid next to me yelled, "Yuck." Then I saw what he had seen too, a pool of urine spreading across the floor. The girl's socks were soaked, and Sister yelled for her to grab paper towels to clean it up.

Judging by Mom's audible gasp, she was mortified by the story, and I suddenly saw my mistake: the outcome of the swatting had shocked her enough that she might talk to Mrs. Toronto about the situation at parent-teacher conferences. It had been a long time since I cried, but I did then because I didn't know how to roll my words back and tell her that the timeline and the teacher in my story were lies.

"You poor thing," Mom told me.

She brought me water, and even in the dim light, I could see her worry lines. She didn't say much about what I'd told her, but she insisted that the nuns and lay teachers she had gone to school with were always so kind, and I told her that the girl was still in my classroom and for a time she sat in front of me and she had puffy skin and a red wine stain shaped like a piece of cocktail shrimp on the back of her neck. Mom listened and stroked my hair until I stopped crying and the pain in my stomach eased. Then she told me to go back to sleep. She went to the door, and just as my head hit the pillow, she said the worst thing I could imagine. "Try not to worry about that girl in your class. Only the worst kids get paddled like that."

She said "worst," but I heard "brown." My mother, with her light skin and pretty face, had always been able to pass, and I resented it that night. Dad always said I was light, but I wasn't as light as Mom, and I resented her for blaming the girl instead of our puritanical teacher.

I climbed out of bed and got on my knees. Because it felt like a sin to hate Mrs. Toronto, because I didn't want to sacrifice who I was to succeed, because I wanted my parents to be proud of me, I prayed. I prayed for the F on my math test to become an A, and for Mrs. Toronto to tell Mom I was an academic star, a kid certain to be okay.

Mom reached under the table at Pancake Alley and pinched my leg again. "Tell your father about Chuckie!" she said.

"I didn't do it!" I hissed back, emboldened by the mention of his name.

Just then the waitress arrived with two hamburgers and two grilled cheese sandwiches. I'm sure she saw the drama going on at our table, yet she cleared her throat and inserted herself into our conversation with a determined professionalism. "Who ordered the onion rings?"

Mom blushed, her eyes still puffy, and her nose running. "That would be her," she said, nodding at Monica. "Doesn't that look yummy?" Her voice sounded weird anytime she tried to hide her anger. Her deep tenor pitched high and phony, but at least she knew how to play nice with white people.

I stared at the waitress's hairline to avoid Mom's glare and the feeling that everyone in the restaurant was watching us. It looked like the waitress had worn so many tight ponytails, she had yanked most of it out. She slid Monica's plate across the table, stretching in front of Dad. As she leaned across his lap, she said, "Excuse me."

"*Squeeze* me?" Dad shouted, like he couldn't believe what he'd heard.

The "squeeze me" joke was Dad's favorite, especially in uptight moments. He liked to feign offense that women were trying to pick him up. When things got awkward, he'd wait for the perfect moment, when the waitress in question was reaching across the table, her attention fixed on someone else, before he shouted his line. Comedy was the tomahawk he used to slice through subliminal tension.

After jumping like she'd seen a scorpion curled up in the stainless steel creamer, the waitress laughed along with Dad. "Got you!" he said, his smile revealing the lucky gap between his teeth. He turned to me and winked, his face changing from tough disciplinarian to naughty kid, and I realized that he was trying to lighten Mom's mood.

Mom turned sideways in the booth and punched Dad on the shoulder. "Just ignore the big dummy," she said to the waitress. "He's always goofing off." Then she sighed and looked at me, and I could see the tension on her face break and calm down. She took her food from the waitress. "We'll talk about this later," she told me, and everyone started eating.

But despite Mom's promise to wait until later, she kept hinting that I was in trouble. She brought up the lie about Mrs. Toronto making my classmate pee. How could she believe anything I told her? Dad interjected to ask about my semester math grade—like the grade was most important—and Mom said the fact that the F only lowered my grade to a B didn't matter because character was more important than grades. Dad said to "go easy" and Mom said he had "no right to talk" and Dad grew quiet because he knew better than to side with us when Mom was on the warpath. In fact, all of us knew when she got on her high horse he couldn't intervene. Then Monica said they would believe me if either of them saw Chuckie, and Lori started laughing, and Joan started humming that stupid Rickie Lee Jones's song again.

When the waitress came back at the end of the meal, she had the check and another plate. "We've got a new cook who can't get the hang of the

Mickey Mouse pancakes," she said. Sure enough, Mickey's ears and head were lumpy and misshapen.

"Thanks, but we don't let the kids eat sweets," Dad told her.

My sisters laughed and rolled their eyes, but he said to get up. It was time to go home. Mom slid out of the booth, straightened her dress, and swung her new purse over her shoulder. A woman at a nearby table stared, and Mom stared back until the woman looked away. Dinner had returned her to her full strength. I saw it in her walk as she headed toward the door, the keys to her sports car dangling from one finger.

When we got to our coats, Dad took the Thunderbird keys and gave them to Joan, who had just received her learner's permit at fourteen. "Take your sisters home," he said, before looking at me. "Not you. You're coming with me and Mom."

Mom wasn't sure about letting Joan drive in the snow with only a learner's permit, but Dad said the roads weren't icy, they were just wet, and besides, he had taught her how to pump the brakes in a snow-packed parking lot at Christmas.

As Dad and I followed Mom toward the van, I imagined what she must have looked like in my classroom, sitting in a small chair next to Mrs. Toronto's large desk, lectured about her skills as a mother, flashing back to her own feelings of inadequacy in childhood. I knew she had wounds from her teachers. It was no secret that her family had relied on Catholic charity. In the nuns' eyes, she had been a poor girl dragging ten little brothers behind her, all of them wearing raggedy hand-me-down clothes.

But she wanted to believe she was beyond that now. We were not a scholarship family. She was a homeowner who drove a fancy sports car and a twelve-seater club van. Her kids excelled in their studies. If she was pissed, she was pissed because she knew how to behave around white people, and she thought it should protect her from being treated poorly. Defending me when I didn't deserve it made her feel small, and no knife on God's green earth cut deeper than losing progress.

So many things happened afterward that I never expected. Dad grounding me until I raised my grade. Mom expecting me to apologize to Mrs. Toronto. I hung my head and listened as we drove, even though I was too young to grasp that my parents pressured me for different reasons. Dad felt like we had sacrificed everything—if we were giving up the reservation, I had to excel. Otherwise, what had it been worth?

Mom, however, felt fear. She couldn't help but internalize Mrs. Toronto's impression of us. She blamed me because she thought my dark skin and lies might drag us down and reflect poorly on the family. A nascent realization rose in my brain: Mom had an inferiority complex with whites like Dad did with Navajos.

As a small girl, I donned both versions of this oppression, and that's why I was always nervous in public. I had developed a "less than" perspective about Navajo people, yet I also feared that I wasn't as "good" as whites. At the age of ten, I started feeling confused about where I might belong in Farmington and took on the worst visions of two different worlds.

We were sitting at a red light when they started fighting. Dad said the main problem was the grade. Mom said it was the cheating and lying. Dad said he needed his kids to do well and go to college, that there was no way he could have us grow up and become incompetent welfare recipients. Mom took this personally. She was always afraid to be thought of as lazy. She said it wasn't her fault she wasn't Betty Crocker; she was raised in a generation that didn't think like that anymore.

We drove down Twentieth Street as I listened to them argue, but I couldn't really enjoy the fact that I'd become invisible in the backseat. We passed Brookside Park, and I spotted the Thunderbird pulled over by the playground. "Look!" I yelled. Joan, Lori, and Monica were scooping up snowballs and running around in the field.

"I told Joan to go straight home," Mom said.

Dad pulled the van over and got out. Mom rolled down the window and yelled that they weren't dressed warm enough to be playing in the snow. Then Dad came around to the sliding door and pulled it open. "Let's go," he told me.

"I don't have the right kind of shoes," I answered, but he was wearing boots and he lifted me over the dirty exhaust-pipe slush that lined the road and set me down in the clean wet piles of snow behind it.

Mom was yelling that Joan was in trouble, and we were going to get sick, but Dad bounded across the field scooping snowballs anyway. "It's kind of dry, don't you think?" he yelled.

I felt the snow sinking into my sneakers, but we played until Monica's lips turned blue, and Dad said it was time to go. Then we jumped in the warm van, and Joan got scolded by Mom, and I knew I'd been given a reprieve.

Mom rolled down the window to yell at Dad, who was still outside. "You drive the Thunderbird," she said. "We're going home."

"Look!" he responded, then fell straight on his back, flapping his wings.

BOARDING SCHOOL

(1980)

✛

That year, Dad had been waking up at the crack of dawn to sit in the kitchen and study for his high school equivalency exam. Unfortunately for me, his early morning hours never made him too tired to run softball drills at our neighborhood field after work. He hit us hard balls and grounders, taught us to choke up on the bat, fake bunts, and get under pop flies. If a rock sent the ball for a crooked bounce that pounded my shin, he marched out onto the field and rubbed the wound. Most days, we played until the sun set and I could barely see the ball.

He had been coaching two teams every summer since we moved to Farmington, picking all the Native, Mexican, and Black girls in the draft. Mom's youngest sister, Annie, grew four inches the year after we started, and from that moment on Dad insisted on driving her up from Yuma every June so she could play on Joan and Lori's team. Monica and I had started with tee ball, and unlike his older fast-pitch team, we would often lose. Dad lectured us continually about developing "killer instincts" like Lori and Joan.

Every time Dad used the phrase "killer instincts," I cringed. Playing ball was a Yuma tradition, and everyone remembered how insanely hyper-competitive he and his brothers had been when they were young. Mom seemed to think his crazy yelling on the field was good. She was the one who had talked him into being a coach in the first place. She said he needed to resurrect one of his healthier hobbies from back home. She'd signed us all up without asking, after which Dad spent the better part of my childhood creating lineups, calling practices, and obsessing over coaching books he found at the library.

Tee ball was a sport none of us had ever played, and Dad memorized the rule book like it was a new religion. He'd discovered that the game had an unorthodox position called the roamer. The roamer was mobile, and Dad assigned the role to the only girl on our team who could reliably catch the ball. She advanced around the infield ahead of the runners, standing with one foot on whatever base Dad told her to take. Then she forced girls out by catching the wild throws the rest of us tossed her after we'd fielded the batter's ball. By the end of the season, copycat coaches in the league had adopted the strategy as well.

I'd nearly died of shame at my first tee ball game when we killed the competition 91–2. The other team, a bunch of unsuspecting blond girls from the rich side of town, had watched us cycle through our batting lineup multiple times, their faces growing red because they couldn't get us out. Their catcher, a girl from my class at school, had even started crying, after which the opposing parents had booed us in the stands. Dad refused to show mercy even after I begged him to stop. The day after the game, the league's president had called the house to say he never wanted to see a final score like that again.

Yet I loved the stadium bleachers, the smell of grass clippings, and the sight of Mom keeping score in her lawn chair. It reminded me of the Dust Devils, the team Grandpa Ed had started for Dad, his brothers, and cousins back in Yuma. For generations the Jackson family had earned their tough reputation on the field, and it made me proud to rattle the fence and cheer for Lori and Joan during championship games. I even felt proud when an umpire expelled Lori, the team's catcher, for tripping a girl as she ran across home plate. But when I stepped onto the diamond myself, I hated the public pressure, and the feeling that there was something to prove. The academic imperative, the athletic demands, our family tension was a moving target, the softball field a substitute for war.

Just before Joan's ninth-grade graduation, Grandma Mary arrived in Farmington with our youngest aunts: Annie and Kathy. We normally drove to Yuma to pick Annie up for softball season, but Dad had been promoted to foreman, and he was working overtime, so they took a Greyhound bus instead.

We'd just bought a single-story ranch home, with big bins out back where we could store wood for our fireplace in the den, and Mom made us vacuum and dust while Dad went to get them at the station. After seeing Dad's income, the Realtor had taken us to a neighborhood with two-story homes that I loved, but Mom said she was just trying to get a bigger sale, and Dad said it would be embarrassing to have our family visit a house so big and grand.

I heard the car door slam, and Annie came busting through the door. She ran down the hall to find Lori and Joan. Aunt Kathy entered and immediately collapsed on the couch. She was twenty and looked chubbier than I remembered. When I asked her how the trip was, she said, "Long."

Grandma Mary entered with Dad. She wore a rosary made of pressed rose petals and a blouse with shoulder pads that made her frame look even lankier. Mom was an obsessive shopper, and our new home had been furnished in the ubiquitous southwestern style, with both Indian-made items bought at the flea market in Shiprock, and inauthentic knockoffs found at furniture stores all over the state. Our living room drapes were printed with kachinas. We had sand paintings on the wall and Acoma pottery displayed on the fireplace.

"Lots of Indian stuff," Grandma said.

"Yes," Mom answered.

Dad told Grandma that we could spend the weekend fishing at one of our favorite lakes in southern Colorado or even Utah. I'd been secretly hoping we would go to Arches National Park, so I could run off and boulder while they ate lunch. Hiking in Telluride wouldn't have been bad either. But Grandma said they weren't up for an outdoor adventure, and as if on cue, Kathy ran to the bathroom to throw up.

"The flu?" Mom asked.

Grandma shook her head. "It's just motion sickness from the drive."

After serving lunch, Mom shot Dad a look, and they slipped into the utility room to whisper about how much Kathy had changed. "What happened to her straight hair?" Mom asked.

Her hippie look had been replaced with feathered flaps. Her eyebrows were plucked and peaked into a thin line. Even her vocabulary had expanded with words like *pachucos*, *cholas*, and *la Raza*. She called herself Chicana now and bragged about the lowrider her boyfriend's uncle drove.

Kathy was fifteen years younger than Mom. As a teenager, she'd caught the tail end of the Vietnam War protests, the pot-smoking, buckskin-wearing zeitgeist. Now her style reflected nationalistic pride. The Chicano Rights Movement was big in Yuma, not only because the city was known as the lettuce capital of the world and played host to Mexican immigrants who crossed the border to pick crops but also because it was the birthplace of the labor leader César Chávez, who was born to a woman named Juana Estrada. Dad's brother Bill had married César's cousin Ruth Estrada, and when I grew older, I imagined their family histories, involving generations of political anger, had played into the attraction.

Kathy had grown up with peers whose families were reclaiming their Aztec, Toltec, Mayan, and Yaqui lineages via "*la causa*." The United Farm Workers' flag, a black Aztec eagle, was common in Yuma, as was the phrase "*sí, se puede*," or "yes, we can." Local priests who were inspired by liberation theology spoke of César at mass. So, even though Grandma always noted how different border Spanish was from her own New Mexican tongue, Kathy's new alliance wasn't surprising. She'd always been different from Mom and Annie. She was ebony to their ivory, and like all the darker siblings in the Herrera family, she sometimes suffered in Grandma's view because of it.

"Kathy's hair looks fine," Dad answered.

Mom's brow was wrinkled with concern. "I worry about that guy she's dating," she said.

As they talked in the utility room, I listened from the den. Things were just getting interesting when the phone rang. Mom went to answer it, and Dad spotted me eavesdropping from the doorway. "Why are you always the one spying?" he asked.

When Mom returned, she said it was the PTO secretary, calling to alert them of an emergency meeting the following night. The nuns were planning to shut down the high school because of financial difficulties. Junior High ran from seventh to ninth grade, while tenth through twelfth were high school. Lori would be safe for another year because she was in the eighth grade, but Joan was in the ninth, and if Sacred Heart shut down, she'd have to go to public school.

"Over my dead body," Dad said.

The next night, Mom and Dad got dressed in their Sunday best and headed to Sacred Heart to fight the nuns' decision to discontinue the higher grades. In their minds, there was no alternative. New Mexican schools were the worst in the nation, and they were scared to expose Joan to the riffraff in Farmington.

Grandma was watching television and Kathy was sleeping when Annie came and found me for a séance. Monica and I were playing a game, but hers sounded more exciting, so we said yes. Mom's new beagle, Lady, had given birth to puppies a couple of months prior, and we dragged two of them into the closet with us. At first Joan said to leave them, but Annie said it was good to bring them in because their mom had died after delivering them and they were close to the spirit world as a result.

The runt of the litter was my favorite. She had a white star on her forehead, and she sat on my lap as Annie lit a candle in the center of our circle. There was some debate about whom we should contact, but Annie said she was the *curandera*, so she got to decide.

"John F. Kennedy . . . John F. Kennedy . . . are you here?"

We closed our eyes as she'd instructed. She called to him repeatedly in a voice that sounded like she was telling ghost stories, and then she said, "If you can hear us, blow out the candle."

The candle went out—of course, what fun would it have been if it hadn't—and everyone stampeded out of the closet. I hugged my puppy close, trying to prevent her from getting trampled, and crawled out last. The first person I saw when I emerged was Grandma, with her hands on her hips, glaring.

"¿Qué demonios estás hacienda?" When she was angry, she spoke in Spanish.

"We were holding a séance," Monica blurted out, and Grandma Mary went nuts.

"¡Eso es adorar al diablo!" She yanked at our braids with her left hand and did the sign of the cross with her right. If she'd had holy water, she would have poured it on us.

Annie cried and said she knew it was evil, but she was afraid to tell us no. The devil tempted good people; Grandma always told us. When we lived in Yuma, she used to say Annie was special and might be a saint someday. "It was their idea," Annie said.

For a parent to be as gullible as Grandma felt crazy. I laughed out loud, and she turned on me, saying, "I knew you were the ringleader in this!"

When my parents arrived home, they were angry.

"Stop crying or I'll give you something to cry about," Mom said. "Tomorrow night is our last chance to convince the nuns, and since you can't behave, you're going to have to come with us." If Bloody Mary, séances, Ouija boards, and tarot cards had always felt like harmless kid's games, they didn't now. Grandma Mary squinted at me from behind a cloud of cigarette smoke. "That one is just like Kathy," she said, pointing toward me with her long nail. "She can never be trusted to do the right thing."

The next night, still angry about the injustice of it all, but not necessarily disappointed to be away from Grandma at home, I rode over to Sacred Heart with Mom and Dad and followed them into the Knights of Columbus Hall. Over the course of the next half hour, I saw all kinds of parents beg and bargain at the microphone. The nuns sat onstage, refusing to budge. Dad got up to speak early, but he did not ask them to reconsider.

"I can tell you that my daughter Joan will never attend a public high school in Farmington," he said. "And I'm wondering if you can give us the names of some Catholic boarding schools where we might be able to send her for a decent education?"

The nuns leaned their heads together before Sister said St. Scholastica in Cañon City, Colorado, was a wonderful—albeit expensive—option for an all-girls school.

I didn't know how far Cañon City was from Farmington, but the idea of Joan going there, to live in dorms with strange girls, felt like a punch in the gut.

I got up from my seat and whispered in Mom's ear. "I'm going out to the playground."

"Don't wander far," she told me.

Across the way, the Sacred Heart church was unlocked, and since I knew it would be quieter than sitting on the monkey bars with a bunch of kids, I pushed the door open. It had been some time since I had entered the church when it was empty. I remembered when we first moved to Farmington, and Mom used to take us to weekday mass. No one else attended but students, and it felt like we were alone at the back of the church. And then a few years later, once I'd started school myself, I remembered the way Katy Randolph used to faint when we knelt for too long; the way the dust mites used to float in the light of the stained-glass windows and make me feel calm. I loved choir practice, "Ave Maria" rising into the rafters.

I had forgotten the respite the daily masses had offered me in a difficult period. When we were newcomers to Farmington, and Mom was always crying, and Dad was always stressed-out, it was the only place where I felt the world could be quiet, where the nuns and my parents left me alone. I remembered feeling warm and safe in the pews, even as I zoned out and didn't listen to Father's homily. I remembered how comforting it was to belong to a class, to sit and stand on cue.

Losing Joan to an out-of-state boarding school felt wrong. Even though Grandma Esther had said that Phoenix Indian School "wasn't that bad"—and Uncle Gene had sought the opportunity to go to two of them before getting expelled at each—the idea of a fragmented family scared me. I sat and thumbed through a hymnal, hearing Dad's voice in my head. According to him, a focus on learning and an obsession with mainstream schools were the things that made his grandparents different from other tribal members in their generation. Granny Ethel had forced him and his siblings to walk across the river into Yuma to attend Immaculate Conception Elementary in the 1940s. She'd argued that teachers on the reservation would only turn them into janitors and dirt diggers, and in her mind, those jobs were beneath them. When her grandkids protested, Granny Ethel insisted, claiming they needed a Western education if they wanted to avoid being swindled by unethical people who weaponized numbers and words.

During the school year Mom was always shushing Dad's reservation stories. But in the summer, when we spent time outdoors—camping, horseback riding, hiking, fishing—she ceded ground. Then it was his world, and she let him talk.

"The smoke always bends toward the Indian princess," Dad would tease us when the wind kicked up the campfire.

We'd cringe and move out of the smoke as soon as he said the words "Indian princess." It was the moniker Sarah Winnemucca—Granny Ethel's Paiute aunt and the black sheep of the family—had used as a stage name as a performer in the late 1800s. Throughout my childhood, we made fun of Sarah around the campfire, even though none of us, including Dad, knew much about her. My sisters and I had been embarrassed about her for years, ever since Dad told us he'd made the mistake of mentioning her to his Navajo coworkers at the plant and they'd mocked him for being relatives with a "a white man's Indian." After that, he'd advised us never to mention Sarah to our Navajo friends, unless we wanted to be told that we came from a family of traitors. We likened her to Tiger Lily in Peter Pan, or the historically inaccurate version of Pocahontas. I had no idea, really, why her name was well known, and for many years, I didn't want to ask.

Our willful ignorance about her arose from a healthy dose of generational infighting and shame. We'd lost touch with Granny Ethel. The men in our family, including Dad, disliked her—he never wanted to stop by her house when we visited the reservation. All their lives, they had mistrusted her version of Aunt Sarah's story, choosing to believe the slander spread about the Winnemucca family by their coworkers and friends instead. When I finally did approach Dad's brother Mike, who would one day become the Quechan (Yuma) tribal president, he told me he thought Sarah had been a guide for Lewis and Clark, which I knew wasn't true because that expedition had taken placed forty years before she was born.

Sarah was born near the Humboldt River in western Nevada in 1844, and served as a bilingual translator at Fort McDermitt during the Shoshone-Paiute wars. True, she had favored a peaceful coexistence with settlers early on. She had also expressed an unpopular belief that Native people fared better under the U.S. military than under the Bureau of Indian Affairs. But labeling her a traitor for her "Indian Princess" stage performances ignored Sarah's savvy: she had used the moniker to draw white crowds and white pocketbooks into her orbit. She'd spent the money she earned from the book's sale and a speaking tour to build a school for Paiute children at Pyramid Lake, Nevada. After seeing her people survive war, relocation, and starvation, she was adamant about them needing a Western education if they were ever going to thrive. The belief our family placed in the power of a mainstream education began with her, and continued through Granny Ethel and her daughters, who were proud of her. Struggling financially, Sarah operated the school that she opened for less than two years before it shut down. The Indian Affairs Commissioner had prevented her from being a teacher at the very educational institute she founded. She died just as poor and discouraged as any other Native person working for change in her generation, despite having lectured about government agent corruption, and inequities in federal Indian policy. But her activism did impact my family, as her teachings carried down through the generations. She was the reason we went to private schools.

Dad and his siblings were rare, some of the only Yuma Indian kids to go to town for their education. Most of his childhood buddies didn't start crossing until the 1950s, and even then, it was only because there was no high school on the reservation. He said his friends stuck to him like glue once they started coming to town, because they wanted him to introduce them around. His voice revealed pride when he remembered the way they clung to his side, and I could imagine how it had made him feel sophisticated and ahead.

I walked over to the confessional booth and slipped in, like I did when I went to receive the sacrament of reconciliation. Facing the screen, I knew the priest wasn't there, but the act of examining my conscience was reflexive. It was disrespectful to question Mom and Dad's motive for sending Joan away, but I couldn't help it. On one hand, I felt grateful that they cared about what happened to us, but on the other hand I resented them for it. Now that they were talking about boarding school for Joan, I found myself thinking their focus was outsize. Their dreams of grandeur didn't make sense. No one on either side of the family had taken a traditional route from high school to college. Their educational talk was all theoretical, and because I didn't know Granny Ethel and Sarah's histories it felt suspect, even a bit fraudulent, like my parents were trying to live vicariously through us.

When Mom and Dad came out of the meeting, I was waiting on the playground. Mom was walking like a stiff old church lady without the white gloves. Her body was rigid, and she had Sister hot on her heels.

"You know what happens to girls who go to coed schools," Sister had said. She was trying to convince Mom to send Joan away to the boarding school in Colorado.

I wanted to lower my head and impale her like a triceratops, but instead I stood frozen in place. I looked at Mom's and Dad's faces, but they were stiff as masks, impossible to read or understand.

Not long after, the decision about Joan's boarding school was made official. She would be leaving in the fall. Mom and Dad told us about their decision just as we were walking into the mall to see *E.T.* We whined, but once we arrived at the theater, and stood in line to buy popcorn, the worry faded. The start of school felt like a long time away.

But I did think about it when we got home, and I knew I wanted to spend what little time we had left with my sister. The summer had just started, and Joan and Lori were once again spending most of their time on the softball field with Dad and his older team. In the past, I'd done what I could to avoid their practices. But that summer, I hung around the field and shagged balls for them. At my own practice, I went all in. I sprinted for pop flies, dove for grounders. And then one day in late July, I even convinced Dad to let me pitch.

Fast-pitch softball requires both speed and accuracy, and as soon as I got on the mound, I realized that I had overestimated my ability. Throwing in the backyard with my sisters catching for me was nothing like pitching to a batter. Having someone in the box made everything more complicated.

I threw the ball over the backstop twice. Even worse, the other team was hitting and scoring, and we still didn't have a single out. I waved at Dad, signaling that I should probably come out of the game, but he wouldn't put our usual pitcher back in. "Figure it out!" he yelled.

I was desperate to quit and asked the umpire for a time-out. Dad folded his arms across his chest and glared at me as I walked over to the dugout.

"Who told you to call a time-out?" he asked. We were playing the worst team in the league, and yet we had gone from a twenty-point lead to a five-point lead in a single inning. I was walking them around the bases, and my sisters were watching. It was humiliating.

"I don't want to pitch," I pleaded. I told him my shoulder hurt, even though it didn't. I was trying to throw fastballs, and the harder I slung them the wilder they became. I had hit the last batter in the ankle, and the bases were loaded.

He shook his head. "Figure it out," he repeated, and sent me back to the pitcher's mound.

The next batter approached the box with a grin on her face. I lobbed a changeup across the plate, but far from being fooled she looked like she expected it. She lifted her back elbow in an exaggerated motion to time her delay, then stepped into the ball and swung for the fence, rounding the bases for a grand slam.

When we were ten points down, Dad finally took me out. I wasn't switched to second base or even right field after my fiasco. He sat me on the bench, where my face burned red with humiliation. After the game we went to the van with Joan and Lori telling me to walk on the other side of the parking lot so people wouldn't associate me with them.

Only Kathy was kind. Her stomach was growing immense, and it made her soft and squishy. Within days of Grandma Mary's departure for Yuma, I finally understood what everyone seemed to have intuited but me. Kathy was pregnant. Grandma had brought her to Farmington because an unwed mother in a Catholic family was an embarrassment.

Mom acted like Kathy had committed a sin. She told Dad, if Kathy asked, that our family could keep the baby. I was horrified that anyone thought Kathy would want to give her child away. I sat by her every night in the den, and she was excited about becoming a mother. She thought our fireplace was fancy and sat in front of the flames more often than she sat in front of the TV.

We got along. I could talk to her, and she listened. Sometimes I stopped, thinking she was bored, but then she would urge me on. I asked her about her friends back home, and she taught me words the tough cholas used on the street. "Don't call any Mexican girls that," she said, laughing, when I'd committed the words to memory. "Unless you want to get jumped."

I felt embarrassed when she told me not to use my new vocabulary because that's exactly what I'd been thinking I might do: try on a new identity, just like she had. I told her I had a hard time fitting in at school, and she said it was because I looked too brown to white people, and too white to brown people.

She held her arm next to mine to show how much darker than me she was. "Probably because the sun is always out in Yuma," she said.

One night I asked if I could feel the baby moving, and it was like she woke up from a dream. "What did you say?" she asked.

"Can I touch your belly to feel the baby moving?" I repeated.

She tilted her head to the side and put her hands on her stomach. "The baby's not moving right now," she answered. Then her voice quavered, and she asked, "Don't you have an early practice tomorrow?"

Her weepiness wasn't unusual, and I didn't think anything of it until the next day, when we came home from the field and found Mom alone in the house. She said she had taken Aunt Kathy to the hospital, where the doctors had failed to find a heartbeat for the baby.

For an entire day, Aunt Kathy knew that the baby she carried was gone. It was devastating to live adjacent to her loss, but even worse was the way Mom whispered about God's wisdom.

Mom's brothers Chris and Tommy drove Grandma back to Farmington so she could be with Aunt Kathy when she was induced. She gave birth to a stillborn boy, and while his burial was being sorted out, they brought him home in a small coffin that sat in Mom's bedroom.

Aunt Kathy wanted to open the casket and hold her baby. Uncle Tommy was still a teenager, but Uncle Chris was in his midtwenties, and he worked as a firefighter. Grandma said he'd seen plenty of death on the job, and she asked him to go down the hall and peek inside the coffin to see if the baby looked okay.

I hovered near Aunt Kathy, standing behind the couch where she sat. I wanted to touch her shoulder, but she looked too fragile to sustain the weight of my hand. Uncle Chris returned to the living room and said it was a bad idea. Aunt Kathy cried when he said it, and I didn't want to believe him. I wished Grandma Mary had sent a woman to check on the baby instead.

Aunt Kathy cried even harder when she learned there would be no mass for her baby. Grandma said babies who died before being baptized didn't get to go to heaven. According to Catholic dogma, they were like virtuous pagans who went to a place called limbo because they had died before the "original sin" could be wiped from their souls. For the first time in my life, righteous anger toward the Church flared up in my belly. I glared at Grandma Mary, resenting her, the priests, the nuns, and the catechism, for putting such terrible sentiments into words.

My parents purchased a cemetery plot, and we went to bury the baby the next day. Mom said we would visit his grave if Aunt Kathy promised to visit my older brother's grave back in Yuma. They hugged each other, agreeing to swap memorial visits, since neither of them could be close to the sons each of them had lost.

That afternoon Grandma, Aunt Kathy, Uncle Chris, and Uncle Tommy climbed into the car and left for Yuma. Only Aunt Annie stayed, since district finals for softball were coming up, and she had to finish the season. Dad said we would drive her home after the tournaments were over. Little did I know that I would run inside Grandma Mary's house when we got there, only to discover that Kathy had moved out with her boyfriend, rarely to be seen by us when we visited again.

A week after Aunt Kathy left, Mom started gathering Joan's supplies for boarding school. She piled twin sheets, a twin comforter, a shower caddy, shower shoes, a laundry bag, and other stuff on the dining room table, and we were thrown by the realization that her departure date would arrive. Monica cried and Joan fought the decision. We all did. But our parents refused to budge.

Cañon City was six hours away, beyond the Sangre de Cristo Mountains and Wolf Creek Pass. We would only be seeing her at Christmas break because they didn't have the money to fly her home for the lesser holidays. I thought of Halloween. It was the last year Mom would let me trick-or-treat, and now Joan wouldn't be there to take me.

For more than an hour, my sisters and I sat at the dinner table, crying and begging. I couldn't believe they had decided to send Joan away. It was like repetition compulsion, knowing Dad's parents had been forcibly sent back in the day. She would be going to school, playing sports, and living with a new set of girls, and it felt like we were being replaced. But Mom and Dad would only repeat the pitch from the school brochure. They said it was an old military school, and the nuns who ran it sent their girls to the best universities.

The next day district finals began for the softball league I played in. We drove to the field, but when we parked, Joan and Lori refused to get out of the van. Joan looked sad. Lori said I was an embarrassment. Lori's words smarted worse than Joan's refusal to come and watch. The two of us never did get along, and I wondered what it would be like without Joan around to serve as a buffer.

I felt completely numb as my team took the field. It was like I was trapped inside a snow globe, watching my once familiar world through the glass. Mom kept score from her lawn chair. Dad stood on the third-base line and signaled for me to bunt. At first my errors weren't purposeful. I stood at home plate and genuinely didn't remember what his signals meant.

When I struck out, he came to the dugout incensed. "Come on," he yelled at me. "She's a wild pitcher. You know the signal to take the walk!"

He pitched my glove at me and sent me out on the field, and suddenly I realized that I knew how to hurt him. I knew how to get back at him for sending Joan away. I started to strike out on purpose. On the field, I began to intentionally fumble, overthrow my teammates, and stumble over dirt when I went to field ground balls.

Our team immediately fell into the loser's bracket that day and had to play another game later than afternoon. After doing all I could to throw that game as well, Dad caught on to what I was doing. He stood in the dugout and told me it was poor character to purposely let your teammates down. I cried like I was having a psychotic break and yelled so everyone could hear. "It's not my fault I suck. You're just mad because I'm not a softball jock like Joan and Lori, and now that you're sending Joan away, you won't have a winning team!"

His face went blank as he looked around to see all the people who were watching. Then he asked me the unthinkable. In our house, we had all been required to play on Dad's softball team, but my plan to fail had worked.

"Do you want to quit?" he asked. He didn't even look at me as he spoke the words. He just started throwing bats and balls into his equipment bag faster than I'd ever seen him in my life.

"Yes," I replied, feeling the tightness in my chest relax.

"Done deal," he replied. Then he walked toward the parking lot and never looked back. And I never played softball again.

PART

3

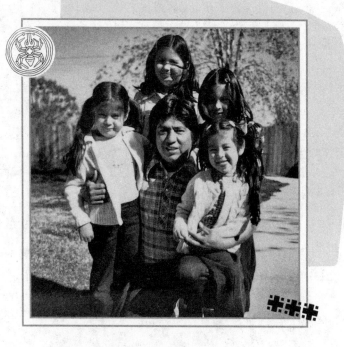

The author (*front left*) with her sister
Lori; her father, Edmond; and her
sisters Joan and Monica, circa 1976, in
Farmington, New Mexico.

The recurring nightmare came with certain fevers in my childhood, the heat making my eyes sink so deep into my head that I couldn't open them. No matter how hard I tried to stay awake, I became blinded to the outside world, able to see only the back of my glowing red eyelids like they were a big movie screen.

The dream starts with the outline of a girl on a Friday after school. She's a new classmate, a stranger who asks me to spend the night at her place. I beg my mother to let me go, but once we arrive at her house, and I walk through the front door alone, I know that I've been tricked. The walls fall away to reveal a long cave, and the girl, seeing how the cave makes me sick, says she knows that it hurts but someone is coming. She puts me in an old hospital bed with an iron frame like the kind we keep on the Cry House grounds. She leans over the bed to stare, her dark eyes and scary smile spinning past me like her face is in a flip-book. I lie on the sickbed, too weak and frightened to fight back. My fingers grope the cave wall. Its texture reminds me of clay, and the gumminess is threaded with something that feels like hair. I touch it, and as I touch it, I taste it like iron in my mouth. I curl into a fetal position, my hands feeling and my teeth gnawing on the wall like it's gum. A tall stick man enters the cave. He puts a cold hand on my forehead and talks to me in a language that I can't understand. There are generations of sadness here. I've never felt such nostalgia in my life. When I wake, I feel his cold hand still. But then I realize it's Mom, using an icy compress to cool me off so I can come home.

HALL OF MIRRORS

(1981)

✚

Everything changed when my eldest sister, Joan, left for boarding school. On her own for the first time, she started drinking and partying, and when Mom unearthed the letter that revealed this fact, Joan said we were fools for letting Mom find it and refused to write us anymore. Shortly thereafter, Mom found out she was pregnant and spent the winter laid up on the sofa, sugar high and sick with gestational diabetes.

Lori disappeared too. She made varsity softball not long after Joan left, which meant she had to be carpooled from the junior high to the high school every afternoon, and a gang of older white girls on the team started showing up to give her a ride. Normally so conservative about our social lives, Mom broke her own rules and let Lori go everywhere with them because they were so sweet and clean with their short hair and button-up shirts she didn't think they'd be teaching Lori how to drive drunk on shots of Bacardi.

That year Dad stopped coming home again. He wanted extra money for travel to softball tournaments, fishing trips to Colorado, Mom's shopping in Albuquerque, and Joan's tuition, so he became an overtime fiend. Mom gave birth to our little sister, Theresa, and her education became part of his financial plans too. And though Mom said it was his penance to work, as long as they paid him overtime, I knew he preferred spending time with the guys at the plant—it didn't look like he suffered.

Meanwhile, to fill the loneliness, Monica and I started reading. Nearly every day, we begged Mom to take us to the library, where we could kill hours sitting cross-legged between the rows of books. Still, by the time Easter rolled around, even the library had lost its appeal. Our family felt broken, and it wasn't long before Mom noticed that Monica had chewed her fingernails down to the quick. She said we needed to go home to Yuma, and pressured Dad to change our next trip to May. This meant, as soon as Joan got home for the summer, we would be off to the reservation, and we'd get there in time for the annual intertribal powwow at San Pasqual High School.

I was pumped that our new vacation schedule lined up with the powwow because it meant we might see our cousins from Los Angeles, who had stayed out west after their parents completed their job training with the federal relocation program. I'd always envied my city cousins. They were all boys with different racial makeups—half-Filipino, half-Mexican, half-Cocopah, half-white—and several of them sang northern drum at powwows around the city. I was excited for us to return to our roots and have all our relatives together, even though Dad told me nothing was certain. He had spoken to a couple of his siblings, and they said it all depended on gas money for the trip.

It was late May when we left for the reservation. Dad loved the early morning and always liked middle-of-the-night starts when we drove to Yuma, so we loaded the van the night before. After dinner, I stood outside with a flashlight, helping him, Joan, and Lori strap luggage to the roof of our Club Wagon van. He removed the long bench in back, threw sleeping bags on the floorboards, then we went inside to sleep a few hours before starting the drive. At three in the morning, we staggered down the driveway to flop onto the sleeping bags in the dark and go back to dreaming while he drove.

The smell of coffee greeted me just before daylight. We vibrated over a cattle guard, and I sat up and looked out the window. A pink line had appeared on the horizon. I crawled up to take a seat and ask what there was to eat. Mom had egg and Spam burritos wrapped in warm tinfoil, and she handed one back. I peeled it open and dug in, hungry and eager to get back to our old stomping grounds. There would be fry bread and red chile stew at the powwow. Our cousins would tell stories and laugh.

We arrived in Yuma just before lunch and dropped Mom and our new baby sister, Theresa, off at Grandma Mary's house. Mom's younger brother Tommy and his girlfriend had been causing trouble, and Mom said it was more important than the powwow. Dad made us go inside and say hello, which made me nervous because I didn't want to miss the start of the festivities: the eagle staff, the flags, the veterans, and the elders who would be leading the Grand Entry. I kept tugging at Dad's arm, and after a while he relented and said we should get back in the van. We drove out to the reservation and parked in the lot behind San Pasqual, where we saw a young dancer sitting on his truck's tailgate changing into moccasins. We walked toward the football field and Dad waved to a couple of kids who were pulling regalia over their basketball shorts near their open car doors.

Even when a powwow is held outdoors, the circle is referred to as the dance arena. It's formed in two concentric rings—the inner circle for the dancers in their jingling dresses and jangling bell bands—the outer for the emcee, arena director, and drummers. At San Pasqual, the powwow was old-school, held under the open sky. Dancers from different tribes would step and spin on the football field for three days. Concession stands popped up near the entrance to the basketball court, and onlookers sat in school bleachers. I ran ahead of Dad and my sisters to find our cousins. I was squeezing through a throng of teens when I heard the three heavy drumbeats that signaled the start of the powwow.

It was too late to say hello now. If our cousins were in town to drum, they would be singing for the Grand Entry, sounding the beats to lead the eagle staff, flags, and elders into the circle followed by a mix of dancers in different regalia—Grass, Jingle, Fancy, Fancy Shawl, and Traditional— behind them. I turned around to look for my sisters, but they were gone, so I went to climb the bleachers, where I could get a better view. The opening songs were long, but people in the stands stayed on their feet out of respect for the dancers, the ancestors, the Creator, and the tradition. The crowd around me oohed, talking about the beautiful display of regalia, the intricate beadwork, the headbands and ribbons, the many colors and styles.

Once the procession of men and boys had entered the arena, the older women came in as well, and behind them the girls. And that's when I saw some of my local cousins lined up, ready to dance into the circle. Their mother, Colis, or as we called her, Babe, was from Oklahoma. She'd met Dad's older brother, Gene, at Concho Indian boarding school, and her beadwork on their regalia lent it an Arapaho flourish. I wondered if they were planning to compete for prize money. If so, their dance style, step accuracy, sportsmanship, and regalia would be judged in their competitions.

When the Grand Entry ended, I felt sad because I hadn't seen any of my Los Angeles cousins in the drum circles or the crowd. I watched the opening category, comprised of older men, but when the Junior Boys Fancy Dance started, I descended the bleachers and headed over to the concession stands to see if I could find my sisters. Joan and Lori had been attached at the hip since Joan arrived home from boarding school, and I knew Monica was most likely with Dad. She always stuck to my parents when we went someplace crowded because she was shy.

As I neared the gym, I spotted the sister of my Uncle Dino's ex-wife in line at a fry bread stand. She was a Yuma tribal member, born and raised, and I always felt uncomfortable around her, because I knew she thought my father and his brothers were no good. "Hi, Auntie," I said, realizing she had spotted me before I spotted her.

"Well, look what the cat dragged in," she said, but she smiled, and I knew she was kidding.

"Have you seen Joan and Lori? Or my dad and Monica?"

"Your sisters came running through a little while ago. They were looking for your Los Angeles cousins and I told them I hadn't seen them, which isn't surprising. Not everyone has money to gas up a big camper van."

Just then, we saw my cousin Bobby walk by. He was squeezing a

nosebleed with his head tilted back and bumped into the corner of a
vendor's table before seeing me. When I said hi, he held up a high five.
"What's up, little cuz?"

"What happened to your nose?" Auntie asked him.

Bobby's eyes looked bloodshot. "It ran into a fist. What do you care?"

"Jackson boys," Auntie said, before rolling her eyes and walking
away.

"I saw your sisters in the Grand Entry," I told him. Bobby and his
sisters were Uncle Gene's kids. "Are they competing?"

"They're just dancing for fun. When did you pull into town?"

"We just got here," I said. "And I already lost Joan and Lori."

"I'm sure they're hanging around in the crowd like you. Come on and
keep me company. I'm running over to my house for a clean shirt."

I couldn't believe my badass older cousin wanted to hang out with a
dorky twelve-year-old in rainbow flip-flops. I knew I was supposed to ask
for Dad's permission before leaving the powwow grounds, but I also
knew he'd be hard to find in the crowd. Jackson Road was only a couple
of miles away, and he likely wouldn't even notice I was missing. "Are you
coming right back?" I asked.

"Why do you think I need a clean shirt?" Bobby replied, showing me
the blood stains on his white tee. "There's a cute girl from Nevada in the
Fancy Shawl competition."

We walked around the parking lot until we found the beater his friend
said he could borrow. The windshield wipers were broken, which meant
they would only stop swiping if you wedged a book of matches into the
wiper handle to keep it in the off position. We climbed into the car, and
the enclosed space made me realize that Bobby smelled like a skunk. I felt
grown-up, knowing what the odor was. Mom's younger brothers listened
to Cheech and Chong and laughed like crazy when they were high. It
didn't scare me. I always figured better giggling on weed than angry on
alcohol.

"Did you really get in a fight?" I asked Bobby.

"With the dry heat," he said, laughing. "I was just giving her shit. I always get a bloody nose when the weather changes. Is Uncle Looney still coaching?"

"What do you think?" I asked.

We left the powwow grounds, hung a right on Picacho Road, then a left onto our family street, where my uncle Gene and my uncle Dino had houses on five-acre plots next to Grandma Esther's old house. My heart sank when we passed her place, empty as a sacred shrine. There were bald patches in the grass and weeds all over the yard. Some old Christmas lights still hung on the porch, and the turquoise paint on the rafters was chipping. Dad said the house belonged to Aunt Vi now, but she had gone upriver for an office position on the Mohave Reservation near Parker, Arizona, and the place looked sad and neglected.

When he parked at his house, we went inside and I followed him down the hallway to his room, where the walls were plastered with posters: the National Indian Youth Council, the Women of All Red Nations on one wall, the Indigenous protest singer Buffy Sainte-Marie, and the leaders of the American Indian Movement (AIM) on another.

"Who's that?" I asked, pointing at Dennis Banks.

"You don't know who that is?" Bobby asked in surprise. "He's like the Indian Malcolm X. And those guys are like the Indian Black Panthers."

My face felt warm with embarrassment. Why did it always feel like my cousins knew things that I didn't? He dug in his drawer for a basketball jersey, threw it on, then went to the bathroom to wash his face.

Bobby said he guessed it wasn't surprising that I didn't know who Dennis Banks was, since I was just a baby during the cultural revolution in the early 1970s. According to him, everything started when our parents' generation moved to cities for the job training programs offered by the Relocation Act. An unforeseen consequence of the act, diverse tribes—led by Ojibwe activists Dennis Banks and Clyde Bellecourt—came together to share their cultures at Urban Indian Centers and, realizing there was power in numbers, engaged in a civil rights uprising fueled by intertribal activism called the Red Power movement.

Bobby finished brushing his teeth and said, "Ask the Los Angeles cousins about the center near their houses in La Mirada and Norwalk. That's where they started drumming and getting into powwows again."

The Red Power movement began at the American Indian Chicago Conference in the summer of 1961. The AICC was the first big intertribal gathering hosted by the National Congress of the American Indian (NCAI), a political organization run by older Natives who continued to hope in democracy. Following two Indigenous conferences organized by John Collier in 1939 and 1940 (the first in Toronto, and the second in Pátzcuaro, Mexico), the NCAI had spent decades fighting for justice by working within the system: lobbying for change and filing court cases. They were patriots who didn't understand what drama they were getting into when they invited the Indian Youth Council (IYC), a group founded the same year in Gallup, New Mexico, to speak in Chicago.

A clash between generations emerged. Like their elders in the NCAI, members of the IYC saw high unemployment, discrimination, and slum housing as secondary struggles. Treaty rights, Indigenous sovereignty, and the return of ancestral lands—issues extraneous to the mainstream civil rights movement—were the main objectives. But the similarities between the two groups ended there. The younger group disliked the strategies of the older organization, calling their faith in litigation "weak." IYC members were impatient and called for a violent transformation of society that went beyond peaceful demands for better treatment.

Cofounders of the IYC, Mel Thom, a Paiute citizen, and Shirley Hill Witt, a Mohawk citizen, accused the NCAI of misrepresenting Indigenous youth with their lenient reaction to federal wrongdoing. Emboldened by the Black Panthers and other extremist groups, the IYC founders called their elders "Uncle Tomahawks" for gifting headdresses to white politicians and engaging in resolutions that never produced change. Their rhetoric lit a fire, and the following decade saw Native Americans shift from patriotism to nationalistic pride with the adoption of more militant tactics: fish-ins in the Pacific Northwest, the takeover of the BIA in DC, and the occupation of Alcatraz the year I was born.

"Too bad a bunch of BIA goons crushed the Red Power movement in its heyday," Bobby said, grabbing his keys to go back to the powwow.

When we left, I noticed Bobby didn't lock the door, and I felt a pang of jealousy that we didn't live on the reservation anymore. I imagined Dad moving us into Grandma Esther's old house on Jackson Road. It would be cramped, but at least I'd feel less lonely. As we drove back to San Pasqual high school and the powwow grounds, Bobby kept scolding me like he was my teacher.

"Man, Dennis Banks and those guys are badasses. You know their boy Leonard Peltier is still in prison for the shit that went down after Wounded Knee? My dad always says if your dad had been sent away after we got our religious freedom in the Indian Civil Rights Movement, he would have been taken care of by medicine men and sweat lodge people in prison, and he would have turned out completely different."

When we got back to the powwow grounds, Bobby walked me back to the stands before taking off with his friends, and I sat on the lowest rung of the bleachers, watching the Fancy Shawl dancers begin their competition. The cultural reverberations of the Indian Relocation Act were all around me: Kiowa boys learning Apache War Dances, Mohave citizens wearing Lakota beadwork designs. The intertribal powwow circuit had been birthed by urban migration, but I wasn't old enough to register all the changes.

Somewhere on the powwow grounds, Dad was talking with old friends. Maybe they were debating the pan-Indian protests I was considered too little to hear them discuss: the Occupation of Alcatraz and Wounded Knee. I had overheard them at past powwows, arguing about the effectiveness of the Red Power movement's militant strategy.

Now, I watched the crowd with new eyes, remembering how Dad had compared AIM tactics with the nonviolence advocated by his parents. Many people, including Bobby, believed Native protests began with the American Indian Movement in 1968. But a radical pan-Indian voice first emerged in Chicago in 1961. Despite our many distinct languages and cultures, in the 1960s and 1970s, people came together. For the first time, we were politically united and able to capture the media's attention. Predictably, the feds worked to label pan-Indian organizations as inauthentic and vowed to engage only with tribal governments.

It would be years before I understood my grandfather's involvement with the NCAI because Dad never talked politics with us. And the pan-Indian and Red Power movements didn't reach us in Navajo country, even when AIM came to town after the Jewelry Box murders in Chokecherry Canyon, because the Navajo didn't like the idea of cultural homogenization. When big-city AIM members came to our corner of New Mexico talking about sweat lodges and confrontation politics, the Navajo people felt that their revitalization efforts would only water down richer beliefs. They had their own ceremonies and did not feel the need to fill in any gaps. My cousins said, even in Los Angeles, Navajo transplants formed their own clubs rather than partaking in the pan-Indian ones. Thus, the community involvement and hope that was being offered to my cousins on the reservation, and at the Los Angeles Indian Center, eluded me in Farmington. As a minority Indian in Navajo country, the pan-Indian movement was not accessible to me.

The next day at the powwow, as I watched the drummers circle their lawn chairs to sing, I was hit with nostalgia. It wasn't just that our cousins hadn't come, or that Joan and Lori were acting too old for me. It was the music bouncing off the drum to vibrate my bones. It was the dancers with their grace, the men nodding as they spun, knees bent deep, thighs parallel to the ground. It was the women, their eagle fans held high as they bounced, toes touching the earth in time with the thrumming bass. I looked at the colorful ribbons streaming off a grass dancer, and I felt lost. I didn't own traditional regalia, and it made me sad. I missed Grandma Esther. I missed the crazy big feelings of my earliest childhood, when our family had the biggest parties in town. But I could also still feel the drumbeat moving through the ground, connecting me with everyone in the circle.

During the next social song—a song when everyone was invited to dance—my knees lifted all by themselves, like I was a puppet on an ancestor's string. When the drummers' voices rose in the sky, my heart quickened, and I realized the feeling of homesickness was a longing for Native culture. I wanted a deeper sense of belonging and more knowledge about our history, and it brought tears to my eyes. An old auntie saw me filled with emotion and invited me into the arena.

I stepped around the circle in my blue jeans, not recognizing half the people around me but feeling happy just the same. Suddenly, I looked up and saw Dad at the edge of the crowd watching me move to the beat of the drums. His eyes were blazing, his body attentive—like it was when he stood on the first-base line coaching, and when he saw that I'd seen him in the crowd, his face broke into a smile.

On the final afternoon of the powwow, after my big sisters had gossiped with every kid they could find, they finally deigned to fill me in on what they'd learned. Dad was frustrated with Uncle Gene because he wouldn't stop drinking and the doctors at the Indian Hospital had warned him that his liver was going bad. Lori said Aunt Vi had called Dad at the hotel the night before to beg him to drive out to Jackson Road and talk some sense into Gene before we left town.

We still had one more day in Yuma, and I expected we would spend it visiting relatives, though there was always a debate about who to privilege first because, with such a large family, it was impossible to see everyone. We were leaving our favorite breakfast spot when Lori and Joan got so involved in the fight about who we should see that Lori accidentally slammed the van's sliding door on Monica's thumb. Dad cursed at how deep the cut was, and Monica—who was initially too stunned to do anything—turned bright red and cried so hard she couldn't breathe.

The next thing I knew, we were driving up the steep hill to the Indian Hospital, which meant hours of waiting, hot and bored, because the reservation medical team was understaffed. After the triage nurse said she needed stitches, Monica freaked out, and Dad said there was nothing the rest of us could do so maybe we should go outside. Mom said yes, she didn't want to see our faces because Lori wasn't even acting sorry for what she did to her little sister.

"Come on," Dad said.

Other than the hospital, the dental trailer, the church, and the tribal police station, I'd never been in any buildings on Indian Hill. Old military barracks, they were mostly empty. We walked by the defunct library with a plaque dedicating it to Edmond Jackson, Dad's father, and I peeked in the window, hoping to see that some books had magically appeared. We crossed the street and were making our way to the overlook, where we could see the Colorado River down below, when Lori said, "The museum is open."

She was right. In all our years of visiting, we'd never caught anyone inside. But now the door was open, and Dad said, "Let's go," so we walked up the handicap ramp to see.

"Randy!" Dad called when he saw an old friend. "I haven't seen your ugly face in forever."

They bumped fists and talked while I walked around with my sisters. There was a mannequin with a placard explaining our ancestors were water people who fought aggressively to maintain their delta farmland at the confluence of two rivers: the Colorado and the Gila. There was a map that showed how close we had been to the Gulf of California before the dams were built, and travelogues by Spanish explorers who had arrived at the river's mouth in galleons, describing how deep the water had been. I learned that the surface area of the Gulf of California was roughly the same size as the Sonoran Desert. Thinking about Dad's love of fishing, and what great swimmers my sisters and I were, the discovery made me proud. Our ancestors once controlled the only desert in North America that was also half maritime.

I learned that Indian Hill was situated on a tight bend in the Colorado River known as the Yuma Crossing. Before the dams, when the river was still swift flowing and dangerous, the shore beneath Indian Hill was the sole place to safely cross for hundreds of miles. A topographical deviation, the sharp bend slowed the flow of the river, making the Yuma Crossing a godsend to forty-niners. Gold seekers wanting to protect their wagons, cattle, and family were obligated to march through our land, and when they first appeared, Quechan men helped them across. But soon, the number of gold seekers swelled.

Like a great human locust storm, the forty-niners trampled my tribe's squash, corn, pumpkin, and beans. Facing hardship themselves, they let their cattle graze on the tribe's provisions, leaving behind crushed plants, and a desperate population on the brink of starvation. The Glanton brothers, a group of outlaws, arrived to steal from the gold miners. Violence erupted, and it grew so terrible that the U.S. government sent troops to establish Fort Yuma and keep the peace. The army garrison, on top of Indian Hill, eventually became part of our reservation.

Dad found us reading about the history in the second room, and said it was time to go. His friend Randy was just the janitor, and we weren't supposed to be inside. As we left, he walked fast, heading to the overlook, where we could see the river. I tried talking to him about what I discovered in the museum, but he was irritable. Years later, Uncle Mike would explain that Gene and Dad had sometimes battled other Indians for calling them "hang around the fort" Indians. Geronimo had been a regional hero who fought without getting captured until 1886, while our tribe had accepted help from the U.S. Army to avoid starvation.

My sisters and I trotted to keep up with Dad. We were crunching through the gravel in front of St. Thomas Indian Mission when he stopped at the memorial to Father Barreneche and Father Garcés, a couple of priests who had been clubbed to death by the tribe in 1781, decades before the gold rush. Angry at the Spanish colonization and forced Christian conversion on their land, our ancestors had revolted, murdering hundreds of Spanish settlers and burning the original Catholic Church on Indian Hill to the ground.

Dad had never once spoken a word about the Yuma massacre, as historians called it, but he did now. "We received our strength from these ancestors. Fearless people who beat their enemies to death before giving in. Don't forget where you came from."

My face felt hot. He would never have made this statement if Mom was around. I wanted to learn about our traditions, ceremonies, and beliefs, and I was happy that we'd seen the museum, but, for some reason, I was embarrassed to talk to Dad about my feelings. He was sure of himself on the reservation—like it was his world—and Mom, my sisters, and I only marginally belonged to it. Maybe I had to insist. Maybe Mom was making him hold back. Maybe if I asked the right question, a door would open: an easy shortcut to discovering my true self. But before anyone could say anything, Dad changed his route and walked away. Rather than taking us to the overlook, he headed back to the hospital. "Let's go watch your little sister get her stitches," he said.

We left Yuma the next morning, and our final stop before leaving was Uncle Gene's house. Mom reached across the aisle from her captain's seat to give Dad's arm a squeeze. He sighed and turned around to look at us in the back of the van, saying, "You guys wait here." Then he hopped out, slammed his driver's door, and walked up the driveway, slowing down to admire an old Lincoln Continental parked in front of the house. He was checking the tires out when Uncle Gene's giant frame appeared in the doorway, and he came outside.

Uncle Gene hesitated when he saw Dad. I don't know how long it had been since they had been together, just the two of them, but when I started to roll down the window Mom said not to. They lifted their chins, then they turned their bodies to lean their backs against the Lincoln with their arms crossed.

I squirmed my way to the front of the van and begged Mom to let me get out, but she shot me her evil eye, and I knew I was stuck. Tension smoked between Dad and his brother like wet wood on a fire. Dad spoke and Uncle Gene shook his head. Dad tried again and Uncle Gene sneered. Their conversation ended quickly. Uncle Gene walked back into the house and Dad got into the van. As we pulled away, Mom exhaled loudly.

Halfway to Gila Bend, Mom and my sisters had already fallen asleep. I unbuckled myself and crawled up front to sit on the ice chest Mom kept between their seats. Long-distance trips had always been an opportunity to talk to Dad, to ask questions under cover of darkness when the night felt quiet and safe.

"Why doesn't Mom like powwows?" I blurted the question out.

"What makes you think she doesn't like them?" Dad asked.

"She always makes an excuse to stay at Grandma Mary's."

Dad was quiet for a minute before answering, "Powwows didn't use to be dry. Back in the day, there was alcohol, and when Indians get drunk it's a problem."

After an uncomfortable silence, I tried again. "Why didn't you learn to speak Keres from Grandma Esther?"

Dad sighed. "I was like lots of teenagers, I guess. I thought my parents were dorky. By the time I was old enough to *want* to ask questions, she was gone."

He wasn't his usual talkative self. Normally, when we were traveling long distances, he was game to talk about everything. Tonight, a dark cloud hung over us, and I understood that I should leave him alone. I crawled back to my seat and put on my Walkman.

I looked out at the desert and felt sad again. I was bummed with my mother and jealous of my cousins. They were cooler, edgier, more Indian. I wanted to emulate them without understanding that their lives were just as hard as mine. What did they think of us? I imagined how we looked to my cousins, pulling up at the powwow in our big van. Maybe they didn't think I belonged on the reservation either.

Not once on our drive back to Farmington did I think Dad might have been quiet because he was worried about Gene. We wended up the highway past a series of sandstone formations, the powwow's colorful regalia still fresh in my mind. I cracked a window and felt the fresh air blow in, imagining my own ribbons and fancy dance shawl twirling in the wind.

A few weeks after the new school year started, Aunt Vi called to say that Uncle Gene had walked on. He drank until his vision left him: the world washing white in a flash as he tried to sober up in the shower. He collapsed, and Bobby wrapped him in a towel, but his liver bled out before the doctors could save him.

Dad's company had a small corporate plane that flew from our local airport, San Juan Regional, to Phoenix and Yuma, where they had other generating stations. I was throwing clothes into my backpack for the trip when I heard Dad talking to Mom about the flight. Apparently, his boss offered him a seat so he could get down to the reservation and back without missing too much work.

I burst out of my bedroom. "You mean we're not driving down together?"

"You have school," Mom said, shaking her head.

I couldn't believe it. Skipping a family funeral contradicted everything Dad had ever said about being there for family. I remembered Uncle Gene in his black boots, his rough-and-tumble style just like the Red Nation guys in Bobby's protest posters; only just like Uncle Johnny, the way he dissented from the system was like yelling into the void. It hurt only him and his family. Compared to his brothers, Dad appeared so compliant and resolved, getting on a corporate plane to go to his brother's funeral.

I watched Dad leave with my fingernails digging into my palms. He was robbing me of a formative experience, time with the family, a chance to practice my tribal traditions. Lori went to her after-school job. Mom took Monica to see a friend. I threw myself on my bed and cried, stupidly believing Dad had lost respect for our roots, that he valued our culture less because he was trying to provide for us and our futures. If Dad's brothers had spent their lives focused on their rights—enraged over the way our people had been abused, maligned, and legally wronged—Dad controlled his anger by focusing on his duties, and right then, I hated him for it.

Dad was so wrecked after the funeral that he got drunk at a bar during his layover in Phoenix, fell asleep at his gate, and missed his flight home. When he arrived at the house three days later, he smelled like he hadn't showered in weeks. His hair was unkempt, and his eyes were red-rimmed. I followed him down the hall to his room, bombarding him with questions, but Mom yanked my ponytail.

"Leave him alone," she said

The following week, when Dad had recovered from the trip, he told me he was sorry for refusing to talk on the drive back from Yuma, and I knew he was thinking about the last time he saw Uncle Gene after the powwow. He patted the couch, inviting me to sit, and told me he meant what he'd said. "I wish I had listened more to my parents, but I got sent away, and then I got married, and they both died so young." He asked me what I wanted to know, and I said I wished he'd talk more about our tribal beliefs.

It was autumn, and the leaves were falling. We'd just come in from raking and bagging the mess from the trees in our yard. Lori was at her part-time job and Monica was helping Mom give a bath to Theresa. Dad started a fire in the woodstove and said he could tell me the Quechan origin story if I wanted to hear it.

He told me, "In the beginning, there was only water. There was no land, no sky, no shoreline, no sun or moon, no clouds. With nothing to mirror the water, the world was invisible.

"Then out of the waters came a mist to form the sky. And in the water Kokomaht, the Creator, became. He thought about the mist. He thought about the sky, and he had his first idea. From his bodiless state, he thought to emerge. From the watery world he would rise up. But he was only half of a whole.

"The waters boiled. Out of the bubbles, like a giant tree of ash, Kokomaht came up and stretched his arms. With his eyes closed to protect his sight, he sliced through the water to stand. Each of his steps along its surface crashed like thunder. He threw back his watery dreadlocks, opened his eyes, and said, 'I name myself Kokomaht, all powerful yet dual.' And that's when a voice from beneath the water called out to Kokomaht. 'Tell me, brother, did you rise with your eyes open or closed?'

"No one else was there to hear the voice of his twin, but Kokomaht heard, and he had his second idea. He knew his twin's intentions were evil and so he lied to him. 'I came with my eyes open,' he said.

"And this is how his twin emerged, jostled by the waves his brother's birth had caused, with his eyes wide open to the world. He was immediately blinded, and this is how Kokomaht held him in check until he sank back into the water in despair, throwing up a spray of confusion. Ever since we've had misunderstandings, illness, death, and hearts that circle from love to sadness."

When he finished, Dad said he'd never met a kid who wanted to connect to their tribal roots as much as me. "I guess my generation was different," he said. "Now go finish your homework."

We were finding surface areas of triangles in geometry, but I couldn't concentrate. What kind of brother would hurt his own twin? I understood that one brother was good and the other was bad—but how could I trust that the second was the evil one? The way he'd been blinded, the story felt paradoxical. I asked Dad if the story made him feel confused too, and he laughed and said the whole point was figuring it out for myself.

LAB WORK

(1982)

✛

My head was throbbing, and my lip was swollen. I'd been heading up the stairs at my new public junior high school when I was jumped from behind. An older girl named Juanita had yanked me backward down the stairwell by my hair. I'd fallen hard, hitting my head and dropping my books. I caught a glimpse of upside-down bodies before her fist caught my nose. Once. Twice. She connected with my lip on the third punch, even as I dodged and twisted, trying to get upright on the stairs. Finally, my seventh-grade English teacher arrived and pulled her off.

Now, Juanita sat next to me in our vice principal's office with a smile on her face. Her knuckles were bloodied from having punched the stairs beneath me. Otherwise, she looked unharmed. I closed my eyes, remembering how the crowd had parted for us to pass through on our way to the office. I'd seen other kids take that walk of shame. "I think she broke your nose," José had mocked me as we passed, and I knew he'd been egging her on.

"What the hell is going on?" our vice principal, Mr. Flynn, asked.

"She was mouthing off," Juanita said.

My head hurt too much to speak. While it was true that we had argued, we'd exchanged words hours before she jumped me. I'd been heading to the gym, before the first bell of the day, when I saw her berating a girl I knew from Sacred Heart. "Give her a break, Juanita," I'd said.

"You got a problem with me picking on this redneck?"

"Yeah, I do."

"Well," Juanita had answered. "Now I got a problem with you."

She'd challenged me to a fight after my volleyball game on Friday and I wasn't about to back down. I'd only ever been beaten up by my sisters, but I hid my fear beneath a layer of bravado. Luckily, it was only Monday. I figured I had all week to settle her down.

Mr. Flynn dialed my mother to say I'd been suspended for fighting. She didn't have to leave home to pick me up early. He'd keep me in his office for the final forty-five minutes of school and let me out at the normal time.

When I went outside after the bell, I saw Mom parked down the street. Monica was already in the van, next to Theresa in her infant car seat. When I climbed in, Mom's mouth was tight, and I knew she was mad. Her pregnant stomach was bulging and pressed against the steering wheel. She was expecting a boy this time, and she had gestational diabetes again, which meant she had no patience for my thirteen-year-old shenanigans.

Monica took one look at my cuts and bruises and started crying, but Mom was having none of it. She put a palm in my face as soon as I started talking, saying she didn't want to hear my excuses. I could save it for Dad. She was tired, and I was only making it worse.

"Go to your room," she said when we pulled into the driveway at home.

I lay on my bottom bunk bed and stared at the wallpaper until I finally heard my father come in. Hours had passed, and other than having Mom yell at me, I still hadn't been asked to tell anyone what happened. I hadn't felt safe talking to Mr. Flynn, and Mom didn't want to listen. But I trusted in Dad's willingness to hear me out.

True to form, he walked in the room and asked, "What happened?

I told him Juanita and I had argued before school. We'd agreed on a time to fight off school grounds, but it wasn't until Friday, and I thought she would cool off before then. My stomach had been a ball of nerves all day, and just before my last class she attacked me from behind on the "up" stairs. When I finished, he shook his head. He said there were rules when it came to street fights and that this was an assault. I could have been seriously hurt and Mr. Flynn had some balls trying to suspend me.

At first, I felt relieved. But my initial relief gave way to horror when I realized that Dad was planning to fight Mr. Flynn's decision. He said a responsible educator would have separated me and Juanita to investigate what happened, and that Flynn was wrong if he thought we were going to sit back and accept my suspension. Mom had always insisted I take punishments from authority figures without complaint, yet Dad was telling me I'd messed up by being too meek and quiet when I was taken to the office.

Before I knew it there were police officers in our living room asking me what had happened. I didn't want to talk, but Dad pulled me into the kitchen. "This is the best way to help Juanita," he said. "A scare now may stop her from getting into bigger trouble down the line."

After the cops left, Dad got a bag of frozen corn out of the freezer and tossed it to me across the table. "Put this on your lip," he told me. As I did my homework, he paced like an agitated mountain lion. He said Mom should have listened to my story, taken me into the school, and confronted Mr. Flynn immediately. Now he would have to drive me the following morning. It would make him late for work, and he didn't like being late for work.

I was terrified that Mr. Flynn would see Dad as a restless Native; that pushing back against his rules would get us in trouble and make all my teachers dislike me. Hadn't my parents always said people expected us to follow higher standards? Wasn't this the moment to turn the other cheek? I tried to convince Dad that Mr. Flynn wouldn't budge, then I went down the hall to look in the mirror. The ice had shrunk the size of my lip, and my nose looked fine. Other than a small bruise under my right eye, and a massive headache, there was little evidence of the assault.

Dad followed me down the hallway and stood in the bathroom door.

"If he still wants you suspended, he's going to have to stop me from taking you to class."

I pictured Dad pushing by Mr. Flynn to take me to biology class. I imagined my classmates gawking as the cops came and handcuffed him for disturbing the peace. It was a nightmare, and I knew I never wanted to play tough girl again. The world was a struggle, but I'd have to find another way to do battle because I didn't have the stomach for cops, violence, and especially for seeing my father get hurt or in trouble on my behalf.

When we pulled up at the school the following morning it felt like everybody was standing outside. I saw my first crush, Rusty, a popular basketball player who was half-Navajo and half-white. The first bell hadn't rung, and the students were not allowed inside yet, but Dad dragged me through the doors like he owned the place.

The vice principal still hadn't arrived, but his secretary led us into his office, and we sat in the same seats where Juanita and I had sat the day before. A framed photo of Mr. Flynn, with his arm around a blond lady who looked like his sister, sat on the desk in front of us.

"Is that him?" Dad asked, looking at the picture.

"Yes," I said.

Just as I answered, Flynn walked into the room. He gave us a gruff hello before beginning a lecture about rules, saying good students didn't require lessons in civility, while bad ones always resisted the teachings that they needed to be upstanding citizens. He spoke like my parents hadn't taught me to respect others, and his rationale, I would discover years later, was the same one the government used when they created Indian boarding schools. White kids were innately civil, while brown kids—and brown parents who protested injustices—needed to have good manners imposed.

The fear I had felt about coming to school that day turned to anger at my vice principal and embarrassment for not trusting Dad to bring me in. I hated the way Mr. Flynn treated my father like he was presumptuous, like it was uppity for him to want to advocate for his daughter. And I was proud of the way Dad kept his anger under control. For the first time in my life, I understood that civility was used to silence less powerful people when they wanted to address a wrong.

"It's unreasonable to expect special treatment," Mr. Flynn said. "There are *rules*, and you showing up to pressure me is disrespectful and rude."

There was a heavy silence when Mr. Flynn finished, and the longer Dad sat without saying a word, the redder Mr. Flynn's neck became. Finally, after what felt like a century, Dad pushed the police report across the desk and said, "I don't appreciate my daughter being punished for getting jumped at school. She could have been killed on those stairs."

Mr. Flynn unfolded the paperwork and read it, understanding for the first time that I'd been attacked from behind hours after the verbal disagreement. When he started talking about Juanita, my father shook his head. He said he wasn't asking Mr. Flynn to protect me from Juanita. He simply wanted the suspension revoked, and any evidence of it taken off my school records. Mr. Flynn stuttered when he agreed, and as we left the room for me to go to class, I saw that he was seething.

When the nuns announced that Sacred Heart wouldn't educate older kids anymore, Mom and Dad suspected the curricula at our local public schools would be a problem. Then they realized the behavioral problems were a danger too. Before Juanita, I'd dodged the violence. The all-white teaching staff had weeded out the "tough" kids, separating us into two groups: achieving and nonachieving. As an achiever, I'd been fine. I'd even babysat for my English teacher. But after getting jumped in the stairwell, my teachers never treated me the same.

Dad gave me a high five as we walked out of Flynn's office. "See you tonight," he said, taking off for his truck. As I walked toward biology class, José found me and asked me how I escaped my suspension. I told him my father said there were rules when it came to fights. He scowled, like he thought I was calling Juanita a coward, and I turned away and ran to class.

Coach Sanders, the basketball coach, was my biology teacher. He was a transplant from the East Coast. He had us scheduled to start our first lab that day, and as soon as I took my seat, he singled out the Native kids for an announcement. The school board was requiring him to offer a research option for those of us who didn't want to do labs.

"The principal was receiving complaints from your parents," he said. "Mr. Flynn met with me and the board, and we conceded that killing insects and dissecting frogs and fetal pigs infringes on Native beliefs."

A few laughs popped up in the back of the room. I turned around and saw that some of the white boys were shaking their heads and rolling their eyes. I wondered what Coach Sanders thought about the research option. Did he think Native traditions were backward or did he think we should be allowed to stay out of the lab?

"It's up to you," Coach Sanders continued.

I felt a rush of irritation knowing Mr. Flynn had weighed in on the decision. I imagined him smirking like the boys at the back of the room. But the hatred I felt toward Flynn and the boys changed to anger at myself when I realized I cared what Coach Sanders thought. I wanted to be a defensive starter on his basketball team, and I admired his education as a scientist. Would he think it was stupid if I opted out?

The class watched as Coach Sanders went to his desk to write down the names of anyone who wanted to do the research paper instead of the labs. A third of the Navajo kids raised their hands, including Rusty, the Navajo-white basketball player who I was infatuated with, but I froze up. I just sat there in my chair and let the coach assume that I was confident in my decision.

A few weeks later, when I was sent to catch insects, I found that the process both attracted and repelled me. I hated watching them die in the ammonia, but I also liked the knowledge and control that came with pinning each bug to the board with a label. I worked on my bug board for weeks, catching and labeling tiger beetles, velvet ants, camel crickets, honeybees, ambush bugs, bark beetles, backswimmers, stink bugs, water boatmen, walking sticks, sucking lice, and giant silkworm moths.

Later in the semester, when my insect project was done, I went ahead with the dissections as well. I dumped my fetal pig out of its stinking formaldehyde bag and took a scalpel to its flesh. I cracked open its rib cage to examine its polished little heart with a feeling of terror and wonder. Half the Indian kids in my school never saw what was beneath the skin in those fetal pigs, and even though none of my Navajo friends criticized me, I felt worried that they were judging me for my decision.

My big sisters laughed when I told them my concerns. They knew some of our Navajo friends had strict ideas about who was authentically Native and who wasn't. They accepted that the more traditional kids were gatekeepers who judged us because we couldn't speak our tribal languages. When I asked them if they envied our friends for having grandparents with dirt hogans, they rolled their eyes like I was dumb. The one time they heard me speaking with an exaggerated "ndn" accent to fit in with some Native friends, they found it fake and performative, like I was trying to commodify our culture.

Joan and Lori were who they were, and they didn't apologize for not wanting to resurrect our family's traditional ways. They wanted a mainstream life: frat parties and senior trips to Mazatlán. They liked listening to pop music on the radio, while my teen taste leaned toward new wave and punk rock. They boiled hot dogs while I read about and committed to vegetarianism. They entered the 1980s with an uncanny sense of belonging, mocking my ozone layer worries and my interest in genealogy. Sometimes they even berated me for prizing Dad's lineage over Mom's, and at the time, I didn't know how to stand up for myself. I didn't have the language and couldn't explain why I didn't like "passing."

To be born to a people with no written histories can feel like a kind of cultural amnesia. I had to choose my own path when the bread crumbs leading home had been eaten. I envied the traditional Navajo students in my class because I thought they didn't share my identity crisis, my complex inner life. I wish I had understood earlier what a privilege it is to have the freedom to choose: to mold your own face, choose your own values, and carve your own monsters and gods.

Two weeks after getting jumped, I found Juanita and José waiting for me after my Friday night volleyball game. Her shoulders were slumped, and she had a bruise on her jaw. She told me her father had hit her after the cops stopped by their house.

"I thought we were friends," she said, glumly.

Fighting was often the gateway to friendship for girls at my school, but I wasn't feeling much trust. She made me promise that we weren't going to press charges, that my father was going to let things drop. When I said that was the plan, she wanted us to go to Party Cove together, to show our classmates the bad blood was over.

"José's driving," she said, hooking her elbow through mine.

Utility roads for Farmington's natural gas industry stretched through the foothills on the outskirts of town. When we were kids, Dad used to take us hiking in the sandstone canyons. As I got older, I often went alone. I loved the sand washes that ran through the arroyos, and I'd heard my sisters talk about Party Cove, though I wasn't old enough to drink or party out there myself. I'd often identified the remnants of weekend bonfires, from the beer cans and plastic trash on my hikes. I hated seeing the sage, rabbit brush, and cacti crushed by four-wheel-drive vehicles, but I couldn't help being curious when I got into José's car.

My parents were going to be mad that I didn't come home after the game. I had no idea how I was going to explain my behavior, except to say that I had to be nice to Juanita to bury the hatchet. Party Cove was a cave beneath two tall bluffs, and our classmates had a fire going when we arrived. Some cheerleaders were sucking nitrous oxide out of whipped cream cans when we got there, and my palms stopped sweating when a couple of them said hello. Juanita laughed when she saw me relax. "See?" she said. "No one's going to bite."

A short time later, José was already too drunk to drive me home. Feeling awkward with the upper classmen at the party, I headed toward the back of the cave. The walls there narrowed and formed a crevasse where a person could use the opposing sides of sandstone to shimmy up thirty feet and stand on top of the bluffs. Every couple of years someone died rock climbing without a harness in the foothills, probably because they'd been drinking. But I'd spent a lot of time hiking and bouldering with Dad in my childhood, and I climbed with confidence, wanting to be alone at the top of the canyon.

I pulled myself up and stood overlooking the sandstone canyon below. Without a bonfire, the stars grew bright in the sky. I could hear the faraway sound of music and laughter below, and I assumed I was alone, but as I moved away from the ledge to sit, I heard voices in the darkness. It was Rusty with a group of basketball players and a couple of his Navajo cousins.

"You shouldn't be climbing in the dark," one of them said. "Now how do you plan to get down?"

I shrugged. "Do you guys know what time it is?" I asked.

I knew my parents were worried about me already, but when one of the basketball players asked if I wanted a beer I said yes because I wanted to impress them.

"Almost eleven," Rusty told me.

They were talking about the boys' basketball coach. There were rumors that he was sleeping with a student while his wife was pregnant at home. I was thankful when Rusty changed the subject.

"Doesn't your dad work out at the power plant?" he asked.

"Yeah, he started as a plate welder and worked his way up," I said.

"Pat's uncle and dad work there," Rusty said, nudging one of his cousins.

"What's your dad's name?" Pat asked.

"Ed Jackson," I told him.

He stood up and staggered over, putting his face inches from mine. "Did you say Ed Jackson?"

"Yes," I said. "Ed Jackson."

Pat sprayed me with spit as he spoke. "Well, a lot of people at the plant don't like your dad. They say he thinks he's better than everyone else because he's a foreman."

Everyone stopped talking. The moon was a tiny sliver, and even though my eyes had adjusted to the dark, I couldn't see the faces of the rest of the guys. Were they as angry as Pat? I wanted to stick up for my father, but I was afraid. I thought of Juanita attacking me on the stairs, and José happy to see me beat up. I couldn't believe these guys were ganging up on me too.

Rusty told Pat to sit down, but he didn't. He stayed right in my face. He was standing so close I could smell a mixture of alcohol and deodorant coming from his body. I'd heard older Navajos criticize their tribal government for building the Navajo coal mine and Four Corners power plant on their reservation near Farmington, but Pat was much younger. He dressed in preppy clothes and drove a nice car. I didn't peg him as a traditionalist and was therefore surprised that he was acting this way, especially when his dad and uncle worked at the power plant as well. Without saying a word, I took off running along the top of the bluff.

"Where are you going?" I heard Rusty call, but I didn't respond. I felt scared and ashamed. I couldn't trust anyone who hated my family. It would take hours to go the length of the bluff instead of climbing down the crevice with their help. The descent into the canyon would be gradual, and once I hit pavement it would take me another hour to get home. Still, I started running and didn't stop.

As I darted between piñon and juniper trees, I kept hearing Pat in my mind, saying no one liked my father. It was painful because I feared people didn't like me either. I had always been an "in between" person, bouncing among friend groups. Being an outsider terrified me, and the farther I ran the more my anger shifted from Pat to my father. I kept stumbling over rocks, and after several miles I finally allowed myself to walk.

Dad had taken me to the power plant with him one time on visitors' day. I wore a hard hat, and he introduced me to the Navajo and Apache guys on his crew. He said they climbed the metal staircase to the top of the generating station every morning. They stood together on a platform twelve stories high to greet the sunrise, and one of the guys said a prayer in Navajo before they headed inside to clean fly ash and weld.

Dad loved his coworkers. He said he owed his success to the guys who worked for him. His supervisor couldn't figure out how he always picked the best welders for his crew, and he said his secret was listening. The more he heard them grinding or cutting cold metal off their welds, the less expert he knew they were at creating fine sutures. A good weld was clean. A bumpy weld had air bubbles inside that made the metal weak. High-pressure pipes could explode if vulnerable, and Dad would go down at the end of the day and catch the poor welds, even when he hadn't been on the floor. He just went to x-ray the areas where he'd heard a lot of cutting and grinding.

"I don't discriminate against non-Navajos," Dad had said, "but on my crew the Navajo guys are always the best welders."

Dad had won awards for quick repairs on tube leaks that lost electricity and cost the company thousands of dollars an hour. His boss flagged him to fix the outdated systems on the older side of the plant. He added cleaning scrubbers and changed out filters to protect the air quality and bring the power plant in line with new EPA regulations. He built twenty-four compartments with 560 filters per slot—he was particularly proud of handling that job. He said all his guys were happy about it because it was supposed to cut down on pollution.

I'd been proud of him doing that job, but after my run-in with Pat I felt confused. I knew that the Relocation Act had made Dad and his generation "different," but now I wondered about the jobs they took to get ahead. I thought about Rusty walking out of biology class to go do research instead of trapping bugs. Everyone in Farmington lived in modern homes with electricity. We switched our lights on without knowing how it worked, while Dad was out at the plant producing electricity that got sold to five western states.

I knew Dad's job was dangerous. His friend Beltran once shut down a breaker without using the correct protocol. Dad saw him racking the switch down and ran, though the explosion still sent him flying through the door. Dad said Beltran's skin was smoking and peeling, and his body's shadow was imprinted on the wall until someone painted it over. Dad's other coworker Glen drowned in a room full of fly ash. He was accidentally closed inside the bag house while checking the insulation covers on some ducts. I thought about the way the rest of us want light and voilà, but none of us cared about the sacrifices and work it took to create it.

It must have been nearly 3:00 A.M. by the time I rounded the corner at the top of my street. I was still in my volleyball uniform, and the kneepads around my ankles were covered in dust. I was thinking about the spare key hidden alongside the house when I spotted someone sitting on our front porch.

As I drew near, I realized it was Dad. He was wrapped in a blanket with his fishing thermos at his feet. As I opened the gate and walked toward the house, he asked, "What time do I get up for work?"

"Four o'clock," I said. He was running a maintenance outage, and if he didn't get enough sleep, and have his wits about him at work, someone on his crew could get hurt.

Without mentioning Juanita, I told him what Pat had said about him at the party. "He claims the guys on your crew hate you," I said, hearing my voice catch. But once I'd spoken the accusation, I couldn't stop, and I heard myself saying I was embarrassed that he worked at the plant.

He snorted and shook his head. Lori and Joan called Dad a broken record because he always dealt with us by telling stories, and he only told his favorites.

Rather than responding to me about his job, Dad started recounting a tale I'd heard a hundred times before. "When my father lost his arm in that car accident, he got all poor me. He nearly drank himself to death and made Mom work like crazy at the laundromat. She was basically a single parent for five years," he said.

"One day when I was nine, I went swimming in the All-American Canal with my brothers. My sister came running to tell us Dad had shot himself. We swam to shore and ran toward our house, and as I was running, I was thinking, What's going to happen to us? When I reached the yard my mother and other sisters were outside. They said Dad had come home drunk. He argued with Mom, and when he went for his rifle, they ran outside. When they got to the yard, they heard a shot, and they were afraid to go back inside. Mom said, 'Eddie, go see.' She was shaking."

"I went to the door and crawled into the kitchen where I saw Dad bent forward in his chair. The rifle was on the floor, and he was breathing. I looked for blood but there was none. I stood up and shook his shoulder. He looked at me with glazed eyes and said something in Quechan. I went to the door and told Mom he'd shot a hole in the ceiling, but he was okay. 'Thank God,' she said, then we all went inside to put him to bed. That's the last time I saw him drink alcohol."

I sat quietly at his feet and didn't reply. The last time he'd told me the story, it was different. He'd described hurrying home, true. But halfway there he'd stopped running. He was panting along when he thought maybe they'd be better off without their father. His siblings passed him, but he walked. He *walked*—and I felt frustrated that he was leaving that part out now. I didn't understand that he wanted to emphasize a greater truth: he loved his father and knew there was more to him than the alcohol and pain.

"Whatever," I told him. It didn't seem like his story had anything to do with Pat's comment. I apologized, mainly to get away from his broken record stories and go inside, but for the first time in my life he told me something new.

"Joan was just a baby when my father got sick with pneumonia," Dad said. "And I guess he was depressed, because he wouldn't get off the couch to go to the hospital. My brothers finally came to get me in Yuma when they realized he was dying. His face had turned gray, and he was hardly breathing, but they were afraid to take him to the doctor.

"He was just like your grandma Esther. Neither of them liked hospitals. Remember how she refused chemotherapy when she got sick? He was the same way. Only this wasn't cancer, it was pneumonia, and I knew it could be treated with antibiotics. My father always said he didn't want to die in some white hospital room with fluorescent lighting. He claimed it took the dignity out of death, and I agree.

"I was the only kid in my family who wasn't afraid of him, and my brothers knew it. That's why they came for me. They were afraid to make him go to the hospital, but I wasn't. I went over to the house and dragged him off the couch. I loaded him in the car and drove him up to the Indian Hospital in Yuma. The nurses took one look at him and sent him in an ambulance to Phoenix. My brothers and I followed the ambulance all the way there to get him admitted. He was lying on a hospital gurney and said he was going to be okay. He said to go home. It took us three hours to get back to the reservation, and as soon as we pulled up in Mom's front yard she came out and said the hospital called to say he didn't make it."

He turned to look at me for the first time all night. "I went against my own father. He was only forty-nine years old, and I wanted him to choose life, even though I also wished I could honor his beliefs. And you think after going through all that I'm going to worry about what some stupid high school kid has to say about me?"

"Well, why'd Pat say it if it wasn't true?"

Dad sighed. He said, "When I first started at the power plant most Indian guys were only hired in entry-level jobs. Navajos started as janitors, and white guys started in the mail room. There were a lot of bigots. We weren't exactly accepted, and before I became a foreman none of the Navajos wanted to bid for promotions. Indians aren't supposed to climb through the ranks. It breaks tradition to place yourself above your clan and cousins.

"Unemployment in Navajo country was terrible in the late 1960s. Their tribe offered money and tax bonuses to investors, and one of the biggest semiconductor manufacturers in the world arrived in Shiprock to build the Fairchild electronics plant. They said they'd pay employees a million dollars, but all the money was going to high-level workers who were white. Twenty armed protesters with the American Indian Movement took the plant by force the year we moved to Farmington. They demanded better pay and promotions, and a lot of Navajo people disliked their radical tactics. The American Indian Movement protesters thought Fairchild would fold to their pressure, but instead the company closed the plant and left town. A machinist on my crew lost his job and had to come and work at the Four Corners Power Plant."

Now Dad sounded mad. "No one agrees about how to make Indian lives better, kid. AIM fights for promotions when some people don't want them. Some Navajos hate outside industries, others say they are necessary. I used to get irritated when Navajo guys refused to advance because they had a cousin on the crew. They were all so afraid of acting uppity, but I wasn't afraid. And I wasn't embarrassed to fight with them about it. Some of them ended up hating me, it's true. But you know what? I was the first Indian foreman in the history of my plant, and now six out of fifteen foreman positions are held by Indian men."

"Are you mad at me?" I asked him.

"There you go," he said. "If you've got one problem, that's it. You worry too damn much about pleasing everyone else. You never make choices for yourself. You've got to learn to stand alone. Have the courage to become an individual."

He shook his head and went inside.

I sat out on the porch and cried. I hated Pat, and I hated my father's job for making me look bad in the eyes of Indian kids I respected. I hated that the power plant was dirty and polluting and that I was the same, a half-breed soiled by colonialism. I hated that, despite being half-white, Rusty was accepted when I wasn't because he was a Navajo in his homeland. But most of all, I hated the story Dad told me about his father. It hurt to imagine my grandfather dying in the very place, and in the very way, he had so fervently opposed.

I paced around on the porch, acknowledging the way everyone feels squeezed between the old and the new. I knew Dad was telling me I had to make my own choices. I hated the pressure and feared choosing wrong. The task was no less than building a life, and before I went inside to bed, I thought of my grandpa Ed and swore that I would never go against my tribal traditions. But even after my vow, it was complicated, because just as my head hit the pillow, I remembered the wonder of the fetal pig's heart, polished and still as a stone in my hands.

ALL SAINTS

(1983)

I don't remember which of Mom's brothers first came to stay with us in Farmington the year I turned fourteen. I have no idea if they were invited, or they simply showed up. They never overlapped, and their dreams of reinvention didn't last long. They were grown men, spiritually adrift and hurt by poor luck and bad decisions. They were set in their ways and always brought trouble they couldn't outrun.

When the first brother came, Dad split our enormous utility room in two. After installing a thin wall, he put in a single bed, an old dresser, and a remnant piece of rug. It was a thoughtful effort, even though the room lacked insulation and the space heater barely warmed things up. The washer and dryer swished and spun at all hours, loud enough to sound like an industrial laundry was sitting at the foot of the bed.

Out of all of Mom's brothers, Uncle Albert was my favorite. He was a mailman with a sweet family and the biggest vocabulary I'd ever heard. When Mom spotted him stepping off the bus in Farmington on the heels of his divorce, she told me his tongue was slick as a slip-and-slide, but she said it with admiration. In confidence though, Dad told us the Vietnam War had messed him up.

My parents asked around—Mom at church, Dad at work—and someone found Uncle Albert a job at an all-night diner downtown. For weeks, he flipped pancakes and burgers on the swing shift, and after he was trained, my parents took us down to eat at his restaurant. I remember he came out of the kitchen in his white apron to ask if we liked the way our meat was cooked, which made Mom beam with pride.

Only a couple months after he arrived though, Dad found a needle and spoon on Albert's bedside table. We were on our way to the movies, loaded up in the van, when Dad came out to tell us what he'd seen.

"What are we going to do?" Mom asked.

"I shook him awake and told him he had to go back to Yuma tomorrow," Dad said.

When Uncle Ritchie arrived a month later, he didn't hide his drug use as well as Uncle Albert had. Dad got him a job washing dishes at a Mexican restaurant, and during the day his friends dropped by to smoke cigarettes on the back patio. They had sleepy eyes and slow laughs. The longer they sat, the lower their eyelids drooped.

One of Uncle Ritchie's friends was creepy. I was only in the eighth grade, but he called me over one day when Monica went out to the patio to get our bikes. "Your sisters are burritos," he said. "And burritos aren't bad, but you, girl, are a taco with all the fixings." He grossed me out and I didn't know why a nice guy like Uncle Ritchie was hanging out with him.

Mom never seemed to worry about her brother's weird friends. Having another baby—my little brother, Ted—made her tired and spacey, and even though I liked Uncle Ritchie, I was relieved when, six weeks later, he got homesick and left and our family had privacy again. I told Monica it was lucky he had a magnet that drew him home to Yuma.

Most of Mom's brothers worked as firefighters, sanitation workers, and store managers in Yuma. They never came to stay with us in New Mexico. But then there were five siblings she needed to help: the lost and struggling ones. When we were little kids and still living in Yuma, they were the brothers who babysat us when Mom's and Dad's sisters were busy. They didn't have jobs or extracurricular activities. They were always hanging out at Grandma Mary's, and I hated it when most of them came over, not because they were mean, but because they ignored us.

As soon as Mom left us in their care, they raided the pantry and parked

themselves in front of the TV. Joan said they were only there to eat, because the more Dad worked, the more packaged food we could afford. It
wasn't just beans and rice at our house, and they knew it. We had chips,
snack cakes, and boxes of cereal. Lori claimed it was the main reason they
agreed to come over.

You might say our mother was a cereal aficionado. Having a bit of
money after getting married, she didn't end up buying clothes. In those
early years, she discovered junk food and purchased Lucky Charms, Cap'n
Crunch, and Cocoa Puffs by the pound. She loaded the grocery cart with
single-serving variety packs like they were status symbols.

Anytime we went over to pick up one of Mom's brothers to babysit it
played out like an extreme sport. If they were outside, she rolled down
the window and yelled that she needed help for the day, and they rushed
the car like they were being chased by the bulls in Pamplona. When one
of them jumped in the front seat to win their spot, Mom pulled away from
the curb, and I stuck my tongue out at the losers while dangling my small
box of Cocoa Puffs out the window to torture them. Monica danced her
box around in the back window as we drove away. We yelled, "They're
cuckoo for Cocoa Puffs!" and cackled like crazy.

All these years later, when Mom's brothers got on or off the Greyhound bus in Farmington, it made me emotional. When they were arriving, it made me sad because it meant they'd screwed up in Yuma. When
they were leaving, I misted up because they'd failed in Farmington too.
The revolving door of possibility spun too quickly for them, and I was
embarrassed to feel pity for grown men. My old cruelties implicated me,
as if the sugar cereal I had dangled before them in my memory was some
sort of gateway drug.

Or maybe I felt upset because I feared their failures might be genetic.
They were my uncles, after all. I could see the family resemblance, and
that made their hangdog expressions feel infectious. Mom commented
on the middle kids in the "birth order" when Uncle Ritchie left. Maybe
Joan and Lori, the eldest kids in our family, would scale all the ladders,
while my future held nothing but chutes. Maybe my youngest siblings

would thrive and consume all our parents' affection, while I lived my life, forgotten.

By the eighth grade, my pride was worn thin. I'd begged to play the trumpet like Dad's father and grandfather, but Mom had insisted on the French horn, and I got my first D in band. I was no longer the star pupil, the girl asked to tutor slower students, the one who got picked for the lead in school plays. I'd long since learned Andrew Jackson was a jerk, and the image I'd once had of myself as class valedictorian was spent. Through the years, so many adults had declared that I was talented, I just knew I'd grow up to be an artist, writer, lawyer, or judge. Now I fretted and brooded over the smallest setbacks. If I couldn't succeed in Podunk, New Mexico, what good could the future have in store?

That summer Joan graduated from high school, and the whole family drove north to Cañon City for her "Class of 1983" celebration. She'd received scholarships to a couple of East Coast schools, but she wanted to attend Pepperdine in Malibu. All year long, she and Lori had gabbed on the phone about sororities until our parents got involved and a debate about money ensued. Mom said Joan should stay local to get to know our newest siblings. Joan was heartbroken, but her fate was decided. She would go to Fort Lewis College in Durango, Colorado, because it was only an hour north of Farmington, and because its status as a land grant school meant tuition for Native students was free.

Not long after we brought Joan home from Cañon City that summer, Grandma Mary called to say that Uncle Tommy had gone missing. The two of them had been fighting all year, and at first Mom rolled her eyes at Grandma's panic. Grandma had been blaming Tommy's new girlfriend for turning him against the church, but I knew lots of young people in Tommy's generation found Catholicism too stifling.

I'd always liked Tommy. He was the king of the younger kids in Mom's family. For many years, when we visited Yuma, he organized our games. He was five years older than Joan, but still deigned to hang out with us when we visited. More than once, he led us into the desert to a sand dune called Mount Baldy, where he built a rich fantasy world with his stories.

Now Tommy was reaching his midtwenties, and Mom said Grandma had to stop treating him like a baby. When the girlfriend told Tommy she was transferring from the local community college to Arizona State University in Phoenix, Tommy claimed it was Grandma who scared her away. That's why, when he went missing, it made sense for everyone to assume he'd gone to Phoenix to find her.

A couple of days passed with no one knowing what happened to him, and Grandma Mary was so worried that Mom started talking about a possible trip to Yuma. Later we would find out that Tommy had gone to the bus station, just like everyone thought, but as he was standing in line to purchase his fare, a couple of bearded men wandered in. They chatted Tommy up and asked him where he wanted to go. They needed a bit of gas money, they said, and were willing to give him a ride in their van. Tommy told them he was heading east toward Gila Bend with a final stop at the ASU campus in Tempe.

"You're in luck, man," they said. "Just pitch in a fiver and we'll drop you off."

No one knows for sure, but Grandma Mary said they gave Tommy LSD when he got in the van. I'm not sure why drugs had to be part of the story because what happened next made sense even without him getting high. The vanload of strangers drove an hour into the desert, took a highway exit toward nowhere, stole Tommy's wallet, and left him on a dirt road miles away from Gila Bend.

It was a hundred-degree day in the middle of the Sonoran Desert, and it took Tommy hours to reach pavement where he could flag somebody down. His tongue grew swollen from dehydration and his skin developed blisters. By the time he was rescued by a Lutheran pastor and his wife, he was sunburned beyond recognition and could barely talk to get his story out. They were heading west and took him to a hospital in Yuma. He was catatonic by the time they arrived, and it took the doctors another day to figure out who he was.

The kind couple got a hotel and waited. When Tommy's identity was unearthed, they called Grandma Mary, who told them she didn't have a car and asked if they could drive Tommy to the house. By the time they pulled up in front of Grandma Mary's house with Tommy in the backseat, she was hysterical. Dad said mothers have a sixth sense about when their children are in danger, and that we should have listened to her. She knew something was wrong, and it was. Tommy never recovered. He remembered her, but he could barely speak, and moved like a robot.

Hearing about it from a distance, Mom and Dad didn't know what to think, and their confusion amplified my own. We'd lost uncles and grandparents and family friends. I understood death as a departure, but what did "crazy" mean? It sounded like the essence of Tommy was missing and only a shell was left behind, but if that was true, where had his personality, mind, and spirit gone?

When Grandma Mary took Tommy back to the doctors, they diagnosed him with schizophrenia, and she called Mom from the hospital, crying. They would eventually give him shock therapy and put him in a home, but that fall he stayed with her and the family while taking a medley of medications. In December, when we drove to Yuma for Christmas, only Dad remained optimistic.

I think he felt sure that we could beckon Tommy back.

Grandma was sitting with him in the front yard when we arrived. His lips were chapped and peeling, and even though I couldn't attribute it to his time in the desert, their cracking felt like a sign of his prolonged wounding. His body moved differently. Tommy had always been quick. He was the family's stealthiest photo bomber, but now he was stiff and clunky.

Mom's younger brother Phillip tried to make light of the situation by telling Dad he should install a pinball machine for Tommy—only no one laughed at his joke. "Don't you get it?" Phillip asked, before singing "Pinball Wizard," by the Who in an off-key approximation. "That deaf, dumb, and blind kid, sure plays a mean pinball."

He had always fancied himself a stand-up comedian, but given the shocking situation his dark humor wasn't working. Mom wrapped Tommy in a hug, her face turned to the side against his chest, and I could see that she was trying not to weep.

For ten minutes, Dad talked to Tommy about the good old days, birthday parties we'd held for him when he was young. He teased him about his tenth or eleventh, when we bought him a skateboard and he was so happy he cried. Joan, Lori, Monica, and I talked to him next, but no matter how hard anyone tried, the Tommy we knew and loved would never reemerge.

The mystery of what had happened to Tommy's mind terrified me. Sitting there with him was worse than any funeral, and I worried that I'd never feel comfortable around him again. He moved only when he was ordered. Grandma Mary had to tell him where to go. If you told him to eat, he ate in a way that suggested he wasn't even sure if he was hungry. He observed the world with shell-shocked eyes.

Our drive back to Farmington that Sunday felt haunted. I looked out the window and remembered Tommy when we were kids. He used to love to play with cicadas. Every summer the bugs crawled up the mesquite trees near Mount Baldy, only to be hunted by Tommy. Many times, I watched him pin a cicada wing down while cupping the bug with his opposite hand. He plucked the wings off and tied lengths of thread around their bodies for whirly toys spun like lassos. He shoved them into aluminum cans to play marching band.

Thinking about Tommy and the cicadas on our drive home from Yuma left me feeling heartsick. His vacant stare somehow reminded me of the clear shells the cicadas shed when their wings hardened and they backed out of their skin like snakes, leaving perfect replicas of their old bodies behind, baked golden and crisp in the sun. I used to hate playing with the mutilated cicadas, but I loved knocking their shells out of the mesquite tree to step on like they were dry autumn leaves.

Dad and Mom were wrecked. For weeks after our return, they stared at the kitchen cabinets like they didn't remember how to open them. Every night we bought and ate takeout. Every morning Mom went to the church to sit in the Eucharistic Chapel and pray.

For a long time, Dad stayed silent. But then one day, about a month after we got back from Yuma, Dad's El Camino ran out of gas while he and I were on our way home from the grocery store. Dad thought it was a mystery how we'd run out so quickly when he'd just filled up the tank on Sunday, but I knew I was likely responsible. I'd been stealing the car for joyrides when nobody was home, even though I didn't have a driver's license yet. I felt cooped up and angry about Tommy, and driving was the only way I could stop thinking about the rotten guys who had abandoned him to die in the desert. In the alley near where we stopped, there were chunks of concrete broken loose from a retaining wall and I kicked one into some weeds as we hoofed it home. I was wearing sandals and the concrete cut my right foot. My toenail started to bleed, but I pretended like I didn't feel a thing.

If Dad noticed my false bravado and anger, he didn't mention it. For most of the walk, he seemed to be deep in thought, working out a problem in his mind. I resigned myself to silence, but then he asked if I'd ever heard of the Native American Church. Apparently, when he'd learned about Tommy, a Navajo friend at Dad's work had invited us to attend.

The friend said Tommy might have started down a new path, one that we couldn't reach with everyday thoughts, words, or reason. He said Tommy could have entered the realm of the medicine man—a world different yet connected to our own—and there he'd gotten tangled up in the desert's phenomena of heat and light. In the Laguna Pueblo culture, Old Spider Woman, Tse-che-nako, weaves the multiverse. She sits in her kiva and thinks, and whatever she thinks about appears. In the beginning she spun a web, laced it with dew, and threw it in the sky for stars. She was power. She was story. And Tommy had been beckoned to a part of her web that we couldn't see.

Dad said only a fool would hope for this calling—not because it meant a life of service—but because it was dangerous. He said Granny Ethel always told him that these types of people were marked, sometimes by an unusual event like the one that happened to Tommy, sometimes from the moment they were born. There could be a sign when they emerged from their mother, or maybe they had seizures or deformities. Others were two-spirit or transgender. They stood on the threshold between worlds, and like the schizophrenic, they encountered supernatural beings.

The more Dad talked, the more his words began to build hope in me. After the powwow, I'd started reading Native mythologies. I was asking more questions, and it felt like my interest in our traditions, and the tragedy that had befallen Tommy, had set off a homing beacon in Dad. For the first time since we'd returned from Yuma, he sounded like he was turning toward tribal beliefs to lessen suffering, the nightmare scenario, and the postapocalyptic difficulties we were enduring. He was the one who had always saved us, and it was soothing to hear him say that Western doctors weren't the only way, that Granny Ethel would have said that no illness, depression, or nightmares were beyond traditional medicine, and that Native plants had healing potential. Today scientists know that psychedelics like peyote create neuroplasticity or a re-wiring of the brain. When a person's thinking gets trapped in a cycle of illness or pain, these plants can give them space to step outside of themselves and heal. This wisdom has been around in Native America for a very long time. Grandfather Peyote has been used as a sacrament by Indigenous Americans for nearly six thousand years, according to anthropologists—long before the Native American Church as a "Christian religion with the practice of the Peyote Sacrament" was founded in 1918. Even though I'd barely known the Native American Church, a pan-Indian church with peyote as a sacrament, existed, my step felt lighter hearing Dad talk about Navajo medicine men who might teach me about Indigenous forms of wisdom.

When we reached our house, we found the lights off, the television on, and Mom dozing in her recliner. In the kitchen, the sink was full of dishes. Dad picked up the phone to order us some pizzas and then rolled up his sleeves to start washing plates. "Don't say anything to Mom yet," he told me. "I'll talk to her about it tomorrow. Tonight, me and Joan need to go pick up some gas for the El Camino."

After eating pizza, I went to bed, but I couldn't stop thinking about Dad's plan. I didn't know if the invitation he'd received was a coincidence, or if he'd sought it out, but I thought the opportunity was brilliant and didn't want to pass it up. He said that Grandfather Peyote was a medicine that helped with spiritual balance, mental clarity, and physical well-being. Old myths about the practice come from the Kiowa and Comanche tribes who lived in the desert where the cactus grew. The story tells of a people trying to survive a drought. Dehydrated and starving, a grandmother and grandson refuse to die without seeking food, and they wander into the desert where they eventually collapse. Just as the life is leaving their bodies, they hear a voice urging them to eat. With no one around to give them further instructions, they can only see a patch of peyote, so they eat it before passing out, and when they wake, they feel nourished, even as they are in the power of the psychoactive medicine. It saves them, and they take the valuable plant home to save their community as well. For this reason, peyote has a reputation for being a medicine that teaches people how to survive. Even after Dad explained that the ceremony required participants to sit up all night, praying from sunset to sunrise, I wanted to go.

But the next night after dinner, Mom said we weren't allowed. Attending a non-Catholic church was a sin, and she wasn't going to watch us go to hell for some devilish plant that might make us lose our minds. I'd anticipated her resistance. After all, she'd once refused to let Joan go to a Lutheran service for the same reason. But I thought I had prepared a convincing argument. That morning in homeroom, I'd asked my old Sacred Heart School friend, Robert, about the Native American Church, and he'd told me, as I explained to my mother, to think of the ceremony as a practice, not a religion. Like Buddhist meditation, people from many different belief systems could benefit from the healing it offered.

Mom cut me off. She said we needed to keep our eyes on heaven. We had to have faith in God's plan for Tommy, instead of thinking we could find a cure. We had to accept God's *will*. She was livid with resistance.

She couldn't abide by me "worshipping" plants or talking about the earth like I was an animist. I thought Dad would be on my side, but he told me to respect my mother and listen. She had a point. President Carter had passed the American Indian Religious Freedom Act in 1978, but there were also state laws, and sometimes local policemen arrested Native people for taking the sacrament of peyote.

I told Dad that the cops on the Navajo reservation were all Native, and no one was going to get in trouble, but Mom wouldn't stop talking. Her voice grew louder and drowned mine out. It became clear that she believed every bit of slander the Catholic Church had slung at Native practices over the centuries. For centuries, Indigenous people who disobeyed the edict were brutally punished, even murdered.

I sat beneath Mom's words like a scalding shower, thinking of my grandparents Grandma Esther and Grandpa Ed, another example of a diverse marriage. They came from very different cultures, yet they'd been willing to compromise in their beliefs. Grandma Esther had committed to the Quechan cremation ceremony, even against the wishes of a priest, and Grandpa Ed had respected that Grandma's tribe was matrilineal—even as his was patrilineal—allowing her to enroll their kids and grandkids as citizens of Laguna rather than the Quechan Nation.

I wished Mom would compromise with us, but she was terrified of complexity. With her, there was only black-and-white: she loved us and wanted to protect us from hell. I could see that she hated the way Dad was flattered by my interest in Indigenous traditions. I thought maybe I was a pawn in a power struggle between them.

"You used to be such a nice girl," she said, her face looking weary. "I don't even know who you are anymore."

"I'll tell you who I am," I said. "I'm not you. I'm nothing like you, and that's why you don't like me."

"Don't you dare talk back to me," she said.

"You can't stop me from going to the Native American Church," I told her.

"Watch me."

Dad said to settle down. Mom's lips were set, and she put her hand on his arm to signal that they were a team. I shifted gears and started begging. "Dad's friend isn't asking us to throw Jesus away, he's a Christian too. I have no problem with Jesus. I just want to learn. . . ." My voice fizzled out.

I meant what I said about Jesus. What could possibly be wrong with such a humble man? I loved the idea of him born in a manger under the night's brightest star. I loved that he stuck up for slaves and the poor and scolded the rich for their greed. I loved that he cared for people, even when they reviled him. If I had a problem with anyone, I had a problem with his racist followers.

"Stop trying to convince me," Mom said. "There is no way you're going to that church with your father."

"I thought you said you believed in miracles," I said. I reminded her about an old Catholic friend of ours, a young girl with cancer, who had gone to a faith healer with her family, after which her cancer went into remission. Mom acknowledged her belief in Amy's miracle, and so I pressed her, asking why she believed so selectively. Why did she discount Native myths and miracles when they had helped us survive for centuries? The world was changing, or I wanted to believe it was. Mom might have wanted to live for the promise of the next world. But I wanted to live in a better world now.

When she said my words were blasphemous, I scoffed. I couldn't understand why we had to adopt her version of God while excluding our ancestral practices—a lot of the other attendees of Native American Church were Christians. Couldn't there be a God that was a God to both sides? Why couldn't she see the beauty of our culture instead of pronouncing it sinful? I told her it was embarrassing how much shame she had been handed with her rosary.

Her jaw dropped open, but I kept talking. I called her a hypocrite for believing only white people could hear the voice of God. If I'd understood then that she was *genízaro*, I would have had more compassion for her. Instead, I told her it was terrible that she pretended to be white and wanted to make me be white too. And that's when Dad told me, "Enough."

By then she was crying, and I realized I had gone too far. I ran outside and jumped on my bike, feeling betrayed by both of my parents. I peddled as fast as I could, down to the river walk, where there were no streetlights and the stars shone bright in the sky. I chained my bike to a lamppost and walked through the cottonwoods to the water.

I sat on a bench in the dark and thought about the Native American Church. There was no way Mom could stop me from going, and there was no way she could make me believe that Grandfather Peyote was like the needle Dad found next to Uncle Albert's bed. The sky was immense, and for the first time since I was a small child, I could feel what a mystery the universe was. My neck tingled. The hair on my arms stood up. The night felt spooky, and I understood that Mom tried to flatten the enormity of the sky, of the universe, out of fear. She needed two-dimensional constellations, easy explanations without anomalies, simple stories to feel like she could control the enormity of life, while Dad's people could see that the universe wasn't two-dimensional at all. There was more to life than we were living. There was a better solution for Tommy and all of us. And I resented the way Mom wanted us to squeeze the terrific and terrifying into a set of linear, simple, and mind-numbing rules.

The autumn came early that year, but even when it was chilly outside, I spent long hours circling the neighborhood on my bike. I found it depressing in the house; maybe I had always found it depressing.

Lori was excited about buying a dress for the homecoming dance. Joan had saved money and kept writing home about a senior trip to Cancún for spring break. For Monica, it was a learner's permit to drive. My sisters were excited about these rites of passage, but for me they felt void of meaning, and it made me feel sad.

Every time I returned home from a bike ride, I felt suffocated and estranged. Lungs fresh, cheeks tingling, I'd enter the house, where the heat was too high, and the air was stifling. Mom would be plopped on the couch watching broadcasters talk about crack cocaine and IRA bombs. The living room was dark, and her face blinked in the television's glare.

The screen had always been her giant pacifier. We were all saturated in historic trauma, yet she was too numb to notice our loss.

I was struck by a memory of myself in preschool, hiding in the bathroom with my ear against the door, playing a game I called "Spy." It was a make-believe game that involved the discovery, via my eavesdropping, that my family wasn't really my family. Now, looking back on the memory, it seemed like I had always recognized that the American culture we donned was a set of ill-fitting clothes, borrowed from someone else. After hearing about Indigenous healing ceremonies from Dad, I wanted more than the Western world could offer. "Study hard" and "go to college" everyone said, but I didn't want to become the type of person who only chased after material things, status, and money. The idea of finding an elder who could teach me about Native traditions, the idea of existing as part of a non-Westernized community of thinking became the only thing that mattered. Dad had a Native American community at work, men who lived connected lives, and I suddenly understood why he liked to spend time there: they tied him to Indigenous worlds by extension.

I rode my bike until winter arrived and the ice prevented me from pedaling around the block anymore. Then I sat and watched Mom in front of the television, resenting the way she had robbed us of a chance for healing and a more beautiful way to connect to the world. After seeing what happened to Tommy, I knew that tragedy and death could come for any of us at any time. The Indigenous worldview was spiritual and had more depth than the capitalist perspective could offer—we were meant to live symbolic and symbiotic lives. I didn't care if Mom refused to accept the esoteric knowledge, the plant wisdom, and the medicinal traditions of our people. Her opinion didn't make them wrong. She could make the rules in our family, but she couldn't control my mind. I wanted to seek the wisdom beyond facts, a singular faith that wasn't tied to dogma, but I didn't know how to return to our ancestral ways when the government had wiped our generational memories clean. Dad said we each had an inner teacher, and if we listened it would tell us what we needed to heal and be real human beings. For the first time in my life, I thought I was hearing mine.

POCAHOTTIE

(1984)

The cheerleaders said they called Josie "Lumpy" because they liked her. A wild Apache girl with a crooked grin and braided hair, she'd been a little on the heavy side as a kid, but by our freshman year of high school she'd picked up a meth habit and lost most of the fat. We were at the same party that night, at Jay's house, in the foothills by the community college. His parents were out of town (an art gallery opening for their friend), and my half-Korean pal, Kira, had invited me to join in. Like Jay, Kira had been born in New York City, and I loved being in her orbit. It made it easier to imagine getting out of Farmington.

Josie had been invited to the party to sell weed, and I knew as soon as she swapped the skunk in her pocket for cash, she'd disappear. She disdained most kids at our high school: the popular crowd, the smart ones, the shy Navajo girls who stuck to each other like glue in the lunchroom. She was irreverent and moody, and the longer I knew her, the more her wildness felt traditional to me.

The month before, a rumor had torn through the school, a story about Josie going ballistic one night when she caught some skinny white boy rolling a drunk Navajo downtown. People said she'd broken a bottle and sent him running, threatening to spank his veins good. In my book the story made her a hero, but the jocks, cheerleaders, and self-identifying mods at the party cared less about the reason she did it and more about how dangerous it made her seem. After I heard the story, I started to feel drawn to her, just like I'd been to Uncle Gene.

"She started that rumor herself," Kira told me, before walking out on the patio to smoke with Jay. I watched them light cigarettes through the window, knowing they'd talk about Motown, jazz, ska, and London-based bands unfamiliar to me. Afraid to sound stupid, I stayed inside and nursed a lukewarm beer until Josie came over to pick on me.

"What's *she* doing here?" she shouted over the music, making sure everyone would hear.

Josie called me Pocahottie, El Malinche, Thocmetone, a traitor by friendship and blood. All she could see was my half-breed body. She hated me because my mother was a Spanish siren with a leopard-skin jacket and almond eyes—a prima donna who refused to be called Indígena. It didn't matter that I felt repulsed and betrayed by Mom's thinking; she could smell the Lopez-Herrera lineage on me. It was in my pale winter skin, my private school vocabulary, and my enunciated way of talking.

To Josie and the other badass Native girls at my public school, I was mainstream enough to be considered white. Maybe they thought my family had too much money, or I acted too confident around our teachers. But regardless of what they thought—that my mother canceled out my father—I also knew the one-drop rule was real, and that to most people in Farmington I would always be Indian.

Josie and I had met in the seventh grade, when I was new to public school and still eager to raise my hand in class. That fall, the boys on the basketball team had tried, unsuccessfully, to recruit me as a cheerleader (my father called it demeaning), and I was the only Native girl, other than Josie, who got invited to sit with the pretty white girls in the lunchroom. Josie was friends with the popular crowd (girls my old Catholic friends called "trailer trash") then because she'd attended elementary school with them. At first, we'd been the same: two shameless sycophants stressed by our changing bodies—dying, to our childhood selves—hoping to fit in.

There were three junior highs in Farmington, but only one high school, so just a quarter of my girlfriends from Sacred Heart had landed in these new hallways of learning. They were white and Hispanic, but it wasn't their ethnic groups that bugged me. If I ignored them in the seventh grade, it was because they were plain Jane girls, bookish and nerdy, and like most kids from highly religious homes, way behind the fashions and time. My high school hopes involved a satin jacket crew like the Pink Ladies in *Grease*—a movie most of them hadn't been allowed to see. The idea of being a nerd mortified me.

Transitioning to public school, I considered myself deserving of popularity. Sheltered by my upbringing, I was naive about how social hierarchies might play out in high school. I'd rarely been required to negotiate the racial tension between townies and reservation folk in Farmington because Dad had always stood sentry. At the roller-skating rink, the mall, and the arcade, I had my older sister Joan, who went toe to toe with any girl who dared to pick on me. During the summer I had my older friends, the Native softball players who Dad hauled to Pizza Hut in our twelve-seater van, my sisters, the Wilson and Benally girls, who braided my hair in the dugout.

I'd tried not to consider what my classmates thought of Indians, but my new school was very mixed, and this made it harder for me to believe what I'd been trained to believe, that hard work would make race invisible. It sounds stupid, but we'd been hiding in plain sight all my life. There were the Big Chief writing tablets, my neighbors' Halloween costumes, the Indian Chief motorcycle commercials, the mascots on so many football fields, the logo on Land O'Lakes butter and Calumet baking powder cans. We had always been both everywhere and nowhere, ubiquitous yet archaic. And New Mexico's educational system had failed us. Without a curriculum to teach us about our state's complex history, my classmates and I were collectively lost. New Mexico was a territory with 29,000 inhabitants when the Navajo Nation was founded in 1868. Ten thousand were Navajos, newly enrolled, and 10,000 were *genízaros* who had been freed by Congress the year before. It should have been obvious that New Mexican families rarely had fully white bloodlines, but it wasn't taught in school, and it would have made my life easier if it was. Instead, my new history teacher taught us that "Indians" had been misnamed because explorers thought they had landed in Hindustan. He didn't say we had 574 federally recognized tribes in the United States, each with distinctive stories, languages, arts, social structures, travel patterns, and spirituality. Celtic speakers alone are clearly defined as the Welsh, Breton, Irish Gaelic, Scots Gaelic, Cornish, and Manx, yet my school taught us nothing about our distinct cultures, much less Canadian, Central, or South American ones. I hated the way we were flattened into "Indians" and suspected it was because a monolithic mythology made it easier to justify stealing our land. Where culture is valued, distinctions matter, but I couldn't articulate any of this back then. The rage I feel today isn't toward my old classmates— social change is a long time coming, and the Reagan years were still full of ugly realities. My rage is against the fear this country has of its own history.

While lacking the ability to voice *why* I wanted to distinguish myself, it felt important to overturn the backward impression people had of us. Now that I was at a mainstream school, I wanted to get off the bench and get into the game, as Dad would say. I wanted to steal the blond girl's boyfriend because I could. I wanted to show my classmates I was there, and not be shy. Josie was the same, and I admired her for it.

By October of my seventh-grade year, I realized all the prettiest girls played dating musical chairs. They held hands with a different boy every couple of weeks, and when they grew bored, they circled back to their old favorite. The queen of these games was a girl named Ariel who had long feathered hair like one of *Charlie's Angels*. Her best friend, Amanda, was a tall brunette with legs as long as an Amazon, and their third wheel had been none other than Josie, who at the age of thirteen hadn't become the drug dealer, Lumpy, yet.

I'd tried out for volleyball first thing that year. Friendly but aloof, Amanda and Ariel also made the JV team. I'd been watching them with Josie every morning, across the street from our school. There was an alley hidden by shrubs that sat against a dead-end street. It was a shortcut on my walk, and at first, I was puzzled that the popular kids convened there before the bell. A middle-aged man sat in his welding truck with a gaggle of girls around his door. He didn't look like a father. Turns out he was selling them skinny joints for a dollar.

There was a tough new parlance in public school. A girl could be a dog, fox, ass, or chick. Boys were studs. There were a hundred ways to imply that a girl was a slut, and when she was, the world acted upon her. Everyone said this girl or that girl wanted to get "laid." I was fascinated by the talk, but I viewed the vocabulary as boastful parroting. Surely their parents were as strict as mine.

Ariel had three boyfriends, played in rotation. An eighth grader named Ron, a seventh grader named Kenny, and a nineteen-year-old who worked at a donut shop called Spudnuts downtown. It was obvious when she was in the older-guy phase of her rotation because he parked outside after school, and she stood by her mother's station wagon, begging to get into his truck. It was during this phase of her rotation that Kenny approached me at lunch.

He asked me if I wanted to be his date at Ariel's fourteenth birthday party. I told him I hadn't been invited. I was sitting with one of my cooler Catholic school friends, Keely Aragon. "My mother would have a *cow*," she whispered when he asked me. My mother would too if she knew Ariel was already dating, but if Kenny could get Ariel to invite me, I was confident I could trick her into letting me go.

The next day, Amanda and Ariel met me at my locker. Ariel said I could come to her birthday party because I was pretty, and Kenny liked me, and it was going to be a boy-girl party. Her parents were going to line a black garbage can in plastic and fill it with jungle juice. They had bought a new double-wide trailer, and she was going to have the party in their old, empty single-wide next door.

She lived out in the county, about halfway between Farmington and Durango. The plan was to meet at three o'clock on Saturday at the school, where her parents would pile kids into their van and station wagon for the twenty-mile ride out to La Plata Highway. It was a slumber party for the girls, and they would return us to the same parking lot the next day.

That Saturday, Mom shook hands with Ariel's mother and asked if we would be supervised. She was imagining me in their family den watching a movie after pizza and cake, not in an empty trailer drinking vodka-doused fruit punch. We started driving, and I asked Ariel where her Apache friend, Josie, was. I'd been hoping to finally get to know her. Rusty hung out with the popular kids, but when I'd asked him if he was going that week, he'd said there was "no way" his mother would let him.

Ariel and Amanda exchanged a look when I asked about Josie. "I didn't invite her," Ariel said. She looked me straight in the eyes and shrugged. "We feel so bad about it," Amanda said, covering a giggle with her hand. "But Ariel's dad trained her dog to attack Indians."

I suddenly realized that she and Amanda hadn't yet met my father and they didn't realize I was Native myself.

Buckled into the back row, my brain blanked, and my seat belt felt like it was choking me. I imagined the dog's teeth sinking into my trembling thighs. I wanted to tell Ariel's mother that I was about to get mauled, but I remembered Joan scolding me once at the roller rink, after some older girls called me a squaw for wearing Indian-beaded hair bar-rettes. "Don't let racists know you're Indian," she'd said, yanking them out of my hair.

An instinct to run kicked in, but by the time it did, we were on the La Plata Highway gathering speed. I felt like crying. It was the same drive we took to fish on the Animas River, a route I usually loved. I tried to reassure myself. If Amanda and Ariel didn't realize I was Native, maybe the dog wouldn't either. Would my long hair be a giveaway? I got a rubber band out of my backpack and pulled it into a bun.

The gravel in their driveway crackled under the tires as we pulled up to the two trailers. Ariel's younger sister opened the screen door of the double-wide, and the dog bounded out, an unruly scruff of hair sticking out around his collar. He approached the cars with a loud bark, and I lingered in my seat until my classmates in the other vehicle got out. Two of the boys started petting the German shepherd and I bolted for the single-wide trailer.

Ariel laughed at how fast I ran, telling everyone later that I couldn't wait to get drunk. "That's why I like Catholic girls," Kenny said. "My brother says they're like racehorses once they get out of the gate."

Everyone laughed, and I laughed too. Mr. Flynn, other grown-ups, teachers, and administrators were easy to hate. With kids my age, I was a coward. I didn't want them to think I was sensitive or touchy. I didn't want to be "uncool." Native or white, when the boys wore Washington Redskin or Kansas City Chief jerseys, I wanted to act like I didn't care. For the bulk of junior high, I did all I could to prove I "could take a joke." When they called me "easygoing," I took it as a compliment. It meant I was hip, game, funny. Even if they didn't know I was Native, I knew what kind of breed I wanted to be—a cool one who was capable of laughing at their "edgy" humor. At that age, it was like I was carrying around a big sign that read: I'M AN IDIOT, GO AHEAD AND MAKE FUN OF ME. Ariel gave me a cup of jungle juice. I drank one, and then two. It was easier than I thought to forget.

The trailer was cold and dark, lit only by fairy lights. I sat on a beanbag in the corner and knew that my little sister Monica would have cried and asked to go home. Joan would have punched someone. And Lori would have drunk them all under the table to prove she was cool.

Halfway through the party, Ariel's parents came in smelling like booze and weed. They found Ariel and her boyfriend double zipped in a sleeping bag, and for some reason, they were shocked. Later, Ariel told me they had strict rules that she couldn't sleep with a boy until she turned sixteen.

Before leaving that night, Kenny bit my neck, giving me a hickey in jest. I knew it was stupid, but I was dizzy from my first-time drinking, and too dehumanized by my fear of Ariel's dog to care. The following morning, when Mom picked me up, she nearly had a stroke over the red bruise, and I felt too ashamed to tell her that it was worse, that I'd been wounded and marked in ways she couldn't see.

My old friends from Sacred Heart would whisper, but that hurt less than Josie's clenched jaw when she saw me. It wasn't like she feared I

would steal her friends, because I rarely hung out with Ariel and Amanda
again. It wasn't that she had learned I was at the party when she hadn't
been invited. It was the embarrassment I felt when I saw her, which to her
must have felt like pity. It felt terrible that I had "passed," even temporarily
with Ariel and Amanda. I felt guilty about my light skin, and she knew it,
and she would never, from that day forward, let either of us forget it again.

The "good white kids" in that town slept with teachers, did drugs, ran away
from home, got abortions, and failed out of school, but it never seemed
to hurt their reputations. I wanted their power, status, and ease. I think I
hoped their ability to break rules and still maintain clean faces would rub
off on me. But by my freshman year, confronted by Josie in the foyer at Jay's
house, I'd lost my confidence with socializing. That's why I had teamed
up with Kira. Being half-Korean and half-white, she understood what it
felt like to straddle two worlds not knowing who to trust. In a racist border
town like Farmington, being on the fence felt dangerous, like every day
held the threat of more scratches and barbs.

I could see a group of cheerleaders smoking a joint near the fireplace
in the living room. I knew they'd heard Josie's insult, "What's *she* doing
here?" But it wasn't their job to worry about our politics, and even if they'd
asked, I'd never have admitted why Josie hated me.

I could hear my sister Joan in my head, warning me to expect hazing
in high school. Tough Indian girls were going to test me, and it was dumb
to argue that I was just as Native as them. "Let the fools try to 'out-Indian'
each other," she'd said. We had our certificate of Indian blood cards and
our family on the reservation. We knew we were authentic citizens of our
nations. We didn't have to wear buckskin and braids.

It was obviously safer if people assumed we were Hispanic, and my
mother especially couldn't understand why I'd want to deal with discrimination if I didn't have to. Raised in this way, there had been moments, like
at Ariel's house, when I'd kept my mouth shut rather than correcting a
stranger's assumptions. But the older I got, the more my cowardice shamed
me. Dad couldn't pass, so why should I?

Josie had me cornered and wouldn't let me slip by. "Hey, you white bitch, when you moving to Albuquerque?" I had no plans to skip town, and she knew it, but she liked to suggest that I should.

I wanted to tell her about a little blond boy, no older than seven, who had called me a NAPI cow that week on my walk home from school. He was referring to Navajo Agricultural Products Incorporated, and I knew it was unlikely that he'd invented the insult himself. I wanted to shock her, but the slur had struck like a bullet with its specificity, and I felt too embarrassed to repeat it. Instead, I asked, "You think you're the only one who gets called a dirty redskin?"

Josie moved in closer, her nose against mine, her face a sneer as she said something I couldn't hear over my fast-beating heart. I had a flash-back, remembering the day Juanita jumped me in the stairwell. I was afraid, and it made my ears ring—a beautiful and temporary deafness—until I heard a voice saying, "Mind if I borrow her, Lumpy?"

It was a basketball player from the boys' team named Craig. He was a transplant from Boulder, Colorado, who had been asking questions about me since the first week of school. A redheaded kid who I'd known since junior high told me to watch out for Craig, implying that he thought it was stalking. Craig had greasy black hair and a bowlegged gait. Like all transplants from out of town, he was popular, but also regarded as strange. People whispered about how he called his parents by their first names.

If I could time travel back to Jay's, I would tell myself to give Josie a chance, that a small scuffle was worth it. Hadn't I noticed her misguided signs of caring? For years, she'd gone out of her way to bump shoulders with me in the hall. We had matching green windbreakers, and she'd yank at the tag on my neck, saying she needed to check that I hadn't stolen hers in gym. If I'd been more mature, I'd have realized that she was angling to talk, maybe to hash out what had happened with Ariel. But instead of trying to resolve things with her, I let Craig drag me outside.

"Keep your eyes on college," my parents had always said, teaching me that I'd never gain success in the mainstream world if I couldn't socialize in it. Yet even as I headed toward the jocks in the backyard, I had to fight

the urge to turn around and follow Josie to her truck. Her rebellious attitude held an authenticity, an allure, a purpose that felt undeniable to me.
If there was one thing I trusted, it was her anger, which mirrored my own.

Craig started hanging around my locker after Jay's house. He'd ask me out,
and I'd turn him down. Then he'd go on dates with other girls before
coming back around. I didn't especially like him, but the perks of saying
yes sold me on him. Instead of being harassed by whistling oilfield workers
on my walk to school, I had a ride. He wrote me notes and told stupid jokes
and brought me cookies from his mother. It felt good to have a protector,
even though he was friends with gunslinging Republican hunters who
irritated me.

At first, I was naive. Even after what happened with Ariel, the idea that
Craig didn't know I was Native hadn't occurred to me. First, he met my
father, which was awkward, and then the social pressures started.

On one of our first dates, we were sitting in the stands, watching a JV
football game, when we overheard some wrestlers sitting behind us. They
were working out a trip to a liquor store called the Copper Penny.

"The store owner ain't gonna sell you shit without a fake ID," one
kid said.

"Just pay a homeless Navajo guy to buy it," another chimed in, "and
once he gives it to you, steal his money and kick him out of the truck."

Knowing cowboys had once used Indians for target practice in Farmington, these boys and their old family traditions didn't surprise me. I'd
heard secondhand stories about guys "rolling drunk Indians," but I'd never
watched them gather friends to go downtown. The authorities would be
no help here—crooked New Mexico cops were all over the news in my
teenage years too. Robert Early Davis, a former detective, and his epon-
ymous Davis gang, a group of Albuquerque police gone bad, had been
terrorizing the Southwest for a decade. They were infamous for murdering, stealing, beating storeowners, and selling narcotics in Farmington,
Roswell, Colorado Springs, Lubbock, Clovis, Amarillo, and other cities.
They'd been caught robbing a jewelry store in Farmington two years

before, and since then they had busted out of prison more times than I could count. Trained to be silent in the face of established hierarchies, I didn't look at Craig, and he didn't look at me. Not a word passed between us, and after they left, I shook with confusion and rage, unable to believe I hadn't done anything. It was shameful to be a coward in the face of violence, especially when I was standing next to a guy I wanted to trust.

The final quarter of the game felt nauseating. Craig talked to some guys while I walked the track around the football field, trying to catch my breath and think. I'd never known where I fit in Farmington, and now dating was making things worse. My older sisters had taught me nothing about the companionship of boys. Lori had softball, and she sauntered onto campus wearing a varsity letterman jacket on the very first day. She never went out with guys, opting instead to hang out with her lesbian teammates. And Joan's forays into dating at boarding school had been too far away for me to observe.

I stood on the track and scanned the stands for Lori. She'd driven Mom's van to the game, but I couldn't find her. Later I would learn that she had driven out in the canyons to drink with her friends. There, she had grazed a big rock, then come home wasted and gone to bed. The next morning, when Dad went to throw out the trash, he returned inside saying the van had a dent and the gas tank was empty. Knowing it had been parked at the high school all night, he decided some young hooligan had bumped it while siphoning fuel.

Lori was a master at escaping punishment. That summer, she'd thrown a rager while our parents were gone, dancing to Devo in the den, and coloring the wood-paneled walls with blue crayon. Seeing the dark scribbles, I doubted she could fix it, especially since she'd woken up late and hungover. Faded sections of wood emerged from her scrubbing, but while I saw a glaring difference in the walls, my parents never noticed a thing.

Had I talked to Lori at the football game, she would have said the wrestlers were joking, and it would only hurt me if I walked around assuming people were racist all the time. In the mix of Navajo, Hispanic, white trailer park, and oil-industry kids who flew to Telluride on weekends,

I needed to relax. Alcohol would have made her feel like she was living in a multicultural Esprit ad; if we just sang along to the Coke commercial ("I'd like to teach the world to sing in perfect harmony") everyone would melt together in the same American pot.

During my freshman year I kept hoping for companionship, and I saw Josie hoping as well, the two of us both arguing with a procession of jerks we'd been foolish enough to trust in the hall. Like sacral pain, the loneliness I felt among my peers was chronic and debilitating. It made me feel unstable, and uncertain, in my steps. I was beginning to understand the diverse racial dynamics in Farmington. It took me years to realize there were reasons Navajo and Hispanic guys didn't ask me out in high school. At the time, my suitors were overwhelmingly white, and contrary to how that might seem, it had nothing to do with my own self-loathing.

My old crush Rusty flirted with me, but he never asked me out. I'd heard Navajo kids lament the rules that governed marriage in their tribe. Many of the Navajo boys at our school weren't allowed to date Navajo girls from whatever clan they liked. They were held to specific girls, from specific clans, because their parents were traditional and followed tribal customs. This meant, if they couldn't date just any Navajo girl, then they couldn't date me either. As a minority Apache, I figured Josie understood how I felt. I wondered what she thought of Rusty, but the one time I had approached her in the parking lot to talk about him and the other Navajo boys she'd scoffed. "I don't give a damn about those sellouts," she told me.

I knew what she meant. The boys at our school were not badass Diné men who stood in their history with yarn buns and poetry and beautiful turquoise bracelets. As a freshman, Rusty was, like me and Josie, at the edge of the popular crowd. But rather than growing angrier by the year, he was a good sport. He dated white girls, took only the easiest classes, knew when to give a self-deprecating chuckle, and how to tap a keg. Hearing Josie accuse them of wanting to please made me slink away, self-conscious about my own short hair and bland clothes. It was humiliating to realize that she found Rusty and his friends just as obedient and unattractive as me.

I couldn't deny the racial politics in my relationship with Craig—his hand sliding under my blouse when I asked him to stop, his friends making jokes like I was cheap. I had initially given him plenty of second chances, trying to force him to veer toward respect. I wanted to believe I was as worthy as the white girls who bragged about their wonderful dates. "You're too pretty to be Indian," one post-Craig escort had said, drunk and full of disgust. Of course, he had wanted to take my pants off anyway. Craig and I stayed in an on-again-off-again relationship for almost seven months. When I began trying to break away, he would show up uninvited wherever I was, punch fences, act jealous, shove ten-page notes through the slats of my locker, drive his car like a maniac. But even with the abuse, it was hard to let go. I would remember how complimentary he had been at the start, and how much easier it felt to socialize with him around. When I stood next to him, people respected me. Even Josie left me alone. And when I saw how nice he was with Kira, Jay, and other kids I admired, I wondered if I was the problem.

I never talked to anyone about what was happening to me. Still, I knew I needed to escape and found a way, finally, that spring when our classes went to the gym for a pep rally. Every year, our school chose a king and queen for prom—as well as a *Native* king and queen for prom. Rusty, who was half-Navajo and half-white, would eventually win the main prom king title, but that wouldn't be until our senior year. I was with Craig in the gym when a shy Navajo girl sitting behind us tapped me on the shoulder and told me I should run for Native prom queen. Craig glared at her, and I felt irritated by her suggestion too. I hated the separate title, just as I would hate it when President George H. W. Bush designated November as Native America heritage month a few years later. Why should we be fenced off, celebrated for only one month, or crowned by only one portion of society? And yet even though I felt irritated by the dual titles, Craig's reaction made me even angrier, because at that point I'd suffered all his games, and the worst one of all was the way he sought to forget, deny, or stop me from being Native. All my life, I'd referred to myself as Native, even though I was afraid other Native kids might say I wasn't *enough*. Hyperconscious of this struggle, I'd never realized that I had plenty of Hispanic classmates who might have acknowledged their Indigenous bloodlines too but didn't. If I had been taught that even the Catholic Church had sold captive Native children under the pretense that they were paying for the child's education, if I had realized that most of these kids were girls, forced to become concubines, and that their children had been given their father's Spanish surname, and that the surname gave them a higher social position in society than their Native mother, I would have understood why so many of my classmates, like my sisters, wanted to self-identify with their Spanish ancestors over their Native ones. If I had realized that this hierarchy in the state was a real thing, up until the day I was born, with a direct correlation to the jobs that people could get, and the educations they were allowed to have, it would have explained so much about my parents' behavior too. In the 1950s, when Indian people did attend New Mexico colleges and universities, they were refused degrees and given certificates of attendance instead, even after completing the same coursework as their Hispanic peers. These practices greatly discouraged anyone from claiming Native bloodlines. Maybe it was because our curriculum had been so whitewashed, and they didn't know. Or maybe they knew but felt ashamed.

I knew there would be no benefit to outing myself as Native, but I felt determined to embrace my Indian inheritance. Something was shifting in me, and it had started with Josie. I no longer wanted to feel guilty about being a half-breed. I no longer wanted to cede ground to anyone who said I wasn't Native. I no longer wanted to listen to my sisters when they said I was hurting my mother's feelings by playing favorites with Dad's family. I was allowed to feel joy and pride in being Native. And, for sure, it wasn't going to be Craig who stopped me. Confronting this reality saved me because it made me see my way out.

In the weeks after the pep rally, I started talking to Craig about my tribe. Occasionally, I even wore a pair of moccasins handed down to me from Joan. Aside from bugging him, they were comfortable, and I liked the way they upheld my culture in a way that everyone could see. One day I was sitting outside after school, in a small patch of grass between the gym and the football field. I was in a bad mood and hoping not to see Craig, but he came around the building and made a beeline for me just as the baseball team came out of the gym with Coach Mann. Craig was asking where I'd been hiding when they passed, and Coach Mann took the opportunity to yell out at him, "I see you finally got your Navajo under a tree!"

Craig's face grew bright red in response to the baseball team's rowdy laugh.

"I'm not Navajo," I told Coach Mann. It felt important to correct him. I wanted everyone to know that not all Indians were Navajo, and not all tribes had names he and other Americans would recognize. But instead of registering my intent as educational, Coach Mann scoffed like I was denying my heritage and walked off with his team.

After they were gone, I stood up and wiped the grass off my bum. Flustered that an adult could be so ignorant, and angry that my rebuttal had failed, I walked toward the front of the building. Craig didn't follow me. He was too busy staring after Coach Mann, visibly flustered by the teasing.

"Do you have to wear those stupid moccasins?" he called after me.

"Absolutely," I yelled back. My voice shook, but inside I felt relieved. I knew that he would finally stop pursuing me, and we would both be happy it was over.

But, of course, that didn't mean that Craig took the breakup well. He crafted a series of jokes about a porn flick titled *Debbie Does Dallas*. He spread ugly rumors. He harassed my little sister Monica, and when Joan came back to Farmington, he sweet-talked her into being his friend, all just to use her against me. She and I had grown apart after all her years away, and shame prevented me from telling her how badly he'd treated me. It was the beginning of a new existence for me, one as an outcast. I don't mean to imply that I didn't go out in my last three years of high school, but I made only shallow connections. By graduation, I'd decided it was weak to want a boyfriend at all.

During these dark days, I thought about what Lori had told me, and

I tried to open my mind about possible friends. At first, I liked Jay and Kira and their crew of artsy intellectuals. They wore black eyeliner and trench coats and talked about Rastafari. They treated animism and Timothy Leary with curiosity, and together we complained about the Reagan administration. But my admiration for them went sour when Jay claimed their alienation was more sophisticated than mine. Kira disappointed me when she started flirting with a Navajo kid to make him tell her taboo stories about Navajo witches called skin walkers. One evening she dragged me along, and he got mad when he saw me, I guess because he knew what he was doing was wrong.

In the end, Craig's cruelest move against me involved Josie. He knew I wanted to be her friend, so he took her under his wing, in part, I suspected, to make sure that the two of us didn't form an alliance. She would run away from home as a junior, but right up to her disappearance, he drove her to parties to sell her weed. Every time I saw them, I wished she was with me. Whether they were laughing next to their lockers, or shooting hoops on the blacktop, I felt a screwed-up sort of optimism in the scorn and derision she showed me. It sounds pitiful, but back when I was fifteen, it was impossible to see another Native girl with sass and smarts being accepted by mainstream society, and not feel at least a tiny bit of respect, longing, love, and admiration.

When Josie stopped coming to school, I felt both worried and sad. Native women get murdered and go missing all the time in the Four Corners region. In New Mexico alone, Betty Lee hitched a ride to Shiprock with a cowboy who left her sledgehammered body on the side of the road. Loreal Tsingine was picked off by a cop on Easter morning. Fred Martinez, a transgender Navajo girl, was bludgeoned to death by a guy she met at a rodeo. For weeks, I dreamed of Josie the way she used to look in the seventh grade, arms crossed over her boyish chest, head cocked to one side as she smiled. I'd imagine us confiding in each other, laughing, going for walks in the canyons. I'd see her long skinny fingers covering her mouth and wake up hoping she was okay.

THE WOMAN WHO WAS A MIRAGE

(1985)

✠

Some Farmington policemen were manhandling a group of Native women near the downtown library. It wasn't the first time I'd seen Native people getting arrested, but it was the first time I'd seen them fighting back. One officer knelt on a lady while another dragged her friend to their squad car by her braids. I shouted for Mom to stop the car and let me out.

"To do what?" she asked.

Four women were in trouble. Two of them sat handcuffed on the curb, their faces bleeding. As we drove by, I saw that one of the handcuffed women was very young. She had her black hair trimmed in a mullet, and she looked me right in the eyes as we passed.

I twisted around in my seat. There was a crowd of bystanders watching, but they just stood there and stared, like police brutality was something they saw every day.

"How can you not care?" I asked Mom.

She shook her head. "You just worry about yourself," she said.

When we arrived at the library, I jumped out of the van and went sheepishly inside. If my family had protested, I might have too, but instead I kept hearing Mom's voice in the car: "Don't make excuses for them."

According to her, those women weren't trying. And as I paced up and down the rows of books, thinking about the young girl with the mullet, I wondered why they should. You only play nice when you think you have a chance to be accepted. Once you see yourself as an enemy, it becomes your duty to be confrontational.

I'd been coming to the library every week. My parents thought I was doing homework, but I was mostly catching up on sleep or looking at old newspapers in the microfiche machine. I couldn't find much on Quechan history, but I had been piecing together more information on my dad's Shoshone-Paiute grandmother, Granny Ethel's aunt, Sarah Winnemucca—the "Indian Princess"—who he teased and tortured us with around the campfire. Her book, *Life Among the Piutes*, wasn't in the library, but I'd found an excerpt: "I was born somewhere near 1844 but am not sure of the precise time. I was a very small child when the first white people came into our country. They came like a lion, yes, like a roaring lion, and have continued so ever since, and I have never forgotten their first coming."

Dad's grandfather hadn't known his birthday either. Instead, he'd taken his son's birthday, and as soon as I read this quote, I saw a theme in my family history, one of displacement, gaping factual holes, and generational cuts so deep and bloody, it felt like I could never stitch it up. And losing family was only part of it. We'd lost our natural resources, the wealth of the continent, the beauty and inherent value of our ancestral homelands as well. The magnitude of my family's loss was beginning to dawn on me, though the particulars about Granny and her aunt remained elusive until my twenties when I finally started visiting bigger libraries.

Sarah Winnemucca's father was a medicine man, her grandfather the leader of the northern Paiute people. Yet while her father did not trust the newly arrived white men, her grandfather guided their mapmaking in the region, and later fought with them in the Bear War against Mexican control of California. She grew up on this threshold, hearing two opposing views, which gave her the ability to see "on the other hand."

Sarah first met white people when her grandfather took her to Sacramento, California, at age six. Her father refused to go. Given his resistance to settlers, I'm not sure why her father allowed her grandfather to place her in the house of a white man named William Ormsby when she was thirteen. She would live with Ormsby, his wife, and teenage daughter, Lizzie, for a year in Genoa, Nevada—by fourteen, she had learned to read, write, and speak English and Spanish in addition to three Native languages. She would return home briefly when she heard her tribe was being treated poorly by settlers in the region, before entering a convent school in San Jose, California, at sixteen.

White emigration west meant her tribe's lifeways and foodways were being interrupted, and while she was away at the convent in San Jose, things were growing violent. In 1860, two white stagecoach owners kidnapped and raped two Paiute girls. A group of warriors, led by Sarah's cousin, brother, and father, rode to rescue the girls. They burned Williams Station and killed five white men. A hundred settlers decided to retaliate, and they called on William Ormsby, who had hosted Sarah, to lead them. But despite outnumbering the Paiute warriors, they were killed in what came to be known as the First Battle of Pyramid Lake. According to Sarah, her brother Natchez tried to save Ormsby by faking Ormsby's death, but failed.

In 1875, Sarah, her family, and their Paiute band were moved from a survivors' camp in Nevada to the Malheur Reservation in Oregon, which was given to them by President Ulysses S. Grant. For a time, they had a good government agent who allowed them to earn money with their farming, but in 1876 he was replaced by a corrupt man named William Rinehart, who told them the Malheur Reservation was no longer theirs. He refused to pay them for their farm labor and robbed them of their food. He starved them, allowing their best reservation land to be used for grazing by white settlers. The grazing was a serious problem because the bulb of the blue flower known as camassia quamash was a major food staple. Traditionally, the bulbs had been ground into nutritious cakes when rations were scant. Now they were being trampled by cows.

Tribal leaders asked the government to intervene and stop the grazing, but since Camas Prairie was misprinted in their treaty as Kansas

Prairie, the government asserted their rights to ignore the request. The
Paiute responded by leaving the reservation. They rode west, raiding white
settlements in northern Nevada and southern Oregon. The skirmishes
escalated, triggering the Bannock War.

Caught between two cultures during the Paiute Indian Wars, Sarah
was dexterous, capable of listening, understanding, and translating flip
sides of the same argument. Even after her family suffered atrocities—
a Nevada volunteer calvary member murdered her mother and baby
brother in a random raid in 1865—she would use her multilingual skills
to advocate for compromise, still believing the best route was assimilation and peace. Because Sarah spoke and wrote English she was hired as
an interpreter by General Oliver O. Howard of the U.S. Army. Dad was
unfortunately marked by the criticisms nearly everyone in his generation
carried about English-speaking Indigenous women who favored compromise during the Indian wars.

In the early 1880s, Sarah gave more than three hundred talks to white
audiences, and the nature of these performances was part of the reason
Dad's family felt embarrassed about Sarah. She frequently reenacted the
myth of Pocahontas falling in love with John Smith, which was a lie. I suppose she predicted the headline would draw attention. White audiences
came to see her in droves. From packed halls in San Francisco to the Win-
throp Hotel in Boston, she dressed in fake Indian costumes and awakened
wealthy audiences to her people's situation. She did it for a larger cause,
ending every show with a plea for donations to help her people, but it still
played into harmful myths about Native women.

Sarah's reputation was particularly hit by the way she'd argued for
property rights via the heinous Dawes Act of 1887. She met with Senator
Dawes and believed that his proposal would help. She thought she was
fighting for self-determination via citizenship and land rights—she believed that she was working to ensure that the government and her white
neighbors recognized their value and dignity, and their claim to land.
Unable to foresee how the original policy would be distorted into another
colonial land grab—one that would cause the loss of an additional ninety

million acres of land—she supported it. Like many of her peers, she was duped into thinking ownership of land in severalty would prevent further abuses within the ward system. It's no wonder she started drinking. After the money from her book ran out, and her school for Indigenous kids was shut down, she became depressed. Criticized by Natives and reviled by American journalists who loved to make fun of her, she cussed and caroused. She cursed Christianity and threatened an editor's life for publishing an article about an instance of public drunkenness. She was audacious and acted up and died at age forty-seven of tuberculosis, like so many Native people. But she did live longer than the average Native. Until the 1950s, the life expectancy for Natives in this country was only forty-four.

I knew so little about my family history growing up. Who knows what my family would have said if my elders had lived longer, if they hadn't been shell-shocked in their twenties and thirties, if they hadn't been silenced by the trauma of poverty and Indian boarding schools. Granny Ethel did live longer, but she had been orphaned so young, all she had were stories like a sieve. Like lots of old grandmas in her generation, she was hard, impenetrable, and Dad too became a vault full of hidden stories. He never told me that Sarah risked her life by riding over two hundred miles on horseback alone, across hostile territory during the war, to save members of her family and tribe when no man among her people would go to negotiate. He never told me she spoke against wartime rape, or that her people were deemed so violent and untrustworthy, they were forced to march to the Yakama Indian Reservation in Washington territory where many of them died. He never told me that Sarah met with President Rutherford B. Hayes in 1880 to ask that her people be allowed to go home to Malheur at their own expense, or that she returned to address Congress in 1884, after giving more than three hundred talks across the United States, to finally win her people's freedom to go to Pyramid Lake (though not to Malheur).

When Mom came for me at the library, she found me sleeping on a beanbag in the children's section and got mad because I'd missed our pickup time outside. I lied to her, saying that I was fine, that I had finished all my homework when I'd never even started. She drove me home in silence. Back then, there was always silence. I couldn't speak up, I realize now, because protest requires hope.

I was falling asleep in class, at the library, before getting my homework done. I wasn't getting my rest because I was always sneaking out at 4:00 A.M. to get high and hike in the canyons. I'd wake up, pull on my boots, take the screen off my bedroom window, and jump out while it was still dark. Smoking weed before sunrise felt counterculture. Getting messed up early in the day made me feel morally superior to the kids who stayed out late with their friends.

It was a twenty-minute walk through town to my favorite trailhead the next morning. I could hear the electricity buzzing in the overhead streetlamps as I walked. I made my way past executive homes at the edge of town, their curtains open, and their televisions left on while they slept. I hated the way they never turned anything off. I shot at their BMWs with my pointer finger, bam, bam.

At school, my science teacher talked about the ozone layer, even as aerosol hairsprays kept clouding the bathroom stalls. I tried to tell Mom about climate change, but she acted like I was gullible. If I was mad about losing our land, I was even angrier about what they'd done to it. While I still didn't know about the massacres, I knew enough to feel robbed. Manhattan was purchased with beads. Valuable furs had been traded for whiskey. White people used empty promises as tender, and in exchange we Indians got blood quantum, our lineages tracked like thoroughbreds or dogs destined to be turned into glue.

I walked until I hit dirt. I hid in low washes when oilfield trucks passed. I turned down a sandy wash that wove through the base of an arroyo like a ribbon of brown velvet. I saw where a four-wheeler had crushed sage and cacti that had been growing between the sandstone rocks. I saw the remnants of a campfire, crushed beer cans, and somebody's vomit.

The sun was ready to rise over the pinion juniper woodland, the careening bluffs, and cedar trees—so I rested against a boulder and waited.

A raven called and sunshine filtered through the branches of a juniper tree above me. Out in the sandstone canyons, against the earth's history, the millennia revealed in the sandstone's strata, the ephemeral nature of my body was brought into relief. The earth humbled me and reminded me that others had come before, and others would come after. Nothing lasted forever, even the pain I was feeling in my daily life.

Mom called me into the kitchen. I was in my room, which I'd taken over from Lori after she'd left for college. It didn't feel like mine, since she said not to move anything. Her skis, letter jacket, and other junk were where she'd left them. It even smelled like her perfume, Love's Baby Soft, because she had spilled a bottle on the carpet before she left.

Mom told me to take the cordless phone to Dad. "It's Aunt Vi," she said.

Dad was working overtime because of an overhaul at the plant, but he was also working on the house every night because there was a leak in the den. I found him outside, preparing to climb up, and together we learned that Granny Ethel had died. I heard him tell Aunt Vi that we couldn't make the funeral because of his job, then he disappeared up the ladder.

I let some time pass before ascending behind him. On the roof, I followed him around, trying to look purposeful with a broom. There were leaves in the gutters, and I knocked them out while he spread stinky black tar on the stucco.

"Funeral this weekend," Dad said. I detected a small crack in his voice, but I didn't look over.

Granny Ethel was never a citizen of the Yuma Nation, but hearing that she would be cremated with a traditional Yuma burial after living there her whole life didn't surprise me.

His voice faltered. "Vi said they'd finish Sunday morning."

Sunday. They would lift her body out of the casket and set it on the cottonwood pyre with blankets and clothing at sunrise. I remembered. I could see the women dancing. I could smell the tobacco, hear the bird singers, and gourd rattles. I kept sweeping.

"They'll burn her house Friday night with everything, all her clothing, furniture, beadwork, and regalia."

"What?" I'd never seen them do this before. I imagined her house in flames. "I thought the government outlawed burning the house. They didn't do that for Uncle Johnny or Uncle Gene."

I knew that our tribal traditions involved letting go of material possessions, and I remembered how we burned Uncle Johnny's belongings when he passed. But I had never heard of anyone in recent years having their entire house and all their heirlooms burned.

"The feds said it was a waste of money, but there's a grandfather clause. She was ninety-one, the oldest living Indian on the reservation. They can't deny her our tribal traditions."

We worked quietly together until the light started to fade, and it was time to go inside. At the top of the ladder, Dad spun around to face me, stretching his foot down to reach the highest rung. "Her house will be the last one to get burned via our tribal traditions," he said, then his face disappeared down the steps.

I knew that we were supposed to let go, that burning a loved one's belongings when they died was a way of reminding ourselves that we loved the person and not what might be gained by their death, but I couldn't stand to think of losing Granny Ethel's work. She was a seamstress who stitched beadwork into leather, all of which would be gone.

As we washed our hands in the kitchen, my father said, "She was a crabby old lady anyway." But I could tell he was sad.

As we anticipated Granny Ethel's funeral, the school week felt heavy, and the mood at home was dark. I wondered what Granny thought about death, but Dad said he had no idea. I remembered running into her once at Woolworth's in Yuma. We were headed to the powwow, and she had asked us to visit her, but Dad didn't want to go. I couldn't understand why he'd never liked her, why he hated wearing the regalia she'd sewn him as a boy.

That night I confronted him. "Why were you always so angry with Granny?" I asked. He said she was too proud when his father lost his arm. But then he softened and pulled out a picture of her when she was young. She was standing in a troupe of performers for some kind of Wild West show. She had stage makeup painted on in a funny-looking circle. He said he had no idea who the other people were, that none of the faces seemed familiar to him.

When I pressed him for more about Granny Ethel, Dad told me he once looked for her name in the Indian census rolls, but she was only sporadically listed as a child, with names that changed all the time, an "Indian Annie" or an "Indian Jim," and her status always said "roaming." He said some tribes didn't have accurate records. If they weren't Christianized, it was hard. Or if they came from a tribe like Granny's that was one of the last to be confined by the U.S. government.

I said it was weird that her people were recorded without surnames, and he laughed. "You think Jackson was our original last name on my grandpa's side of the family?"

"What?" I asked.

"Our Indian name was Sackhavaum," he told me, spelling it on a piece of paper because he couldn't pronounce it. "I never met him, but my great-grandpa was Chappo Sackhavaum."

I was outraged. I'd never questioned our last name, and it made me feel stupid, but Dad said I should be proud. He said the Yuma families that ended up with a president's name were the ones who resisted when the feds showed up to take our treaty land. Men like Chappo refused to sign, so the officials signed for them with names like Jefferson and Jackson.

I looked back at the photo of Granny Ethel working for the western show. Our family was a black hole, our world a performance that didn't reflect who we were. I demanded that Dad show me more photos, and he promised to dig around in the garage the following day. Everything he was saying now felt like an important discovery. I'd never seen him so willing to talk about Granny, or our family history.

He took the photo back from me and said he couldn't be sure, but he guessed maybe Granny's people had made their bucks performing in her childhood, perhaps because they admired Sarah's performances. I imagined the shows: Indians getting knifed by cowboys during stagecoach attacks; Indians kidnapping innocent pioneer girls. It embarrassed me, but I couldn't blame her. She had to eat, and her hard edges probably had to do with childhood trauma. I felt sure that she'd done what she felt was necessary to survive. Plus, the stage was in her blood via Sarah, and before I went to bed, I heard Dad praise Sarah for the first time.

I walked down the hall to my room that night feeling guilty. Dad had revealed that the name "Winnemucca" meant "mirage" in the northern Paiute language. It felt fitting, given that my impression of Granny Ethel, Aunt Sarah, and everyone on their side of the family had never felt solid or true. It felt like I owed someone an apology, though it was more a feeling than a rational thought. I suppose, the more I learned about how fierce Granny's lineage had been, the more I felt embarrassed about my own stupid forms of rebellion—smoking weed, driving too fast, hanging rebel posters in my room like my cousin Bobby. After learning about the kinds of resistance and activism my ancestors had practiced, I felt my rebellions were weak.

The weekend of Granny Ethel's funeral, Lori drove up from college, and Joan came over to the house. Mom and Dad said it was a day of mourning, which meant only Theresa and Ted were allowed to watch television back in our parents' room. The rest of us played Monopoly, but the dice rolling lasted for hours, and I was relieved when Dad came into the living room with an old photo album.

Lori was taking forever to exchange some houses for a hotel on Indiana Avenue, so I went to join him on the couch. I'd just sat down when Joan told me it was my turn to roll. "I don't want to play anymore," I said.

"I don't want to play either," Monica agreed, going to check on Theresa and Ted.

Joan told me to stop acting like a tribal elder, but I didn't change my mind. The photos were mostly of us on vacation, fishing at the Animas River, or standing next to animal enclosures at the San Diego Zoo. But Dad had found one of the Yuma Marching Band taken when he was a little boy in the 1950s. In the photo, he looked about eight years old, and he was sitting in front of the band with his brothers and cousin. The men in the band, including his father and grandfather, were wearing Plains Indian headdresses made by Granny Ethel.

My sisters and I oohed at the eagle bone whistle and feather Dad was wearing in the photo, but the expression on his face looked so miserable, we had to ask what was going on. He told us, in the nineteenth century, lots of ladies like Granny Ethel appropriated the traditional clothing of their Plains Indian neighbors.

"Yuma Indians didn't wear feather headdresses." He laughed. "I didn't like it because the Lakota kids we saw at powwows and band competitions used to laugh at us."

Dad said he remembered Granny Ethel preparing regalia for Eisenhower's inaugural parade in the early 1950s. Twenty-two Yuma Indian band members, including her son and husband, had traveled east to Washington to perform. She had sewn them plenty of outfits through the years, but never for such an important event, and he remembered how she had been determined to send them off with the finest beadwork.

Granny wasn't in the Yuma Marching Band photo Dad showed us, but I could envision her dreaming about the parade as she sewed. With each threaded bead, she would have imagined the spectators pressed together on the sidewalk. She would have dreamed of them standing on tiptoe to see her husband carrying his trumpet—big-city folk craning their necks to glimpse the Sonoran Desert Indians in Plains Indian regalia blasting John Philip Sousa to the sky.

When the Yuma Indian band wore the regalia Granny made for them, they were connecting with the spirit of our nation's Indigenous ancestors, even as they were outsiders imitating a different tribe. On the night of her funeral, I heard pride in Dad's voice as he described her stringing the beads, sewing the fabric, and signing her name on the inside of each feathered bonnet. He hadn't wanted to wear her work—because he didn't like the idea of playing an old-time Lakota shooting arrows from the back of a horse. But even as I understood why he thought people on the powwow road were too glass-cased for his taste—why he didn't want to be pumped with preservatives—it didn't stop me from appreciating Granny's habit of sewing regalia. I felt grateful that she left evidence of how she had balanced her identity and personality in a modern existence, even if I wasn't sure about the idea of cultural performance.

My favorite photo in the family collection that night was not a photo but a *Yuma Daily Sun* article. A journalist named Frank Love had a column about old Yuma days. Love recounted memories of Christmas Eve, back when he went to hear a middle-aged Indian guy play "Silent Night" on his trumpet in the belfry tower of the St. Thomas Indian Mission before midnight mass. There was a picture of Dad's grandpa at the church in his regalia and headdress.

The same Christmas column remembered not only Grandpa Ed but also a radio disc jockey who worked for a local Yuma radio station. Every year the disc jockey hosted a Christmas party for his listeners, and every year he played Santa and arrived via a new type of transportation. A golf cart, a fire truck, a tractor—the DJ was reaching the end of his options until he found a crop duster who agreed to fly over Yuma and drop off a dummy of Santa in the date groves, after which the DJ would come out. But a parachute that was supposed to deploy above the dummy didn't open, and a crowd of Christmas revelers watched Santa crash in the desert while "Here Comes Santa Claus" blared on the radio station's speakers.

We finished looking through the album, and Dad took it back to its storage spot in the garage. I went down the hall to brush my teeth, imagining the fire, and the way Granny's grave site would smoke at dawn. I thought of her house, the regalia up in flames, total destruction as a living enactment of Yuma culture.

I went to find my younger siblings. I offered to read Theresa a book. I needed her weight in my lap, a distraction to stop the thought of ashes and dust. She ran to her room and came back with her favorite, a Syd Hoff book. After she climbed into my lap, I started to read: "One day Danny went to the museum. He wanted to see what was inside. He saw Indians. He saw bears. He saw Eskimos. He saw guns. He saw swords. And he saw dinosaurs."

A couple of months after Granny Ethel died, I was driving home from a doctor's appointment at the Northern Navajo Medical Center in Shiprock when I saw the girl with the mullet, the one who had been arrested near the library, hitchhiking with a friend. It was cold and starting to rain, so I pulled over on the shoulder and stopped. I could see the two of them running along the highway in the rearview mirror. I unlocked the doors, and they climbed into the car.

Her name was Betty Turtle. She was half-Cheyenne and half-Navajo, and had grown up in Watonga, Oklahoma. She and her friend were trying to get to Aztec, a town past Farmington. They looked cold and tired, maybe hungover, and she asked if I could turn up the heat. Then it grew quiet in the car, and after twenty minutes passed, I assumed we just wouldn't be speaking. But then, out of nowhere, they started talking about their friend: another young woman, who had died the month before. Apparently, the three of them had been hitchhiking when they climbed into the back of a pickup truck with some guys who were drinking. The driver veered off the highway and rolled the truck down an embankment.

"I remember sitting up and calling for you," Betty said, turning in her seat to see her friend.

"Yeah," her friend said, "but when we called for Lynette, she didn't answer."

They told me that the two of them had been thrown to safety, but their friend had been crushed by the cab.

If my mom had been there, I thought, she would have blamed the girl for her own death—that's what you got for hitchhiking and getting into a car with men who'd been drinking. That's what happened when you didn't do the right things and follow the right rules. But that felt unfair to me, the same way it'd felt unfair when she'd blamed the women in the park for the way the police had abused them. I wanted to ask Betty and her friend what had happened to the driver—Had he been arrested? Gone to jail? But just then my mix tape started playing a Modern English song, and they asked me to turn up the volume. Yet again, I was missing out on an opportunity to bond with someone Native and young, to ask how they'd been taught by their people to process death, to find out how they mourned and wonder aloud if any of their practices might help me.

We arrived in Farmington just as it started raining harder. We stopped at the corner of Dustin Road, where I was supposed to turn left to go home. "I live that way," I told her.

Betty zipped her jacket higher, anticipating the cold, and said, "You can drop us at the gas station on the corner," but I glanced over my shoulder and saw that her friend was asleep. She looked even younger than me and Betty, and I didn't have the heart to leave them standing in puddles on the side of the road.

"I'll just drive you all the way to Aztec," I said. It was only fifteen miles farther. I knew Mom would be mad and call me selfish when I was late, because Monica needed the car, but at that moment it didn't matter.

It was as if my kindness finally made Betty see me and my need. She started talking. She asked what tribe I was. She told me her uncle, who was really her mom's new husband and her stepfather, was a Cheyenne holy man. He ran sweats and served as a roadman for the Native American Church. She said he also acted in Hollywood movies on the side, in bit parts mostly, but he knew some famous people. He was old, like in his sixties, and he enjoyed reconnecting lost kids to their culture.

"Especially pretty girls," she said, laughing. "You should give me your phone number so you can meet him."

By the time I dropped her off at her friend's mobile home park, my heart was singing. Neither of them had phones where they were staying. The trailer they went into had the electricity shut off for nonpayment, but they assured me they had lots of blankets. I scribbled my home phone number on a scrap of paper I found in the glove box, gave it to her, and drove away.

Betty said not to be surprised if it took her uncle Eugene time to call. According to her, he worked in mysterious ways and would contact me when he got a sign that I was ready. I was home by the time I saw that her friend had left a plastic shopping bag in the backseat. I carried it inside, took a scolding from Mom, and went to my room to see what it contained.

There was a bag of Frito chips, some trash, a brand-new travel-size whiskey, and an old notebook with a list of furniture and stuff. The rest of the pages in the notebook were empty, except for one that read, "He was high when he said being Indian is feeling like we're not Indian enough." I threw everything in the waste bucket except for the miniature whiskey. That I drank, to celebrate my luck, or maybe to numb my pain. Even after I was buzzed, I wasn't sure which.

PART
4

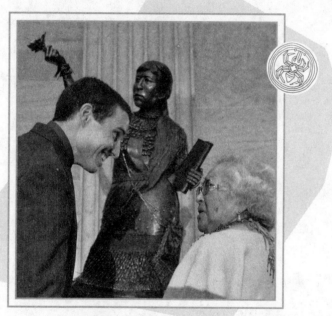

The author's great-aunt Louise Jackson Tannheimer, descendant of Sarah Winnemucca, who fought to see Winnemucca's statue included in the Capitol's collection, shaking hands with sculptor Benjamin Victor, on March 9, 2005, in Washington, D.C. (*Photo by Tom Williams/Roll Call/Getty Images*)

[ ]

I t's nearly sunrise on the Navajo reservation, and I'm in a waking dream, in a teepee set up by a Cheyenne roadman, a medicine man named Blackbear. I sit in a circle of elders on a night with no moon, and listen to a woman sing Wani Wachi Yelo, the sound of the water drum and gourd rattle passing through my body as she prays. An eagle bone whistles as she weeps. On the dirt before us, the road of life, fashioned out of sand to cradle the fire, its flames dancing and leaping, alive.

The roadman passes another dose of the green cacti we call Grandfather Peyote. It has been mashed into a relish, its sour taste hard to send down. Trees and cacti are social beings. The earth's plants use electric signals through a fungal network to warn one another of danger. They watch, keep track, and remember. They nourish the stumps of fallen companions for centuries by feeding them a sugar solution through their roots. They nourish and nurse the sick, including me.

The fire in the center of the teepee, the water I go out to bring in at 3:00 A.M., the cedar thrown on the wood embers, the eagle wing used to fan the incense on my body and purify me as I stand before my community. This ceremony links me to this continent, the plants, animals, and ancestors who came before me. It enables me to release pain, over twenty years of collected trauma. I see the earth breathing. I see the sunrise in the flames on the floor before me. I rest my face on the earth and feel her inhalation, her belly swelling in time with mine. This cactus, this hero's dose, this living relative, this health restorer. This omniscient spirit.

The night following the ceremony I dream. In my sleep, I ascend a mountain. The sky is black. There is a hogan and a barrel of water. A man with coal eyes, all pupils, no white in his gaze, approaches me. He is Grandfather Peyote, and when he hugs me, he squeezes me so hard I can't breathe. He forces an exhalation so complete that when I inhale, I become something new.

THE GHOST DANCE

(1986)

✜

After school one day during my junior year, I drove to Joan's apartment. The door was locked, and nobody answered, so I dug under a loose brick for the spare key and let myself in. Larry, a friend of hers from work, was passed out on the floor. It was the first day of the spring semester and I was already wishing the school year was over.

Joan came out of her room with her hair up in a towel. She was wearing a button-up blouse with padded shoulders, and I could see that she had been putting on her makeup. The television was turned up too loud for her to catch my knocking; I could hear Michael J. Fox on the show *Family Ties* promoting his club of young Republicans.

"Why the long face?" she asked.

"I got my ACT scores back," I told her.

"They can't be that bad," she said.

But they were. Everything had gotten worse that year. My test scores, my grades. In response, I had adopted a new motto: screw academia. I no longer believed college was in my future, and not just because it was beginning to look like I wouldn't be able to get in. I'd spent my whole life trying to succeed in the ways my parents thought would free me—working hard to impress my teachers, studying to get good grades—but I felt more trapped than ever. Heavy and weighted down. And the only moments when I felt anything close to uplifted were the moments when I got the chance to explore the very culture and the history that my parents wanted me to leave behind.

I'd fallen in love with Native poets, Simon Ortiz, Luci Tapahonso, nila northSun, on my trips to the downtown library, and the more I learned the more I resented the absence of Native wisdom and culture in my formal education. Anytime my teachers talked about Native history, it had to do with the conquest of our people. There was absolutely no mention of our successes. There was, in fact, no mention of us as modern people or as a contributing culture at all. The silencing of our history, of all that we'd sacrificed for the United States, burned in my chest.

In my English class, most of the authors we read were dead white guys. In social studies, my teacher didn't mention that the founding fathers took their democratic ideals for the Constitution from the Iroquois Confederacy. My math teacher went off on some tangent about how equal employment opportunities had cured our country of racism. My health teacher claimed Native people were alcoholics because we were biologically inferior in our ability to process booze. My counselor professed "not to see color," like she could somehow miss my melanin.

There was no single moment when I realized that my education would fail to free me. Rather, it had dawned on me slowly and incrementally over the last few years. I was smart. I *knew* I was smart. But the cards were stacked against me, and they had been since the beginning. I was tired of fighting the system. I'd been angry for years, but now that anger felt impossible to hide. To act on it in school and at home energized me.

"Want to know why you're failing?" Joan asked. "Because you're using nine out of your ten brain cells to think about how unfair the world is."

In her opinion, I was a crybaby. I spent too much time reading Native poetry and moaning about our ancestors. Instead, I needed to face facts and work within the confines of the "real world." Hadn't I learned anything from Mom and Dad? She used all their go-to phrases in her scolding: "Be strong." "Get tough." "Stop playing the victim."

But even though she was my older sister—supposedly more experienced in the ways of the "real world"—it was easy to dismiss her. Her boarding school years had turned her into a conservative. She was dating a Rush Limbaugh fan, and so I told myself that Joan didn't know what she was talking about, that she was just a product of the anti-Native education system I was railing against. "Those bastards at school aren't teaching me anything," I said.

The fact that literacy was the tool by which oppression functioned—that my ancestors had been held down precisely because of their inability to understand legalese—hadn't occurred to me yet. Neither had the fact that my bad humor was broadcasting how much I'd invested in a system that betrayed me. I kept saying I didn't care, but the truth was I cared too much.

"You're going to ruin your life," Joan said. But she'd quit college for a manager's job at Domino's Pizza, and aside from disappointing my parents, she seemed to be doing just fine. She had her own apartment and had bought a MR2 Turbo that went from zero to sixty in six seconds. And almost every day, she got to party with her friends, local boys like Larry and Travis, who she'd hired to deliver pizzas.

Joan had a good life. One that I envied. In those days, I was converted, eager to be a badass Jackson girl like my big sisters. But partying required an influx of cash. So that fall, I'd begged Joan for a job, and she'd hired me to work in the kitchen. She wouldn't trust me slinging dough, but I was allowed to sprinkle toppings and cheese. I was nearly always grounded that year, but the job gave me a reprieve. More than that, it gave me friends. Suddenly, I was being invited to hang out with Joan and her buddies, pizza guys in their late twenties who bought me vodka whenever I asked.

"Can you guys shut up?" Larry asked, when our argument about my ACT scores grew loud.

"Get up or you'll be late for work," Joan said, nudging him with her foot. Then she went back into her room like I wasn't even there.

He rolled over on his back, and the smell of alcohol nearly bowled me over. "I'm leaving anyway," I said.

But I didn't want to go home. I'd gone to Joan's apartment looking for a little sympathy, which turned out to be foolish. And expecting any from my parents would have been downright insane. So instead, I wandered around a grocery store near our house until it was late enough to crawl into bed without being noticed. Then, the next morning, I snuck out before dawn to get high in my favorite canyon. Technically, I was grounded, but I knew Dad would let my escape slide if I told him I went hiking. He always said exercising in the morning brought clarity of mind.

As I walked toward the trailhead at the edge of town, I felt a mixture of sadness and rage. I knew I could do better in school, but I couldn't bring myself to try. In my mind, my parents were lying when they said a promising future was within my grasp. How could they deny that most kids in Farmington wouldn't get out? And what did "getting out" even mean? A honeymoon in Hawaii. A tract home in the suburbs. A plastic Christmas tree. I didn't want a white American life. I wanted a life that would make my ancestors proud.

That morning, I walked for hours. My legs twitched and my body grew warm. The sun rose, and I had to take off my jacket and tie it around my waist. I saw tire tracks in the dirt where four-wheeling Jeeps climbed over rock, crushing sage and rabbit brush. I saw the remains of high school parties, the ashes of campfires where the local kids drank and gossiped with friends. Moving through the piñon and juniper trees, I heard the rumble of an oilfield truck come around the bend, the lyrics from "Okie from Muskogee" wafting out the open windows.

"Hey, girl! You been drinking? Do you need a ride?" When I saw the white guys in the truck, I ducked off the trail and started running, my heart pumping with fear that they might hurt me. I darted among cactus and sage, and climbed over sandstone boulders, until my legs felt like rubber, and I was sure no one was following me.

Finally, I sat down at the mouth of a sandstone cave. I was carrying a small backpack, and after catching my breath, I pulled out my stash and my pipe. I brushed sand off the pages of a poetry book I'd checked out at the library, then used its center fold to clean a bud of weed. I smoked and leaned back to see the contrails of jets traveling across the sky.

I was scheduled to work at Domino's that night, and I hoped it would be slow so Joan would let me ride with my favorite coworker, Stefan, when he went to deliver pizzas. He was lanky and queer, easily my favorite for the way he blasted Whitney Houston as we drove. If the order was late, we took the back roads so he could speed. The needle ticked ninety, and it always gave me a buzz whenever he came up too fast on another car and had to pass on double solid yellow lines. On his days off, he sometimes stopped by the restaurant on his motorcycle to give me a ride. I'd climb on without a helmet and lean into the corners with a fearless feeling, staring at the pavement as it rushed up at my face.

Thinking about my rides on the back of Stefan's bike, I suddenly thought of Uncle Gene racing the train, Dad flipping the car, and Uncle Johnny driving off the bridge. The images of their escapades ran through my head, and I sat up with a jolt. I was high, and it felt like a revelation. For the first time in my life, I recognized my own behavior as part of a family tradition.

I remembered Dad telling me a story when Granny Ethel died. He had been near tears, talking about a car accident he had been in with his grandparents when he was twelve. His grandfather had been drinking and Dad got thrown from the car. When he came to, he saw his Granny Ethel trapped in the driver's seat. The engine was smoking, and he pulled her screaming in pain from the wreckage.

It scared me, realizing how much I had come to love speeding, drinking, and the glorification of risky behavior. My impulse control was hanging by a thread. Self-harm was our twentieth-century battle cry. We thought we were being brave, but there was a thin line between courage and stupidity. I fell asleep out there in the canyon, or maybe I would have internalized the lesson. Instead, when I woke up, the realization was like a nightmare that faded the longer I was awake. Risky behavior was addictive. And some lessons must be learned more than once, not

because we're incapable of change, but because maturity takes commitment and time.

The following weekend, Joan talked me into driving up to a bar in Durango.
It had been her favorite hangout back when she was attending school at
Fort Lewis College. She asked an old girlfriend, an Arapaho still attending classes there, to lend me her ID. As we exited the dorms and hopped
in the car, she told me, "Memorize her birthday and remember what
zodiac sign she is. The bouncers like to ask."

"She's a Halloween baby," I told them after examining her driver's
license.

"That makes her a Scorpio," Joan's boyfriend said.

We were with Larry from Joan's pizza crew. He was a sensitive moper
with long eyelashes, and I didn't much like him. He and Stefan were always fighting. At first, I assumed they were dating, or wanted to date, but
after several months I could see that Larry wouldn't admit his attraction.
Sometimes he flirted with Stefan, other times he paraded his girlfriend
around. They had been friends since childhood, and I could see how
painful the situation was for Stefan, especially since Larry's girlfriend had
given birth to his child.

All of which explains why I wasn't nice to Larry on the night we went
dancing in Durango with Joan. When he tried to joke with me, I asked,
"How come you never stay home with your baby and wife?"

"She's not my wife," he said. "And how come you can't mind your
own business?"

A band was playing, and when they went on break, we went out in
the alley to smoke a fat joint. When we went back inside, we danced to
the Violent Femmes, and my ears started ringing from the noise. I tried to
keep pace with Joan and the guys, ducking out every hour to smoke more
weed, but I put up my hand when they kept offering me more drinks. By
the end of the night, the three of them were so messed up they could
hardly stand.

I was snoring in a booth when Joan shook me awake. "It's time to go home," she slurred. We went outside, and Larry tossed me his keys.

"Designated driver," he said. Then the three of them piled in the car and passed out.

It was a scary drive home. I wasn't as drunk as they were, but I still fought to keep my eyes open. The two-lane La Plata Highway wends by a small ski resort called Hesperus before cutting through mountains with running rivers on both sides.

I don't know how many times I jerked awake to find myself cutting around some bend like someone else had their hands on the wheel. One time I caught myself dreaming that it was broad daylight and there was a cow the size of a house in the middle of the road. I slammed on the brakes, and Joan's boyfriend yelled, "Cool it, Debbie!"

The road was never ending. Every time I thought we might be getting closer to the neat streets and lights of town, I was wrong. It was still the rivers and pastures, the Indian paintbrush and trees, the hints of steep cliffs beyond the shoulder of the road. The switchbacks and hairpins just kept coming. It was impossible to figure how any road could keep going without end, or how I was staying between the lines.

The following morning, when I woke up in Joan's apartment, I could barely remember arriving home. It was Sunday. The four of us moaned around all afternoon, nursing queasy stomachs and taking aspirin for our pounding heads. Joan's assistant manager was working for her that night, and as soon as the sun started to set the bottles of booze came out on the table. Larry's brother, Travis, arrived with Stefan and some other friends. A bit later, Larry's girlfriend walked in with their baby daughter.

The thought of more alcohol made me feel like throwing up, and I could see that Stefan was uncomfortable in the company of Larry's girlfriend and baby, so I suggested we go out and grab something greasy to eat. I said it would help soak up the liquor in my gut. He glanced over at Larry, who had been staring at him all night, and agreed to take me to get french fries at a fast-food joint down the street. We used the drive-through, and once we had our order he asked if I minded cruising around town to look for a certain someone he liked.

We circled parking lots outside of restaurants, bars, and movie theaters searching for a red Ford Escort driven by *blank*. Stefan refused to give me a name, and I said he had to nod if I guessed it right. Was it Taylor? Jamie? Frankie? He laughed until he snorted when he heard all the gender-neutral guesses, which made me feel clever and hopeful that one day I'd be his confidante.

About an hour later, we pulled back into the parking lot at Joan's apartment, where I immediately experienced a feeling of dread. I didn't want to go inside. I *really* didn't want to go inside. A warm shower, a bowl of soup, an old VHS movie, even taking the trash out or scrubbing the kitchen for Mom sounded better than more booze. Inside, I knew Joan and her boyfriend would be laughing at Danitra Vance who played Cabrini Green Harlem Watts Jackson, teenage welfare queen, on *Saturday Night Live* that season, and if I walked in and said the skit was a negative stereo- type, they'd call me a Debbie Downer.

"I want to go home," I said to Stefan before he could stop the car.

"Why didn't you tell me before?"

"I didn't realize until we got here."

Stefan pulled around the parking lot and turned his blinker on to leave. Later that night, I'd learn that we were nearly at my house when all hell began breaking loose at Joan's.

Before Stefan could get back to Joan's apartment, Larry had raised a pistol to his temple, pretending to play Russian roulette. Joan said he was trying to impress his girlfriend, who was sitting nearby with their baby, but when she told me later my first thought was that his unresolved attraction to Stefan had made him depressed. They were in the spare bedroom with one of Larry's friends, while Joan and her boyfriend were in the living room watching *Saturday Night Live* like I assumed they would be.

Joan said she heard a shot and then Larry's girlfriend and friend ran out of the bedroom with the baby. Larry's body was toppled over on the carpet when she arrived in the bedroom doorway, and by the time she got back to the living room phone everyone but her boyfriend had gone. She was the only one outside when the cops arrived, mascara dried on her cheeks as she told them about the little round hole in Larry's temple. Only a small trickle of blood flowed out.

The following afternoon, caution tape was stretched across the door of Joan's apartment, and the parking space in front of it was blocked off with orange cones. The night before, the coroner had stopped by to bag Larry's body and take him to the morgue. Dad and I were sitting in the parking lot of the apartment complex after dropping Joan off to get her car. "Just drive," I told him. But Dad stared at the caution tape and refused to move. He kept saying this is exactly why we'd moved away from the reservation—to protect us from violence like this.

"And here we thought the one place you were safe was with your sister," he said.

A blank had killed Larry. I didn't understand how that was possible, but Dad explained that a blank can shatter bone when a handgun with one in its chamber gets placed too close to the skin. When Larry fired, a fragment of his skull had driven into his brain.

Dad stared at me in the passenger seat. "I'm worried about you," he said. "It doesn't seem like you care about anything anymore. You quit volleyball and now Mom's going to make you quit work. You have to have purpose in life if you want to survive!"

I looked out the window and shrugged, not wanting to admit that I'd quit volleyball because it was embarrassing to be benched for bad grades. In my mind, it was better to act like I didn't want to play than admit that I was failing.

As usual, Dad had been working long hours, and he was headed to a leadership conference with the company foremen the next day. Lori had sorority fees, her apartment, and food needs at New Mexico State University in Las Cruces, and Dad still thought he had four kids to put through college. His goals were clear, and he said he needed me to set mine.

"I know I haven't been around as much," he told me. "But that doesn't mean you can hang around with losers and cause your mom trouble. We need to be able to trust you."

I sulked. Larry was dead and Dad was badmouthing him even before he'd been lowered into his grave. Yet even as I considered calling my father callous, I knew it was hypocritical. I'd never taken an interest in Larry. In fact, his death made me realize how lacking in compassion I'd been toward him. I knew he didn't get along with his parents, but I'd never envisioned his lack of support or his fear of condemnation. I felt sad for Joan, terrified for Stefan, and upset by the way I'd failed Larry.

In the days after Larry's funeral, I found I couldn't sleep. All week long, I kept waking to memories of Larry's family and friends mourning at the church. I could feel Stefan's hand in mine, his whole body trembling. I could see Larry's girlfriend, crumpled and puffy. She kept shaking her head when her mother tried to hand her the baby. Every morning that week, I woke exhausted, but Mom insisted I go to school.

My first class on the day after Larry's funeral was American humanities. It was cotaught by two women everyone at the high school dubbed Bruce and Eagle. Eagle was a blond German who dressed like an early pioneer; Bruce was a thick-calved brunette who buzzed around on a Harley-Davidson. Eagle taught history and politics, while Bruce assigned literature from the same era, and after Larry died, Eagle gave us Dee Brown's history book, *Bury My Heart at Wounded Knee*.

I'd never heard of it before, but I went to the front of the room when my row was called to grab a copy. From a distance, I saw a Navajo on the cover, and my interest was piqued. Eagle told us to read two chapters by Friday, then she handed out additional mimeographed readings, and moved on to other things.

That night I went home and pulled the assignment out of my backpack. I sat on the bedroom floor and flipped through the well-thumbed pages. The blurbs on the cover might have made me cautious—reviewers announcing that the author had captured the "grim," "painful," and "shameful" story of how the West was "lost"—but I was eager to finally be handed a nonfiction book that pertained to my life, and I forged ahead without pausing.

Into the morning, I gorged myself on Dee Brown's words. The author had recorded eloquent quotes by Chief Joseph, Sitting Bull, Red Cloud, Little Crow, Geronimo, and others. I clung to their words, even though the sadness in their voices cut deep. I read about how the Lakota received a portion of their land at Fort Laramie in 1868, only to have the treaty revoked when miners struck gold. It reminded me of my own tribe's demise at the hands of the forty-niners—the way our crops were trampled by their rush to get to California—and it made me see the nexus between the extractive industries, religion, and war, that would affect all tribes.

After I finished the two chapters Eagle had assigned as homework, I turned to a chapter that hadn't been assigned and read about the Sand Creek massacre. At first, I thought the atrocities Dee Brown described had to be wrong. I couldn't believe anyone would murder and mutilate unarmed women and children. I couldn't believe the hope the Cheyenne and Arapaho mothers displayed while trying to protect their kids, the way they raised an American flag as a symbol of peace only to be bayoneted to death as they huddled beneath it for protection.

The tribes who fought valiantly broke my heart, but not as much as the ones who tried to trust. The history book depicted Natives from every region trying to assimilate, attempting to prove they were civilized and deserved to stay on their land. The Cherokee created an alphabet for their language and ran a newspaper to show they were capable. Hawaiian rulers installed electricity in Iolani Palace before the White House and Buckingham Palace had it in theirs, so they could impress dignitaries with their civilization. But nothing they did ever garnered them the respect they desired. No matter how obedient they acted, white Americans still took advantage of them. At every turn, the Natives were betrayed, denigrated, assaulted. Reading about the atrocities in the face of attempted assimilation made my face grow hot with shame.

All that night, I kept putting the book down and vowing to go to

sleep, but it glowed like plutonium near my bed. I was too scared of nightmares to rest. Every time I nodded off, I saw guns, the small hole in Larry's
head, little kids lying bloody in the snow. So instead, I paced. History had
never felt so palpable before. So real. So *mine*. Suddenly, the vague sense
of injustice that I'd been struggling with that year began to crystalize.
I wasn't wrong to think that, in Farmington, the cards were stacked
against me. In fact, outside of my reservation, it seemed they would be
stacked against me no matter where I went, just as they had been stacked
against my parents and my grandparents and all my ancestors before me
since my people had first encountered white colonists. We were a persecuted people. The victims of generations of violence and genocide. It was
all right there, written down in black and white before me. So why had
my parents never told me about our collective history?

Sitting there in my bed, I knew it would be better to wait for Dad to
come home from his leadership conference to ask him, but in the moment, Thursday felt too far away. And that's why, against my better judgment, I went down the hall to my Mom's room, hoping I could find the
words to tell her what I was feeling, that I could put into words the pain
I'd been struggling with for years.

At first, I knocked softy on Mom's door. I didn't know what I planned
to say—something about feeling betrayed, something about wanting to
better understand my lineage. But when she didn't answer and I knocked
louder, I heard my little brother let out an angry cry. Mom flung open the
door with her eyes half-closed and sleepy. "I just got him down," she said.
"Get out of here or I'll make you take care of him!"

Dismissed and disappointed, I crawled back into bed. I told myself
that I would wait to read more until Dad got home, but I couldn't stop
myself from reading one more chapter. The last pages I read that night
involved Granny Ethel's people, the Paiute. Apparently, during a solar
eclipse in 1889, a man from her tribe named Wovoka had a vision about
the second coming of an Indian Jesus. He danced the Ghost Dance and
convinced Native people from other tribes to dance the Ghost Dance too.
It was a supernatural prayer, an ecstatic movement, and they couldn't stop

performing it because Wovoka said it was the only way to restore the world to the way it was before colonization.

The Ghost Dancers danced for days. Whole families refused to eat or stop. The media whipped the country into a frenzy, reporting that the Natives had gone mad. Christians could turn wine into blood, yet somehow a religious dance meant war. Just after Christmas, the military arrived with guns. And that's when I put the book down. I didn't have to finish reading to know what happened, and I knew the Ghost Dancers had known what would happen too. It was suicide, I thought, as I closed my eyes and imagined hearing the drums.

Not long after, I finally drifted off to sleep, but I was woken by Mom in the early hours of the morning, who had suddenly found it necessary to clean the carpet in my room. She kept ramming the foot of my bed with the vacuum until I sat up and asked what she was doing. "You woke Ted, and it took me two hours to get him back to sleep," she said. "I'm giving you a taste of your own medicine!"

That Friday, my American humanities teacher launched into a discussion of *Bury My Heart at Wounded Knee*. There was only one other Native American in my class, a Navajo guy by the name of Christian, and I was astounded when our teacher addressed the awkward silence in our classroom by encouraging him to speak first.

"Get your books out," she said, telling us to turn to the page that dealt with the Long Walk so he could start our discussion.

Dee Brown's book was only sixteen years old at that point, which meant my classmates and I were being exposed to content our parents probably didn't know. I'd never heard anyone talk about the genocide of my people before, and I was happy I wasn't the one tasked with starting the conversation.

"Go ahead, Christian," Eagle said. "In 1864, your tribe was forcibly expelled to Bosque Redondo. Why don't you tell the class what you think of that event?"

I looked around to see if anyone else appeared nervous. But their

faces were blank and hard to read. Eagle might have started class by shining a light on our country's failure to account for its past violence. She
might have acknowledged that many of us had never heard about these
atrocities. She might have considered the mental health impact the lesson would have on students like Christian and me. Instead, she made no
attempt to contextualize our discussion.

All week long I had tried to muster the confidence to talk to my
parents about what they knew, but after my failed attempt with Mom, I'd
been reluctant to approach them. The only person who I'd talked to in
my family about the book was Joan, and she told me I had to remember
that things in our country had changed. We lived in a meritocracy now,
which meant we could pull ourselves up if we tried. When I pressed her,
she didn't want to hear my horror stories. She insisted it was better not
to know.

In class, Christian cleared his throat when Eagle told him to begin. He
said his mother had taught him to forgive what the government had done
to his tribe. Grace was a part of his faith, and a hallmark of his family's
resilience. He was smart and soft-spoken, and I'd never heard him say so
much in class. His face was sad, but if he was still bothered by the effects
of white supremacy, he didn't show it.

I couldn't believe he was so calm. It felt like he had the right to be
angry, and even though I had no place, I found his religious platitudes
suspect. What kind of psychic toll did it take for him to forgive? I worried
that he was repressing deeper feelings.

I turned to the front of the room and saw Eagle smiling at Christian.
When he stopped talking, she turned her gaze on me, and I shrank down
in my seat, terrified that she would call on me next. I couldn't speak for
my tribe or my family. I could only speak for myself. And I knew that, on
my own, I would say something angry and be a disappointment.

It turned out that my fear was unwarranted though, because after
Christian spoke other students started speaking. Some of them felt sorry
for the poor Indians (like we weren't sitting next to them in class), while
others sounded excited by the killings. A redheaded baseball player in

back said that it wasn't wrong for the white settlers to take Native land because none of them had been using it anyway.

I wanted to tell the kid my ancestors didn't believe in overusing or injuring the earth. They believed that she was alive, that rocks spoke, and water was sacred. I wanted to quote Simon Ortiz's poem "That's the Place Indians Talk About." I heard the lines in my head, "when we pray, when we sing, when we talk with the stones."

But I froze. I thought about the stories Dad told us as kids: the girl who shape-shifted into a bobcat, the lovers who turned into mountains. I'd loved the myths growing up, but Joan said educated people found those stories naive. She told me about a psychology class she took at Fort Lewis College, where a professor told them that Carl Jung had summed up the Indigenous mentality with the term "participation mystique." To him, the Native identification with the earth was childlike and primitive. A connection with objects denoted we, and our ancestors, had only a partial identity.

For the next hour, I suffered in silence as my classmates debated my ancestors' worth as human beings. And if I'd felt shame in the past few days as I'd wrestled with my newfound knowledge of my people's mistreatment, if I'd struggled with what felt like my family's willful ignorance, well, learning that I lacked the courage to stand up and defend my ancestors wrecked me. That whole year, I'd been thinking that my rebellion against school made me a badass Jackson girl like my sisters. But it turned out that I wasn't a badass girl at all. When push came to shove and it was time to speak, I discovered that I was a coward.

The following day was freezing, but the house felt stuffy and hot. Dad left for work, and Lori went to the ski slopes early. It was Saturday and Mom said she was taking Monica, Theresa, and Ted to a movie at the mall. I didn't want to be left alone. But when I asked if I could join, she was mean as she often was, telling me I wasn't invited, and it made me feel like my deepest suspicions about myself were true. I *was* a disappointment to my family. I felt like a coward and a traitor, and as soon as the house was empty, I went searching for something, anything I could use to numb the pain. At the back of a kitchen cabinet, I found a bottle of Tylenol. I took the pills with me into the bathroom and then I locked the door.

I didn't plan what I was going to do until I was in the middle of doing it, spinning the lid off the bottle with the heel of my hand, pouring the Tylenol out on the counter, collecting the ones that rolled into the sink or fell on the floor. All my life, these little pills had helped ease my aches and pains, and just the sight of them made me feel better.

Still, for a moment I stalled, arranging the Tylenol in patterns and lines. I heard a dog barking and climbed on the edge of the tub to crank open a window and listen. I thought a passing car might be someone in the family. I was eager for one of them to come home and ask me what was wrong. Maybe Dad would quit work early, or maybe Lori had forgotten her gaiters. Maybe all the seats in the movie theater would be taken, or maybe Monica would convince Mom they should come back and get me.

But even though I tried to kill time, no one in my family arrived, so I pushed the pills into a pile and started counting. I thought it would be easy to swallow three or four pills at a time, but they were bitter, and before I knew it, I was waterlogged and sick. Taking them dry made my eyes water, but I told myself I wasn't crying. When I finished, I lay down in the tub. And, because I was so exhausted, I fell asleep.

When I jolted awake with my sinuses burning, I had no idea how long I'd been out. But fear brought me to my feet, the sudden realization that I was dying when I wanted to stay alive, and the feeling that I wasn't alone. Grandma Esther was with me, and she didn't want me to die. I pulled myself to standing, opened the door, and called for help. I could hear a lawn mower buzzing in someone's front yard, and a television with canned laughter in Mom's room. I went down the hall and found Monica home from the mall.

My kindest sister, so innocent and shy, she deserved better from me that day. She sped me to the emergency room in Dad's old truck, a manual ride with "three on the tree," a transmission that shifted on the column. It's not an easy vehicle to drive, and I remember her stripping the teeth off the gears and crying all the way to the emergency room.

The next thing I knew I was vomiting black charcoal at the hospital, and the doctors were saying the poison had entered my bloodstream. Mom arrived first, and I'll never forget her hands over her mouth as she talked to the doctor. She was mortified by what I'd done, and frightened because she thought it might reflect on her as a mother. She wasn't sure if I'd hurt my liver permanently, and she couldn't stop crying. She wandered the halls until Dad arrived and told her he'd take over.

Dad stood by my bed with his usual calm. I've never seen anyone get quieter during a crisis than him. Once I was stabilized and they gave me a regular room, he came and told me it would be a week before they would let me go home. I was queasy and in pain but relieved that everyone knew how depressed I had become. He asked if I was worried about what I had done to my body, and I admitted I was scared.

Then he said I had visited him at the power plant that day. I didn't understand what he meant until he explained that he was looking at some engineering plans when he felt someone yanking on his sleeve. He turned around, but there was no one there. He went back to his work, and it happened again.

"At least your spirit knows you've got something to live for," he said.

I thought about how I had staggered down the hall to find Monica and I knew that my body had some of that wisdom too. I said that I had learned I was wrong. My ancestors didn't want me to die, and I didn't want to die either. Now all I had to do was figure out how to stay alive.

The following morning, a psychiatrist came in to see me. She said she was concerned that I hadn't left a suicide note, which I interpreted as a request to describe my depression succinctly. I scoffed, thinking about what betrayals she might expect me to name: Monica, you shouldn't have thrown my favorite doll out the window. Lori, it's your fault I broke my collarbone. Joan, why did you make friends with Craig? I rolled my eyes and told the psychiatrist I hated mouth breathers, clubbers of baby seals, hairspray-addicted girls, and people with WHAT WOULD REAGAN DO bumper stickers.

I could hear myself being sarcastic, and I felt frightened that I had no way to talk about my grief. My parents, my family, my culture, my country, I didn't know how to put any of it in words—let alone speak those kinds of truths to some white lady.

When Mom returned that afternoon to talk about the two of us receiving counseling from a priest, I told her no. And when she forged on, talking sweet and acting like we were definitely going, I told her no again. That's when she said it was time for us to be honest with each other. Something had happened to her as a child.

"I was walking home from school," she said. "And I saw some cherries hanging on a tree. I was little and I was hungry and I sat in the yard and ate the cherries until the man who owned the house came out and said I was stealing."

She started crying, and I realized she was sharing some sort of genesis, perhaps the origin of her grief, but I couldn't intuit what she meant by it, and she was incapable of describing it further. Even so, I could see that it took a lot for her to tell me the story and she needed me to see her pain and console her in it. It was important that I understand how mortified she had been, how wronged and humiliated she'd felt. All I could do was give her a hug.

The next morning it was Dad's turn to show up. He pulled up a chair and said he wanted to talk. He had been thinking, he said, since coming back from his leadership conference. He said there had been a lot of talk about diversity there, because most of the welders were Navajo, and most of the administration was white, and their miscommunications were costing the company money.

Dad had new vocabulary words: *ethnocentrism*, *xenophobia*, and *cultural pluralism*. He was excited, and I remember thinking he looked like he had been handed a new way of expressing himself. Most importantly, he apologized. He said they'd taught him that culture was automatic, that it affected people's behavior in ways they didn't think about it, and he confessed that he had never realized how hard it was for me to be a half-breed. Apparently, a guy from the instrumentation department had spoken at the conference, a man who was half-Native and half-Chicano like me and my sisters, and his talk had been all about how alienated he felt, never able to fit in either world.

Dad told me, "I always looked at you and thought you were light-skinned and pretty and smart, and I'll admit that I felt relieved because I thought your life would be easier than mine. Now I understand I was wrong."

When Mom had left my side the day before, I'd watched her walk away with a feeling of pity. And now here was Dad looking at me with the same pity I had felt for Mom. I wanted to be thankful for his apology, but when he left, I felt sad. Talking about my half-breed status was missing the point. I didn't give a crap if Dad had some rumored drop of white blood, or Mom had even more. My main concern wasn't bloodlines, rather it was the despicable way our ancestors' ideas had been bled out of our approach to life.

After Dad left, I watched the *Challenger* space shuttle explode in the sky. A nurse had come into the room to turn on the television, saying that the excitement at Cape Canaveral was sure to cheer me up. Instead, I watched the joy melting off the faces of Christa McAuliffe's parents as they went from thinking the booster rockets had separated to realizing their daughter was dead. It was a horrifying spectacle of national grief, and for the first time in forever I cried.

FLIGHT

(1987)

A ton of rain fell the summer after my overdose, which made the waters near our old campground rise and darken. This meant big trout on the feed, and Dad angling to fish every weekend. Each time he suggested a trip, I suspected he just wanted an excuse to check in on me. But I didn't mind. I was happy enough to have a reason to leave the house.

That summer my family circled the wagons. After leaving the hospital, my parents had taken me to a Japanese restaurant all by myself. The restaurant belonged to a friend of my father's and the portions were so tiny, we all came home wanting. Since then, they'd been watching. Even though I told them I felt better, they were concerned. I tried to reassure them. I said a burden had been lifted now that we'd talked. The struggles that had plagued me for years—our family's forced assimilation, and the genocide we'd suffered at the hands of our own government—were in the open, and the silence and shame we'd always agreed upon as a family were gone. My grief had exploded into view. My resentment had been named and spoken, and now that my parents understood the source of my depression, I felt an enormous relief.

They were concerned that I hadn't shared my thoughts in a suicide note though, and worried that I needed the counseling the hospital had recommended, but that our insurance didn't cover it. So instead, they worked hard to make sure I was never left alone. Monica asked if I wanted to hang out with her and her nerdy friends nearly every day that summer, and even Joan and Lori came home to keep me company. They liked singing that ridiculous Melissa Manchester song about the clowns—"Don't cry out loud, just keep it inside, learn how to hide your feelings"—anytime I started acting sad. And on fishing trips with Dad, they always wanted to reminisce about the years we spent growing up in Yuma, back when we oldest four girls called ourselves the "Jackson 4."

On weekends when Dad succeeded in convincing the lot of us to trek up north to Durango, our parents would drive up in the truck with the babies, and the rest of us would follow behind them in the van. One Friday in July I was stretched out on the back bench, blankets, sleeping bags, and book bags on the ground at my feet, when Joan and Lori recalled an old nickname of mine, one they said showed how prescient they had been because it identified me as crazy from the get-go. "Mary Hartman" was a character in a satirical soap opera that spoofed regular soap operas. She was a nervous housewife with major issues. Her friend got paralyzed, her daughter was kidnapped, and the cops arrested her grandfather for being the town flasher, yet all she could think about was the waxy yellow buildup on her floors. At the end of the first season, her tendency to sublimate and appropriate the language used in commercials landed her in the psych ward.

"Oh my god," Joan said, laughing. "Mom was obsessed with that stupid show! Remember that little boy character? What was his name?"

"Jimmy Joe Jeeter!" Lori exclaimed.

Monica couldn't remember, so Lori explained. "He was an eight-year-old evangelist who got electrocuted when a television fell in his bathtub."

"You didn't call me Mary Hartman because you thought I was crazy," I said. "It was because of my hair!"

I distinctly remembered them telling me to go stand by the television when *Mary Hartman, Mary Hartman* was on so they could compare our braids. It was a time when Mom only combed our hair once every two weeks and my braids got loose and bagged out over my ears just like crazy Mary's.

Talking about the show made them remember something else: how we used to draw squares on the ground to play house outside near the carport and everyone called everyone else Mary.

"Mary, can I borrow some flour?"

"Sure, Mary, but why don't you go to the store?"

"Jeez, Mary, didn't you hear the price of beer?"

Sometimes, we would stop and try to convince each other to take a different name. "Why don't you be Sara?"

"You be Sara. I'm Mary."

One time, we got into such a big argument, Monica went inside and came out with her little red belt. She swung it around, just like Dad swung his when he was mad. Only she was ruthless, and she tried to catch our legs with the buckle.

Joan was laughing so hard remembering Monica with her belt, I thought she might wreck the van. "Oh my god! Remember how we ran from her, and she was hitting us and you got a bunch of goat head stickers in your foot?"

Back then, Monica had cracked our ankle bones with her belt buckle, and we'd actually cried from the pain. But once she'd grown tired, we'd decided that playing with the belt was fun, and we'd kept trying to hit each other with it. We had taken turns chasing each other, and the whipping made us laugh just as it was making us laugh now. It had been a long time since I'd thought about that day, but sitting there in the back of the van, I remembered how scary it was to hit them when they gave it to me, scarier than it was to be hit.

It started drizzling outside. Joan turned on the windshield wipers, and we grew quiet, but our memories of Yuma got me thinking. We'd been so little, yet the world had already taught us to accept a beating and brace ourselves for pain. It made me wonder if all Native kids felt so dehumanized by the start of preschool. I couldn't believe how insidious America was at making Native people believe the oppressor's low opinion of us.

As we arrived at our campground and started unloading the van, I vowed to make my life better for the little girl I'd once been. I needed to push the self-doubt out of my heart. I needed to find the courage to get rid of the shame. I needed to resist the conditioning, propaganda, and hate, and make self-love my primary goal.

The following morning, we rented a boat at a natural lake east of our favorite camping spot on the Animas River. I climbed aboard and Dad shoved us offshore while Mom went on a grocery run with my siblings. It was just the two of us on the water, and I tightened the tension spool on my rod as I waited for him to position the boat and start trolling.

The lake beneath us shone like tin in the morning light. We had been fishing about an hour when he said, "When I was your age—" and I cut him off.

"When you were my age, you were in prison," I said.

I knew it was rude, but as happy as I'd been to feel understood by them, maybe for the first time ever, the weeks of their focused attention had begun to wear on me. They wanted more than I could give—more explanation for why I struggled so deeply with assimilation, for why that struggle had sent me over the edge.

We were casting in eddies that swirled in circles along the shoreline. I was kneeling in the well of the boat and could feel the water trembling through its thin shell.

"I know you think you're moving back to the reservation," he said bluntly. "But you can't run around in Yuma like you do in Farmington and expect everything to turn out okay."

I didn't reply or even look up from my line in the water. How did he know what I was planning? In the weeks since my suicide attempt, we'd had a few deep conversations about the Native poetry books I'd been bringing home from Farmington's embarrassingly biased library, and about how angry I was with academia in general. But I hadn't spoken with anyone, not even my sisters, about my plan.

"As I was saying," he continued. "When I was a kid, my brother Gene

268   Deborah Jackson Taffa

left Yuma. He kept saying he wanted to go and live with Grandma Esther's family at Laguna. He got it in his head that it was some kind of promised land, and if he went there, he could fix all his problems. Gene was obsessed with belonging. He hated the way the guys in Yuma called him a half-breed because he wasn't full-blood Quechan. It bothered him that not everyone accepted him, and at some point, he got the idea that maybe he could gain acceptance with Mom's people, so he took a bus to New Mexico and lived with Grandma's brother, but one day when they were out at sheep camp Grandma's brother had a heart attack."

He paused and looked at me to see if I was listening. "Gene carried our uncle all the way out to the freeway, unwilling to admit he was dead. After that, he came home traumatized and was never the same again."

I reeled my line in and set it on the bottom of the boat to signal that I didn't like his story. It was depressing, and it sounded like he was saying I shouldn't romanticize the reservation. Or maybe he was saying an imagined return always failed an actual one. If I had been older, I might have heard him saying that our ancestral traditions were not easy to find; that a physical return didn't necessarily mean a spiritual one.

All summer long, Dad had been telling these little stories, like he was trying to give me advice without actually saying whatever it was he wanted to say. He kept bringing up the family's past and then apologizing for it, which irritated me to no end, in part because at this point in my recovery I couldn't see that I had my own apologies to offer.

"What point are you trying to make with that story?" I asked.

"No point," he said. "You're always complaining that I don't talk enough about my family." Then he reeled his line in too, and I could see that he was just as tired as I was. He was quiet, and he spun the boat around and headed back toward the parking lot and dock.

We buzzed across the river, each of us quiet and lost in private thoughts. If I'd had more empathy for Dad, I might have realized that the desire to belong had hurt him just as much as it had hurt Gene, though maybe in a different way. If Dad had practiced more empathy for me, he might have seen that my generation's pride was a sign that things *could* change, that the resurgence of ceremonies, the revitalization of languages, the restoration of culture were arriving.

Dad knew how rough Yuma was. It was even rowdier than Farmington, and his voice cracked when we pulled up at the dock and got our fishing tackle out of the boat. "I couldn't tell Gene what to do," he said, "just like I can't tell you. We don't get to control the people we love. We only get to forgive them or forgive ourselves if we can't."

When we arrived back at camp, he went to clean the fish, and I went down to the Animas River's shoreline to skip stones. I dangled my feet off the bank, remembering when I was little and Dad used to tell us stories about the lost souls on the water. Back then his story was a campfire tale, but now I knew too much about Native death to treat it like a game. And if I was looking for anyone's soul on the river, it was my own.

A few weeks later, the time came for Lori to return to college. It was a bleak prospect, considering the fun we'd had all summer, watching Rambo and Mad Max flicks and talking about how the four of us would survive the wasteland that came after the apocalypse.

We ate popcorn and rewound the rented VHS tapes to watch the fight scenes a second time, promising each other we would raise an army of dogs and hunt and fish to survive. There was no room for hesitation or doubt in our struggle. The future allowed no room for despair.

Spending time with my sisters had put spunk back in my steps, and I felt jealous of Lori's escape. She wasn't sneaking out a window in the middle of the night or boarding a Greyhound bus after getting caught with drugs. Hers was a modest success, swapping a northern New Mexico town for one seven hours south. But the freedom looked sweet, and I told myself that's how I wanted to get out too. Chin up rather than head down.

The only difference with my escape plan: I wouldn't be going to college. Despite Dad's warning, I still wanted to return to Yuma. But first, I needed to graduate from high school. The only problem was that my grades were so poor at this point, I didn't know if I'd make it. And if I didn't walk across the stage at graduation, my parents would pressure me to reenroll and keep trying for my diploma, which would mean another year in Farmington.

Given how much I hated our town, there was a lot on the line, and the night before my first day of senior year I felt nervous. I laid out my clothes like I was a warrior preparing for battle, then I went to brush my teeth while Psalm Twenty-Three played in my head: "Yea, though I walk through the valley of the shadow of death, I will fear no evil. For thou art with me."

Mom didn't know I still relied on my childhood prayers for support, and that's the way I wanted it. Though I'd spent the summer bonding with my dad and my sisters about my struggles with assimilation, my mom hadn't made as much of an effort to understand me. She still thought that prayer could solve all my problems, but I hated the church's dogma. I couldn't accept their stance on abortion, birth control, or the subservient role of women. Still, she was right about one thing. In moments of crisis, the prayers did help. And while I felt some shame about that, I reminded myself that these were the same prayers Grandma Esther had said with a very different value system.

I was braiding my hair in the mirror when Mom poked her head into the room. "Ready for tomorrow?" she asked.

"Not really," I said.

We looked at each other through the mirror, and I knew there were things she would say if we weren't so prickly and breakable. She stood, watching me braid my hair, for a long time, which bothered me more than I expected. Finally, I looked down and busied myself with a ponytail holder until I heard her walk away.

The next day, to guarantee that I'd graduate on time, I assembled a couple of tutors. Chemistry and trigonometry would be obstacles, and I was relieved when two smart kids at my school, Daniel and Patti, agreed to help me for free. They were sweet kids, slated to be valedictorian and salutatorian, though the order was still in flux.

Mr. Braswell, our psychology teacher, said we could use his room to study. He and his wife were family friends from the years she taught at Sacred Heart, and at that old private school they'd been admired for their faith. The story was that Mrs. Braswell had been pregnant when she was diagnosed with advanced breast cancer. Her doctors advised her to abort the baby for chemo, but she refused. And when both she and her baby survived, they were regarded as miracles by the community.

At the public high school, people laughed at Mr. Braswell. He practiced kindness, and it made him nerdy. He lacked sarcasm and wore thick glasses. I liked him though. He seemed to be one of the only teachers at my school who still took me seriously. All the others, as soon as my grades dropped, acted like I wasn't smart enough to make it. But Mr. Braswell seemed to intuit that my struggles at school had nothing to do with intelligence and continued to make demands.

Sometimes, when we were studying, Daniel would say he had to get home because his mother needed the car to get to work at the Indian Hospital in Shiprock. She was a doctor who treated Navajo citizens at their northern medical facilities west of Farmington and had become something of a role model for me, not because she was a doctor, but because she traveled with the Peace Corps and loved to climb mountains. She had recently returned from a solo trek across the country of Bhutan, and often invited me and Patti on hikes to Dzilth-Na-O-Dith-Hle State Park with her family.

One afternoon late in the semester Patti, Daniel, and I were studying in his family's kitchen when his mother, Dr. Eckerman, asked me, "Have you ever thought about practicing medicine on your reservation?"

"That's a great idea," Patti said.

I knew they meant it as a compliment, but it upset me, because it amplified a big problem with my plan. I would go home to the reservation—and do what? I wanted an education that aligned with the wisdom of my ancestors, but who was still living traditionally? It was nearly Christmas vacation, and I'd spent all semester trying to read about Quechan-Yuma culture at bookstores and libraries. There was so little information about my tribe anywhere in print, it felt like we didn't exist.

If I could have seen into my future, I would have told her that I was too confused to invest in more schooling right after high school. I wanted to sit at the feet of my Native elders; my grandpa Ed still had sisters alive and living on the reservation, and they had always been nice to me. I wanted to dig through the archives at Yuma's historical society. I wanted to get involved in tribal politics and see how traditional Indigenous communities lived. But at the time, I floundered for a response, and felt my face blushing.

After a moment, I found my voice and said I wasn't sure about med school, but I would like to go home and learn how to speak Quechan.

"Wouldn't that be interesting?" Daniel's mother said, before pointing out how unfortunate it was that tribal languages weren't on our standardized tests. "It's sad that learning a language like that won't really get you ahead."

By the spring semester, I was bored. My grades had risen to Cs thanks to Daniel and Patti, and it looked like I would be able to graduate with my class. I deserved a bit of time off, I thought, so I decided to accept an invitation to a birthday party. I was going to spend the night with a couple of my old Catholic friends.

I was standing in my friend's kitchen when she answered the phone and told me it was my dad. My god, I thought, he was never going to stop worrying about me. My first instinct was to think he was checking in to see that I wasn't drinking or self-harming. Maybe he thought I was careening off a cliff into a lake somewhere.

My heart pounded hard when I took the phone, irritated that he thought I was having suicidal ideations again when I assured him repeatedly that I wasn't. But when I got on the line, I realized he wasn't calling about me or worried about what I was doing at all. He was calling about Lori. She had been in a serious car accident, and he needed me to come home immediately.

I grabbed my stuff, my friend asking if I wanted her to drive me. Later, she would tell me that I left her house crying, but I don't remember any details of that night until I arrived home. Joan was in the front yard waiting for me. Her mascara was streaked, and she had lost all semblance of calm. I couldn't stand the way she was screaming, so I went inside to find Mom. She was in the bedroom reciting a rosary aloud as she packed. She didn't want to talk but told me I could find Dad in the den.

I went downstairs and found Dad sitting next to the phone on the couch. He was dry-eyed and didn't try to hide the gravity of Lori's injuries when he recounted what happened.

Lori had been day drinking with her sorority sisters at New Mexico State University in Las Cruces. It was unseasonably warm, and they had decided to go have some fun with a bunch of fraternity guys they knew. A big group of them loaded their ice chests up with drinks and carpooled out to the sloping hills of White Sands National Monument, where they went sledding on toboggans rubbed down with slippery surf wax.

On the way back to the dorms, Lori climbed into a car with a frat boy who drove like a maniac. They were in a Corvette, and he was racing another driver when they flew over the top of a hill and rear-ended a family in a dually truck. The father had just filled up and was moving slowly as he pulled out of a rural gas station. The front passenger side of the Corvette where Lori was seated took most of the impact. She was not buckled in, which ironically saved her life because she slid down into the foot well like a fetus. If she'd stayed sitting, she would have been decapitated when the car's roof on her side was sheared off. Instead, she got encased in metal and the firefighters had to pull her out using the Jaws of Life.

When the emergency room doctor called, Dad told the doctor that he and his wife were getting in the car to drive down right away. But seven hours was a long time away from a phone, and the doctor said they were concerned about bleeding in her brain. It was best if Mom and Dad waited until morning so they could give permission for emergency surgery if it was needed. By then, they would know if she was going to stabilize or not.

The night was long and sleepless, but it didn't seem real. My family and I paced around each other with worry until the doctor called back and said they would need to cut into Lori's skull to relieve the pressure on her brain. She came out of surgery stabilized, and Mom and Dad climbed into the car with Ted and Theresa at sunrise. It was a long drive to the hospital in Las Cruces, where Lori was in the ICU, and they promised to call and send for us once they knew more.

Lori slipped into a coma that day. I wanted to see her, but Mom insisted we stay in school. Joan stopped by the house a couple of times, but for the most part Monica and I were on our own, lonely and frightened. In the evenings, she kept crying, and I told her not to worry. Lori was my superhero, and it was difficult to imagine her hurt.

A mother of a volleyball teammate called my parents and offered to buy me and Monica airplane tickets to fly down to Las Cruces and see Lori. Everyone was talking like we should go and say goodbye. Mom's church friends dropped off casseroles with prayer cards featuring Jude Thaddeus, the patron saint of lost causes. I felt grateful for the tickets to fly down and see Lori, but I couldn't help feeling embarrassed by the car accident. I remembered Dad telling me I cared too much about what everyone thought, and for the first time it felt true. Lori was the only thing that mattered, not what people said about the fact that she had been in a car accident while drinking.

The following week, Monica and I did our laundry and packed our luggage for the trip. She told me that Mom had warned her about Lori's shaved head and deep wounds, and she asked if I was nervous to see her. I told her no; it would alleviate my worries to be there. The following day we rode with Joan to the San Juan Airport, where she dropped us off for our flight.

"Tell stupid I love her," Joan said as we got out of the car. She said she had to work, otherwise she would come down too. But I knew that she and Lori had always been very close, and I could see that she was afraid.

When we arrived at the hospital, I entered the ICU and stood next to Lori's bed. Seeing her with a shaved head, a mangled left ear, and a tube down her throat made me feel sick. Her arm looked scabbed and swollen. The only other person I'd seen this close to death was Grandma Esther. But this was different. My sister was young, and the sound of the machine breathing for her scared me. I tried to see her features beneath the swollen flesh, but it was impossible.

I remembered when we were little and still living in Yuma, lying in our bed beneath the swamp cooler, counting change for the corner store. I could see her six-year-old face hiding between Mom's sheets when we played hide-and-seek. I saw her cheering for our favorite neighborhood mutt, Rocco. Joan, Monica, and I had all acted rowdy, climbed into cars with drunk classmates, which meant it could have been any one of us lying in that bed, and I felt sorry that it was Lori.

I was bending over her bed, telling her I was there, when Mom came into the room. She looked crazy. Her hair was greasy and unkempt. When she saw me standing by the bed, her eyes flashed around the room, like she was looking for something to throw. "What's wrong?" I asked her.

"Take a good look at her," Mom said.

"Why are you mad at me?"

"This is what I've been trying to tell you. You think you're so smart, but it only takes one impulsive moment to become a statistic!"

Her rage was palpable, and I realized she wasn't going to tiptoe around my overdose anymore. "You can't flirt with the devil, unless you want to wind up dead," she said.

I sat down on a chair in the corner and started crying. And as soon as Mom saw me crying, she got even angrier. "Do you remember what happened to Dad right before we left the reservation?"

She was talking about the time he got electrocuted after the pow-wow. As usual he'd been out with his brothers when they got in a fight at a bar downtown. I was too young to remember it, but I had heard the story.

When the cops came, he ran. He cut down an alley and waded across the historic crossing where the water was low, knowing that if he made it up Indian Hill he could hide in Granny Ethel's fry bread trailer. He was soaking wet, and as he climbed the stairs to get inside he grabbed hold of a metal fixture. The generator had faulty wiring, and he was electrocuted.

He said it felt like all his ribs were breaking at once. He hovered above his body and could see himself jerking as he hung on to the metal. "It was so peaceful," he said. He knew he was dying and felt with it, but then the generator kicked off and his body flew back and landed on the packed dirt with a blow. "It hurt so bad I wished I could stop breathing."

All at once it hit me. Mom had saved Dad's life. If he was alive, it was because of her. She had never backed down or abandoned him, even when he did stupid things. She loved him, and she was loyal. Her faith in our family was real.

"All I ever wanted was to keep everyone safe," she said.

I thought about all the orthodontist appointments she'd driven me to. How many times she had kept score at our games and brought cupcakes to my class for my birthday. I remembered how she took my temperature and sat by my bed when I was running a fever. Mom had given up her life and any possibility of a career to raise us, and it was tragic that I had treated her with such disrespect. I saw the black circles under her eyes and felt terrible.

"Dad can't even come in here," she said. "It makes him too upset."

I hugged her, and she started crying. It alarmed me because Mom wasn't the type to indulge in tears.

"Why can't you do what I tell you?" she asked. "You've always been so smart, and we always expected you and your sisters to do well. When are you going to stop being so angry?"

All she had ever been was a mother. After my suicide attempt, when I'd told her how angry I was at our history, she urged me to pray for the grace to forgive. She wanted me to turn the other cheek, follow the rules, and forgive the wrongs, and rather than admire her strength, or respect her beliefs, I had shunned her for them. For the first time, I realized how condescending it was to assume that her faith made her dumb when she had been using it for strength.

I went out into the waiting room and told Monica it was her turn to see Lori, then wandered down the hall to find Dad. Mom said he was in the chapel, that he never left the chapel. I entered the vestibule through the door at the back and found him kneeling before a dozen lit candles in front of the pews. There was a large well of sand that people stood the candles in, and an image of Our Lady of Guadalupe hung before him where he knelt.

He heard me blowing my nose and came to give me a hug, then we sat next to each other in a pew.

"Is Lori going to be okay?" I asked.

"I don't know," he answered.

We sat quietly for a moment before I said how guilty I felt about Mom. I told him how ashamed I was of my anger, but as soon as he heard me talking about shame, he cut me off.

"Stop," he said. "Mom understands you more than you realize. She doesn't want you to feel bad."

He told me how grateful they were that I'd forced them to face issues they couldn't confront as a couple before. He said it wasn't easy being in a mixed-race marriage, and neither was it easy learning to navigate a world in which success required proximity to whiteness, white institutions, and white gatekeepers. They weren't judging me for my anger. When he was young, he had been angry too.

"Even Jesus lost it sometimes," he said. "Remember the money changers in the temple?"

He said maybe Lori drank because she hadn't figured out how to handle her anger either. He said it wasn't healthy to smile and push our feelings down. All the years that I'd argued and challenged him and Mom were helpful, because it made them realize they couldn't keep pretending their kids' societal struggles didn't exist.

"Old habits are hard to break, and Mom's always wanted to force her beliefs on you, but this year she's finally come to realize no one can decide but you."

Listening to him talk, I realized that my parents' faith had made then adaptive, enduring, and strong. They viewed their marriage and their responsibility to their family as something sacred, and I admired their perseverance, but I also wasn't ready to forgive America for its racism, and as I got ready to leave the chapel, I told him that's how I felt.

"Anger can be healthy," he said. "We just don't want it to kill you."

He'd always told me I couldn't depend on anyone to save me or tell me what my purpose might be, and as I left the chapel that day, I realized he was right. I didn't have to agree with Mom, and I didn't have to follow in the footsteps of my sisters. I had to find what felt important to me.

As I went down the hall, I heard him calling. "One more thing," he said. "You're always talking about honoring our ancestors, but just remember, if you can't love your mother on earth who you can see, how can you love the people in the next who you can't?"

I went out to the van alone. There would be a lot of downtime at the hospital, and I wanted to get my bookbag so I could stay caught up on my schoolwork. My plan to graduate and leave Farmington hadn't changed, but defying my parents when I knew they didn't want me to move onto the reservation felt shakier now. They insisted it was a violent place, a place with no economy and no future for me. They feared that I might spiral, drink, grow depressed, and end up like Lori. And maybe they were right. After seeing Lori in a fight for her life, I knew I had to do all I could to never hurt them again.

I found a library book in my backpack. I'd read it the month before. It talked about flesh offerings as prayer in tribal ceremonies. A clip of skin here, a piercing there. On this continent, our ancestors believed the only thing we owned was our body. I saw this in our funeral practices, the idea that one should not cling to the material. Our bodies were all we had, and that night when we got back to the hotel I went for a walk with a pair of scissors in my backpack.

I sat on a boulder in the desert for a long time. The sun started to set, and when the Organ Mountains glowed pink, I cut off a quarter-size piece from my forearm. Then I wrapped the small piece of flesh in a piece of cloth and tied it to a stick in the sand. I knelt beside my offering and bled, praying that me, my family, and especially Lori, would have our wounds heal and be whole.

A few days later, Dad drove us back to the airport. Lori was still not awake, and the mood was grim as we stopped to get gas. We were standing in the station's parking lot after running inside for snacks, when Monica pointed at an open field behind the parking lot and said, "Look!"

An enormous kaleidoscope of monarch butterflies was fluttering around in the grass. Dad said they must be the swarms he had read about in the news, coming all the way back from Mexico. But it seemed early in the year for such a phenomenon, and none of us felt certain. We got back in the car, surprised but happy, and everyone agreed that seeing them was a good omen for Lori.

When we got back to the house, I smudged all our rooms with cedar on a cast-iron skillet like I'd seen my cousins do on the reservation. Monica ran around and opened the windows before me. We felt certain that Lori would wake up that week. We held hands and said a prayer and asked the ancestors to bring her a blessing.

The weekend after our return to Farmington, Lori came out of her coma. When Mom called, she was crying and laughing. She recounted how impressed the doctor was with Lori's strength and she was thrilled that Lori couldn't remember the accident. She sounded less chirpy when she called a few days later and said Lori couldn't remember Yuma either. With each phone call, the issues our sister faced became more apparent. In addition to her memory loss, she was dealing with a lost sense of smell and a drag in her leg when she stepped.

Everyone was devastated about Lori's prospects, especially since she had made so much progress toward getting her engineering degree. But the imminent concern was her memory and sense of identity. The doctor advised that we take her to visit the family in Yuma as soon as she finished her time at a rehabilitation center in Las Cruces.

Nearly three months after her accident, it was spring break, and we

were ready to take Lori home to Yuma. Dad's siblings came in from Los
Angeles, and Mom's family opened their doors. We drove by Senator Wash
and went up to St. Thomas Indian Mission. We circled the block around
the Dolly Madison Store where we used to buy day-old cupcakes and bread.
We bought ice cream at the Tastee-Freez and burritos at Mr. G's. We
walked the block around Grandma Mary's house. We went to the drive-in,
drove out to Jackson Road, and visited our old haunts on the reservation.

It reminded me of how we had all rallied around Tommy when his
life changed. Aunt Annie asked Lori if she remembered the time we were
playing Mouse Trap and she got the marble from the board game stuck
up her nose. The Jackson cousins told Lori it was good that she forgot the
leg warmers she wore everywhere in the early 1980s because they were
bougie. Grandma Mary bought Lori a Rubik's Cube, telling her she was
the only kid she'd ever known to solve one.

Aunt Vi came down from the Mojave Indian reservation near Parker,
Arizona, and while everyone else milled around Grandma Esther's house,
the two of us walked down to the All-American Canal. She had her ex-
ercise tights on and said she needed to stretch her legs to make up for a
missed aerobics class. At fiftysomething years old, she was still pretty. She
had her hair piled in a ballet bun on top of her head.

"Looney looks a decade older after what you girls have put him
through this year," she said. "And now I hear that you're talking about
coming back to live here?"

"Who told you that?" I asked.

She gave me a look that meant I wasn't allowed to ask questions. "You
know, when you were a little kid, you used to use all these big words, and
me and your mother would look at each other and shake our heads. I
always expected you to do something great."

"Not you too," I told her. "I don't know why you and Dad act like
college is the only route to success. I want to learn about our tribal traditions. I don't know why you didn't want to learn about them when you
were a kid."

"All we wanted was enough food in our bellies," she said, laughing.

But then she thought about it for a minute and tried to clarify the difference between her generation and mine. "It was different back then. A lot of people died before they were fifty. Or they didn't talk about the past. Everyone was scarred from Indian boarding school."

I nodded.

"But listen to this story," she said. She told me about a ceremony that was let go in the 1950s. She said that each clan had a contribution of music to make to it, but when one of the families who was meant to provide song at the ceremony lost three members of their family in one year—before they had fully taught the music to their offspring—my great-grandfather and his friends held a meeting and came out saying it was over. Younger generations argued, but they were reminded never to grasp at material things. The world was perpetually in flux, too sacred to tether, and the elders said this change was part of the world's ongoing ceremony. Aunt Vi said it was a reminder that even ceremony was material. There was only true power and endurance in nature.

"What do you think of that?" she asked when she finished. I told her that it made me mad, and she laughed and said it made her mad too. We were quiet for a minute, then she told me she didn't want me to miss the point. She wasn't telling me because she needed to vent her emotions or wanted me to vent mine. She was telling me because she wanted me to understand how complicated it was to stay alive.

We were nearing Grandma Esther's house again, and I could see my cousin's daughter doing cartwheels in the yard. Aunt Vi said, "You know, your father worked hard to give you a good life."

"I know that," I answered.

"Then act like it," she said.

That night we said goodbye and piled into the van. Lori kept saying Dolly Parton visited her in the hospital, but we were growing used to her non-sensical talk, so it wasn't too shocking. It took months for her brain to settle down, and although she would eventually return to full health, and then even become a business owner, she never did finish her degree.

I fell asleep for the first three hours of the trip back, until the city lights in Phoenix woke me up, and I started thinking about my talk with Aunt Vi. Her comment about Dad's work hit hard and made me see how I'd been blaming my parents for issues that were centuries old, and not created by them. This was the insidious thing about colonialism, the way it created factions and tore families apart.

I remembered our old house, which we'd visited earlier that day; the neighbor who had lost his dog to the rattlesnake bite; how I hated everyone for being mean to him and treating him like an outsider because he hadn't gone back to his own reservation. I hated when other Natives policed my identity, acting like I was too assimilated, and yet here I was, judging my parents. My attitude about their work and faith, my snobbery about their choices, my desire to turn them into something they weren't. It was all bound up in an impulse to give them the lives they should have had, the life I felt they deserved.

Especially my father, I had wanted to turn into the crying Indian in the public service announcement against littering, never realizing that injustice was when someone privileged like me, someone who has reaped the benefits of money, comfort, and electricity, turned around and vilified a struggling father for trying to take care of his kids.

I rested my forehead on the bench seat in front of me and felt like I might be carsick. I suddenly realized it was never my parents who had to change. It was me. Dad's method of survival was his business. Now I had to find mine.

Somewhere outside Kayenta I finally fell asleep again and had a dream about the Old World. In it, my ancestors were running across the desert. They were leaping over washes and climbing up boulders with supernatural speed—and they were pulling me alongside them. At first I thought we were trying to escape, but then I realized we were running *toward* rather than away, and the dream became beautiful.

The next thing I knew, Mom was shaking me awake in my seat. We were back home in Farmington. I saw the horizon pink with dawn and knew exactly who my ancestors were. They were not fry bread and commodity cheese eaters. They were not tethered to ceremony, song, or even a government given reservation. They were strong, nomadic, and found awe in the earth. They said I should never hold on to material things, and rather than focusing on the costumes, traditions, and clichés that were romanticized by our oppressors, I vowed to focus on their edicts. I wanted to live as they had lived, healthy and strong. I wanted to value what they had valued, the beauty of the earth. And from that realization my future fell into place.

Early the following morning before the first bell, I went to find my psychology teacher, Mr. Braswell. I remembered a gig he told us he took during college. He'd talked about it a hundred times that year.

"I worked in Yellowstone," he said. "They let me live in the dorm at Old Faithful and I hiked for hundreds of miles all over the park. I climbed mountains in the Grand Tetons and got healthier than I'd ever been in my life. I can't promise you that you'll get a fancy job, but you could probably get a job as a cook or a maid."

His comment had never been directed toward me. He told the whole class, and he said he had been telling his classes for over twenty years. Every year he offered to give an application to any student who wanted one. He offered to help fill it out and promised to provide a letter of recommendation. But no one ever took him up on his offer until me.

That night I went home and told my parents we needed to talk. I brought my backpack to the dining room table and pulled out the application. "It doesn't pay much," I told them. "But getting my foot in the door at the national parks feels like a good thing to do."

At first Mom was upset that I was having doubts about college, but then Dad put up his hand. "Remember how much my fire watch years helped me," he said.

Then I learned something I had never known about Dad. When he was sent away to prison the first time, he ended up on a firefighting crew in Northern California, spotting lightning strikes from lonely lookout towers, and chopping smoldering logs to settle burned ground. He said the guards sometimes made them dig for old Indian pottery at locations they called "dump sites," presumably so they could take the relics and sell them for profit. One time, when Dad was out with his crew, the fire they were fighting crowned, and they had to crawl under the power wagon and radio for help. Dad said one minute they there sweating and the next they were shivering beneath a blanket of man-made snow.

When they didn't have forest fires to fight, they climbed telephone poles to fix insulators that had been damaged by hunters. He said one time he was up on a pole when a black bear appeared beneath him, and he had to wait until it rambled away in the woods.

"It was magical," he said. "I think it was the period in my teenage years that healed me. Being out in the woods away from everyone gave me time to think."

"Why didn't you tell me this before?" I asked.

"I'm telling you now," he said, smiling.

The day after I turned eighteen, I walked across a stage at Farmington High and received my diploma. I didn't win a single honor, but Mom and Dad acted like I was a hero. They gave me camping equipment from REI and they bought me two new books: one about the Natives who once lived in Yellowstone, and another titled *Ceremony* by a Laguna writer named Leslie Marmon Silko.

In the card she gave me with my gift, Mom said that she was proud of me, her family, and the life we had built in Farmington. She wrote, "Stay focused on your family and faith, no matter how you define it," and after I read the card, she took my hand and kissed it.

The morning after my graduation ceremony, we woke up in the middle of the night to start our drive to Yellowstone where I had accepted a job as a maid. It was a humble job that wouldn't earn me gold, but it didn't matter. I was following my heart, and I knew it was the right thing to do. Dad carried Theresa and Ted outside while they were still sleeping and loaded them into the camper shell in the back of the truck. Monica and

I climbed in after them, and the four of us fell asleep on the mattress he had positioned in the truck bed.

Hours later, we pulled to a stop. I'd lost track of how long we'd been driving and sat up wondering where we were. Quietly, so I wouldn't wake my younger siblings, I exited the camper shell. It was sunrise, and we were at a rest stop. At first, I couldn't find Dad, but after using the restroom, I walked behind the building and saw him standing at a lookout.

"Where are we?" I asked, rubbing my eyes.

"Northern Utah," he said. The view was green and grand as a painting. Neither of us had ever been so far from the Southwest. I stood next to Dad and could see how happy he was to be having an adventure someplace new.

"Life's going to be boring without you around to make everything complicated," he said.

I turned my face to hide my emotions. Complicated as my family was, I would miss them.

We walked back to the truck and found Mom awake. "Trade places with me so I can see how the kids are doing in back," she said.

Sitting in the cab next to Dad, I couldn't have guessed that I would spend the next two years widening my gyre, like a falcon forgetting his falconer. Yellowstone would be followed by Hog Island off the coast of Maine, then the far reaches of Alaska, five islands in Indonesia, and three countries in West Africa. I would realize that a quarter of the world was Indigenous, and when I was done, I would end up on the reservation in Yuma, strong, straightened out, and ready to help.

When we arrived in Yellowstone, Dad said, "Look at that!" and I opened my sleepy eyes to see a family of bison walking alongside the road. We got out of the truck and stood on the side of the road, keeping our distance. I watched my parents, Monica, Theresa, and Ted talking reverently about their size, before being grossed out by the clumps of balled hair the bison left behind on the side of the road.

When they dropped me off at orientation in Gardiner, Montana, the whole lot of them looked nervous and out of place in the lobby. Monica cried and said she couldn't believe they were leaving me with strangers. Mom looked around at the other visitors and tugged at her blouse like she wished she had worn something different.

I wanted to tell them we belonged in Montana, just as we belonged in the Southwest. I wanted to tell them that we should think of the United States as one big reservation, that our ancestors' blood and bones permeated the dust at the edge of every sunset, that their spirits existed in the water and air, and there was no place where we weren't welcome.

Instead, I thought it might sound hokey and waved them off, hiding the huge lump in my throat. They climbed in the truck, and I stood on the front porch of the orientation building, watching as they pulled out of the lot. I reminded myself they would have fun on their vacation. Theresa and Ted would scream at the fat marmots on the footbridge near Old Faithful. Monica would take a photo of herself in front of Yellowstone Falls. Mom and Dad would kiss in front of an open field at sunset, a herd of elk grazing behind them in the distance. I watched Dad's truck until it grew small in the distance and disappeared around the bend.

EPILOGUE

✛

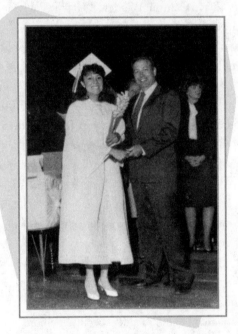

The author receiving her diploma at Farmington High School, May 1987.

A person teaches best what she needs to learn, and reconnecting with my homeland, rediscovering my center as it relates to my past, claiming my inheritance as a woman whose spirituality is deeply rooted in the desert, is what I most needed when I started writing this book. While my life's road did return me to the reservation in my twenties—it also spirited me away to Iowa City and Saint Louis in my thirties and forties. The demands of career and family make us all mobile, but there are seasons to life, and I always knew my ancestors would eventually call me home again.

My Laguna grandmother, Esther, is the one who taught me that a deep intimacy with a homeland requires three things: sensory experiences of particular geographies, a storied history of the trails, and a deep caring about them. I remember her pinning laundry on the clothesline as she recited place names. Start with *Tse-pi'na*: a single word that encompasses the modern stories and old myths, the ponderosa pine and alligator juniper, the wild turkey and mule deer. Her list had other places that readers and lovers of the desert will recognize in English: Hesperus Peak, Aztec Ruins, Wheeler Peak, Chaco Canyon, Window Rock, the Painted Desert, Canyon de Chelly, the Zuni and Kachina Mountains.

Her way of remembering was a constant; it was her way of being in her homeland even as she was absent in Yuma. The word *Tse-pi'na* had power in her life, as it has power in mine now. Not only does it return me to my time with my grandma, but it also returns me to myself. I remember climbing the mountain's western slope with my three children in my twenties. I remember carrying my baby in a cradleboard on my back, while helping my three- and four-year-olds over large roots and fallen trunks at a glacial pace.

Storied histories, sensory experiences, a deep caring, and the desire to be in certain places: my grandmother's commitment to place-names was devotional. It was a way to keep her values intact even as she lived on her husband's reservation. I have remembered this through the years when my homeland felt like a distant memory, difficult to conjure on the page. I remembered that human beings have always tied the most important events in their lives—moments of transcendent beauty, memories that hold numinous meaning, birth, and death experiences—to tangible places. Geography is a shaping force that develops our sense of identity and morality.

If I learned anything by listening to my grandmother's soft voice as she hung her laundry, it is that recitation, poetry, and writing are almost always born of nostalgia. My grandmother walked on long ago. In her lifetime, she never left the desert. While writing this book, I missed her, and I thought of my writing as a way of hanging bedsheets on the clothesline, scribbling words and place-names to remember who I am, just as she taught me to do. Her relationship with the desert was physical, biological, moral, and above all, intimate and reciprocal. All my life, even when I've traveled, I've wanted my relationship with the desert to be that way too.

Barry Lopez wrote, "If you're intimate with a place, a place with whose history you're familiar, and you establish an ethical conversation with it, the implication that follows is this: the place knows you're there. It feels you. You will not be forgotten, cut off, abandoned."

For two decades, I kept this quote in a notebook nearby me as I wrote. I told myself, the land remembers my name. When I felt the words were too difficult to render, I remembered that my ancestors could hear me reciting. I knew that our traditions had to change, not only for us and our grandchildren, but also for the world to hear echoes from the Indigenous past, a time when the pace of life and the wisdom born of our relationship to the earth was still alive. I knew that our people had to change because change is the essence of life. This last year, living through a pandemic, becoming a grandmother for a second time, I began to hear the end of my tale, and it was as if the act of finishing meant the desert could finally call me home.

Perhaps it is always better to write about a place from a distance, as Leslie Marmon Silko said about writing *Ceremony*, because it's only in a state of nostalgia that we see things clearly. I wrote these pages mostly in the Midwest, where I often felt lost and alone, but I am finishing tonight in Santa Fe, New Mexico, where I have been invited to support the next generation of Native writers as the director of the MFA in creative writing at the Institute of American Indian Arts. I don't know how many times I've heard young Native scholars tell me they were trying to remember their ancestral cultures, values, and stories with trepidation in their voices, to which I always say, "Don't worry, your ancestors are keeping track of *you*."

The totem pole, the Bodhi tree, the hearth. We are at home on this planet when we feel the sacred places rising up through our feet, when we embrace the mountains and desert arroyos as holy. The Ancient Ones walk beside us, and all we must do is keep our fingers on the pulse of music. If we listen, we can hear it rising up from the planet: the sound of the spirit that was, is, and always will be.

ACKNOWLEDGMENTS

I first conceived of this book as a kid, and as such, many teachers have helped me along the way. I am grateful to those mentors who plucked me out of workshops to offer praise, and more importantly, who cared enough to offer criticism, thereby showing their investment in my story. In order of appearance in my life, they are the late Ntozake Shange at the Taos Poetry Circus, Sandra Scofield at the Iowa Summer Writing Festival, Kathleen Finneran at Webster and Washington University in Saint Louis, Phillip Lopate at the New York State Summer Writers Institute, John D'Agata at the Nonfiction Writing Program in Iowa City, and Billy-Ray Belcourt at the Tin House Summer Workshop. Additionally, I must thank Mac-Dowell and Hedgebrook for the gift of time, the Ellen Melloy Fund, PEN America, Kranzberg Arts, the Santa Fe Writers Project, the Rona Jaffe Foundation, Chaco Symphony (Gary Gackstatter and R. Carlos Nakai), the Santa Fe International Literary Festival, We Need Diverse Books, the Fine Arts Work Center, the University of Iowa, Brigid Hughes at *A Public Space*, Laguna Pueblo, and the Quechan Nation for their generous grants, opportunities, and financial support.

It takes a tribe to write a book. I am grateful for the good medicine, wisdom, and healing I have received from Dr. Robert Martin and my colleagues at the Institute of American Indian Arts, as well as from Eugene Blackbear; Preston Arrowweed; the late Claudette White; Charlene

2

92 Acknowledgments

Teters; Mike Jackson; John Antonio; the late Louise Jackson Tannheimer; my father, Edmond Jackson; and my mother, the late Lorraine Lopez Herrera. Their lives have reminded me to honor my roots and my ancestors. I am thankful for the writers who went through the Nonfiction Writing Program and Iowa Writers' Workshop in tandem with me. Our intellectual similarities and cultural differences helped develop my voice and my priorities. I thank my agent, Samantha Shea, for the faith she placed in me as we polished this memoir for sale. I thank my primary editor, Jenny Xu, for the quiet grace and authority she brought to its final revision. I thank editor Emily Graff for help with the book cover, and executive editor Adenike Olanrewaju, for taking on an orphan with gusto and belief.

I cherish and thank my partner, Simone, who set sail with a crazy American girl after briefly meeting me in Indonesia when we were both twenty. It's taken a long time to bring this project to fruition, yet you never wavered in your belief that it would happen. Most affectionately, I thank my children: Francesca, Elia, Sonora, Julian, and Miquela. By now you know how important it was for me to tell this story, though when you were young, I'm sure you lamented having a distracted mother. Despite witnessing my trauma, and living with my obsessive writing, you never stopped loving me. You sacrificed time with me, and I feel lucky to have had your support, scholarship, and advice through the years. To my grandsons, Keola and Makoa, I felt your hands guiding me through the final revision. When I imagined you growing old enough to read my words, it drew out the honesty in me.

I would also like to thank my siblings, who survived childhood with me, and with whom I've sometimes disagreed on childhood memories. My older sisters laughed, for example, when I wrote that our beagle had twelve puppies. But whereas I removed that claim, I've kept others, because our memories differ, and I had to be true to my own recollections. Some school acquaintances have had their names and identifying characteristics changed to protect their privacy, and some events have been compressed to help with flow. Any mistakes, cruelties, or failures my people perceive in this book are mine and mine alone.

Finally, I'd like to thank the editors of the following journals, in which five of these essays, in different versions, first appeared: *A Public Space*, the *Los Angeles Review of Books*, *Salon Magazine*, *The Rumpus*, *Huizache* magazine, and *Prairie Schooner*.

ABOUT THE AUTHOR

Deborah Taffa is the director of the MFA creative writing program at the Institute of American Indian Arts in Santa Fe, New Mexico. A member of the Yuma Nation and Laguna Pueblo, she received her MFA from the Nonfiction Writing Program in Iowa City. Her writing can be found in *Salon*, *The Best of Brevity*, the *Boston Review*, the *Los Angeles Review of Books*, the Best American series, *A Public Space*, and other places. She is currently serving as editor in chief at *River Styx* magazine. Learn more at www.deborahtaffa.com.